# ARAB AMERICAN ENCYCLOPEDIA

# ARAB AMERICAN ENCYCLOPEDIA

Arab Community Center for Economic and
Social Services (ACCESS)

Anan Ameri and Dawn Ramey, Editors

U·X·L®

AN IMPRINT OF THE GALE GROUP

DETROIT · SAN FRANCISCO · LONDON
BOSTON · WOODBRIDGE, CT

Arab American Encyclopedia

**Edited by Anan Ameri and Dawn Ramey**

## Staff

Michelle Lee, *U•X•L Editor*
Sonia Benson, *U•X•L Contributing Editor*
Carol DeKane Nagel, *U•X•L Managing Editor*
Thomas L. Romig, *U•X•L Publisher*

Shalice Shah-Caldwell, *Permissions Associate (Pictures)*
Rita Wimberley, *Senior Buyer*
Evi Seoud, *Assistant Production Manager*
Dorothy Maki, *Manufacturing Manager*
Mary Beth Trimper, *Production Director*

Pamela A. E. Galbreath, *Senior Art Director*
Cynthia Baldwin, *Product Design Manager*

Marco Di Vita, Graphics Group, *Typesetting*

The front cover mural was painted by Sari Khoury, photographed by Robert J. Huffman of Field Mark Publications, and reproduced by permission of Field Mark Publications and the Arab Community Center for Economic and Social Services (ACCESS).

**Library of Congress Cataloging-in-Publication Data**

Arab American encyclopedia / Arab Community Center for Economic and Social Services (ACCESS); Anan Ameri and Dawn Ramey, editors.
    p.cm.
    Includes bibliographical references and index.
    Summary: Chapters arranged by subject present information about the history, immigration, economics, languages, religion, holidays, literature, education, jobs, politics, and other aspects of Arab Americans.
    ISBN 0-7876-2952-9
    1. Arab Americans Encyclopedias, Juvenile. [1. Arab Americans.]
    I. Ameri, Anan. II. Ramey, Dawn. III. Arab Community Center for Economic and Social Services.
    E184.A65A48 1999
    973' .04927—dc21
                                      99-37499
                                            CIP

Printed in the United States of America

10 9 8 7 6 5 4 3 2

# Contents

v

**Graduates at Fordson High School in Dearborn, Michigan.** *Reproduced by permission of Millard Berry.*

**An Arab American extended family.** *Reproduced by permission of AP/Wide World Photos.*

**Hamza El Din.** *Reproduced by permission of Jack Vartoogian.*

# Reader's Guide

**A**rab American Encyclopedia explores the history and culture of Arab America, a community of people who trace their roots to one or more of the twenty-one Arab countries. The Encyclopedia is organized into nineteen subject chapters, including immigration, religion, employment, education, family, health, civil rights, music, and literature. The volume contains more than seventy black-and-white photographs and maps and concludes with a subject index. The volume begins with a glossary of terms; words are also defined in a Words to Know box within the chapter in which they appear. Sidebars and Fact Focus boxes provide complementary and engaging information, and a list of sources is provided at the end of each chapter for students who wish to pursue further readings or research. Also included in this volume are a timeline of important events in Arab American history and a list of research and activity ideas.

## Related Reference Sources:

Arab American Biography (two volumes) profiles seventy-five noteworthy Arab Americans. Featured are prominent men and women, both living and deceased, who are notable for their achievements in fields ranging from social activism to sports, academia to politics, entertainment to science, and religion to the military. Early immigrants as well as contemporary figures are among those included. Black-and-white photographs accompany most entries, and a list of sources for further reading is provided at the end of each entry. The volume also includes cross-references, a timeline, a glossary, and a subject index.

*Arab American Voices* (one volume) presents twenty-six full or excerpted speeches, diary entries, newspaper accounts, works of fiction, poems, memoirs, and other materials by and about Arab Americans. Each entry is accompanied by an introduction and biographical and historical information, a document-specific glossary, and sources for further reading. The volume is illustrated with black-and-white photographs and features a timeline and a subject index.

## Comments and Suggestions

We welcome your comments on *Arab American Encyclopedia* and suggestions for topics to be featured in future editions. Please write: Editors, *Arab American Encyclopedia*, U•X•L, 27500 Drake Rd., Farmington Hills, Michigan 48331-3535; call toll-free: 1-800-877-4253; fax to (248) 414-5043; or send e-mail via http://www.galegroup.com.

# Contributors

- The Arab Community Center for Economic and Social Services (ACCESS) is a human service organization committed to the development of the Arab American community in all aspects of its economic, social, and cultural life. Founded in 1972, ACCESS has provided southeast Michigan with a wide range of services, including legal, medical, educational, cultural, and employment training. Additionally, to promote an appreciation for Arab and Arab American culture, ACCESS inaugurated its Cultural Arts Program in 1987. The program offers educational exhibits, seminars, consultations, group tours of ACCESS's Museum of Arab Culture, and numerous performances of Arab and Arab American music, dance, and poetry.

- Anan Ameri is the Cultural Arts Director at the Arab Community Center for Economic and Social Services (ACCESS). She received her B.A. from the Jordanian University in Amman, Jordan, her M.A. from Cairo University in Egypt, and her Ph.D. in Sociology from Wayne State University in Detroit, Michigan. Her career experience includes: researcher at the Palestine Research Center in

Beirut, Lebanon, the Acting Director of the Institute for Jerusalem Studies in Jerusalem, a visiting scholar at the Center for Middle Eastern Studies at Harvard University, a Fellow at the Bunting Institute of Radcliffe College in Cambridge, Massachusetts, and the National President and the Executive Director of the Palestine Aid Society of America. She is also the author of a number of publications, including *Industrial and Agricultural Development in Palestine, 1917-1970.*

• Kenneth K. Ayouby is a doctoral student in Education and Cultural Studies at Wayne State University in Detroit, Michigan. In his role as Student Services Liaison/Hearing Officer in the Dearborn schools' central administration (a suburb of Detroit with a large Arab American student population), Ayouby works with staff, students, and community in areas relating to student discipline as well as cross-cultural issues. Additionally, he is an adjunct lecturer in Arabic Studies at the University of Michigan at Dearborn and a contributing writer and editorial board member of the *Arab American Journal.*

• Louise Cainkar is a Sociologist and Research Assistant Professor with the University of Illinois at Chicago's Great Cities Institute. She received her Ph.D. from Northwestern University in Evanston, Illinois. Cainkar's work focuses on immigrant communities in the United States, especially Arab immigrant communities, and she has published a number of studies on Arab immigrants, on immigrants and the U.S. census, and on race and ethnicity in the labor force. Cainkar also works extensively with community-based organizations and focuses on improving human rights in the Middle East.

• Gary David is an assistant professor of Sociology at Bentley College in Waltham, Massachusetts. He has conducted research on a variety of subject areas in the metropolitan Detroit Arab American community and has been active in numerous community organizations. David's dissertation research examined intercultural communication between Arab and Chaldean American convenience store workers and their customers. He has also studied issues of identity in the Detroit community and is the author of the report *Mosaic of Middle Eastern Communities in Metropolitan Detroit.*

- Rosina Hassoun is an adjunct assistant professor in the Department of Anthropology and the Bailey Scholars Program at Michigan State University in East Lansing. She holds a Ph.D. in Biological/Medical Anthropology from the University of Florida at Gainesville. Hassoun's research focuses on health, nutrition, and acculturation in Arab/Chaldean populations. She is a consultant with the Arab Community Center for Economic and Social Services (ACCESS) in Dearborn. Additionally, Hassoun is participating in the first community needs assessment for ACCESS in Cleveland, Ohio, and conducting regional cultural sensitivity training with the American Cancer Society.

- Alexandra Kalaydjian has an M.A. in Women's Studies with an emphasis on immigrant women from the Middle East. She is currently working on an M.A. in Social Work at the University of Michigan at Ann Arbor. In 1998 and 1999 she served as the Educational Outreach Coordinator at the Arab Community Center for Economic and Social Service (ACCESS).

- Jessica LaBumbard has a B.A. in Sociology and Spanish, and is pursuing an M.A. in Intercultural and International Management. She has worked in the field of human rights both in the United States and abroad. Her work in the United States has entailed representing people in political asylum cases, advocating for a more just immigration policy, and educating the local community on refugee issues. Additionally, she has worked with refugees from Somalia, Sudan, Algeria, Lebanon, Jordan, Palestine, Syria, Iraq, and Kuwait. Her work abroad has consisted of numerous visits to postwar countries in Central America as a member of fact-finding delegations and as a long-term international human rights observer for returned refugees.

- Salwa Mikdadi Nashashibi is the President and Founder of the International Council for Women in the Arts. She is a frequent lecturer and writer on the subject of women artists of the Arab world and is the editor of the award-winning publication *Forces of Change: Women Artists of the Arab World.*

- Dawn Ramey is a Ph.D. candidate in Anthropology at Indiana University. She conducts research on social justice issues for the Arab American community and also has participated in other research projects, including one on Moroccan immigrants in Madrid, Spain. Ramey worked with the Arab Community Center for Economic and Social Services (ACCESS) from 1995 to 1999 and taught anthropology and Spanish at a number of colleges and universities. Additionally, she is interested in the development of multicultural curricular materials for adults and is involved in a number of coalitions and groups with the goal of promoting a more just and humane world.

• Karen Rignall, an Egyptian American, is a trained anthropologist who did her graduate work at the University of Michigan at Ann Arbor and conducted research in Egypt and Morocco. While in Michigan, she worked with the Arab Community Center for Economic and Social Services (ACCESS) in fundraising and cultural arts. Rignall currently resides in New York City, where she is actively involved with the Arab American community.

• Helen Hatab Samhan is Executive Vice President of the Arab American Institute in Washington, D.C., a nonprofit institute representing Arab American issues in politics, elections, leadership training, and public policy. She holds an M.A. in Middle East Studies from the American University of Beirut. Samhan lectures and publishes on Arab American affairs, particularly the immigrant experience of Arabs in the United States, their identity and demographics, the history of anti-Arab racism, political involvement, and Arab American women. Samhan is active in civic affairs in northern Virginia, where she resides, and serves as a Human Rights Commissioner for Fairfax County.

• Loukia K. Sarroub is a Ph.D. candidate in the College of Education at Michigan State University in East Lansing, Michigan, with concentrations in both education policy and social analysis and literacy education. During the 1990s, Sarroub conducted research on classroom-based assessments and on portfolio assessment at a junior high school. Currently, she is examining discourse and literacy practices at home and school among secondary school Yemeni American students. She hopes to understand how students negotiate their home and school worlds and how recent immigrants of Yemeni origin become Americanized in the public schools.

- Janice Terry is a professor of Middle Eastern History at Eastern Michigan University in Ypsilanti. She holds an M.A. in Arab Studies from the American University of Beirut and a Ph.D. from the School of Oriental and African Studies at the University of London. She is the author of *The Arab World from Nationalism to Revolution* (1971) and *The Waft (1919-1952): Cornerstone of Egyptian Political Power* (1982).

- Marvin Wingfield is Director of Education and Outreach for the American-Arab Anti-Discrimination Committee (ADC). ADC's program of "Reaching the Teachers" encourages Arab American parents and others to get involved in their children's schools. This program also assists educators in teaching about the Arab world and developing a better understanding of Arab American students. Wingfield first began working with ADC in 1981. He has a M.A. in Biblical Studies from the Earlham School of Religion, a Quaker school in Richmond, Indiana, and spent two years in the doctoral program in Religious Studies at the Catholic University of America in Washington, D.C.

# Timeline of Important Arab American Events

**1875**    Arab immigration to the United States begins in significant numbers.

**1876**    Philadelphia hosts the Centennial Exposition celebrating one hundred years of U.S. independence. To help celebrate, the city invites people from all over the world to participate in the exhibit. Many Arab merchants arrive and some decide to stay in the country.

**1880**    The age of peddling begins in the United States. Many Arab immigrants go into business as peddlers.

**1892**    The first Arabic language newspaper in the United States, *Kawkab Amrika* (*Star of America*), is published.

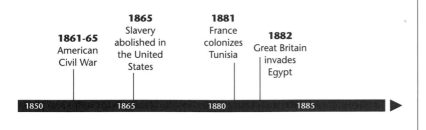

**1861-65** American Civil War

**1865** Slavery abolished in the United States

**1881** France colonizes Tunisia

**1882** Great Britain invades Egypt

1850    1865    1880    1885

**A Syrian man peddles food in the early 1900s.** *Reproduced by permission of Corbis Corporation (Bellevue).*

**A group of Syrian children in New York City, c. 1908-15.** *Reproduced by permission of Corbis Corporation (Bellevue).*

**1893** Chicago's Colombia Exhibit attracts many Arab merchants.

**1899** The Bureau of Immigration acknowledges that most of the increasing flow of "Turks from Asia" are in fact Arabs from Syria and adds the classification "Syrian" to its records.

**1907** Syrians win a case against a judge who denied citizenship to a Syrian, claiming that Syrians belong to the "yellow race."

**1911** Ameen Rihani publishes *The Book of Khalid*, the first Arab American novel.

**1912** Many Arab American textile workers participate in the Bread and Roses Strike in Lawrence, Massachusetts, in the hopes of gaining improved working conditions and higher wages. The workers eventually win the strike, but a young Arab American boy named John Ramey is killed by a federal militiaman.

**1915** The Arabs and the British sign the Sherif Husayn-McMahon Correspondence, which promises the Arabs an independent Arab nation after World War I. This nation was to include the present-day countries of Syria, Jordan, Saudi Arabia, Palestine, and Israel.

**1916** The Arabs rise up in an armed revolt against the Ottoman Empire and fight with the British on the side of the Allies (Great Britain, France, Russia and the United States) for the rest of World War I.

**1916** The British and the French sign the Sakes Picot Agreement, which would divide Turkey among the winning Allies and the Arab world between the British and the French.

**1891**
Britain's Labour Party is founded

**1912**
France colonizes Morocco

**1914-18**
World War I

1890     1900     1905     1910     1915

**1917** The British issue the Balfour Declaration, which promises their support for the establishment of a Jewish state in Palestine.

**1919** The British and the French implement the Sakes Picot Agreement, dividing up the Arab world among themselves in direct contradiction to the British agreement with Sherif Husayn.

**1920** The Pen League, an Arab American writers group, is founded in New York City.

**1921** The first major Hollywood portrayal of an Arab character is Rudolph Valentino's role in *The Sheik,* a movie that distorts Arab culture and promotes stereotypes.

**1923** The first Arab mosque in America is built in Highland Park, Michigan.

**1923** Kahlil Gibran publishes *The Prophet.*

**1924** The Johnson-Reed Quota Act passes, setting limits on how many people can immigrate from certain countries to the United States. Each Arab country receives a maximum quota of one hundred new immigrants per year.

**1936** Palestinians hold a six-month strike protesting British support of the Zionist movement in Palestine.

**1936** The number of Palestinian immigrants in the United States exceeds the number of Syrian and Lebanese immigrants for the first time.

**1947** The newly formed United Nations divides Palestine into a Jewish state and an Arab state.

**1948** Zionists in Palestine declare the independent Jewish state of Israel. War immediately breaks out and some 800,000 Palestinians become refugees. The Israelis win the war and add even more territory to their control.

**Rudolph Valentino holds Agnes Ayers in a still of the 1921 movie *The Sheik.*** *Reproduced by permission of Corbis Corporation (Bellevue).*

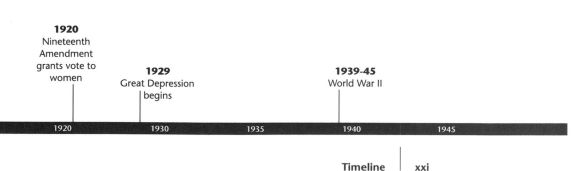

**1920** Nineteenth Amendment grants vote to women

**1929** Great Depression begins

**1939-45** World War II

1920     1930     1935     1940     1945

**Gamal Abdal Nasser.**
*Reproduced by permission of the United Nations.*

**1948**  Sam Maloof begins making furniture.

**1950**  The National Association of Syrian and Lebanese American Clubs is formed.

**1952**  The first Federation of Islamic Associations is founded and calls on Muslim communities in the United States and Canada to organize themselves into local associations to administer to the religious needs of their members.

**1956**  Israel, Britain, and France invade Egypt when Egypt's president, Gamal Abdal Nasser, takes over the Egyptian Suez Canal, previously controlled by Britain and France.

**1965**  A new immigration law in the United States removes the immigration quotas that varied by country, allowing a revitalization of Arab immigration.

**1967**  The third Arab-Israeli war breaks out. Israel occupies the Palestinian territories of East Jerusalem, the West Bank of the Jordan River, and the Gaza Strip on the Mediterranean coast. Israel also takes over parts of Syria and Egypt. This war results in increased immigration of Palestinians to the United States.

**1967**  The Association of Arab-American University Graduates (AAUG) is formed.

**1972**  The Arab Community Center for Economic and Social Services (ACCESS) is founded in Dearborn, Michigan.

**1972**  Arab American actor Jamie Farr begins playing Corporal Klinger on the television series *M*A*S*H.*

**1973**  The fourth Arab-Israeli war begins.

**1973**  Nagi Diafullah, a young Yemeni American, is killed while participating in a United Farm Worker (UFW) protest.

**1973**  The National Association of Arab Americans (NAAA) is formed.

**1954**
U.S. Supreme Court prohibits public school segregation

**1950-53**
Korean War

**1965**
U.S. troops become involved in the Vietnam War

**1969**
Neil Armstrong walks on the moon

1950    1955    1960    1965    1970

**1973** The Supreme Court rules in *Espinoza v. Farah Manufacturing Company* that nothing in the Civil Rights Act of 1964 prohibits discrimination on the basis of citizenship or alien status.

**1974** Congress passes the Equal Educational Opportunity Act, making bilingual education available to public school students whose primary language is not English.

**1975** Civil war breaks out in Lebanon, greatly increasing the number of Lebanese immigrants to the United States.

**1979** Egypt and Israel sign a peace treaty.

**1980** The American-Arab Anti-Discrimination Committee (ADC) is founded by former senator James Abourezk to fight discrimination against Arab Americans.

**1981** President Anwar Sadat of Egypt is assassinated because of the peace treaty he made with Israel in 1979.

**1982** Israel invades and occupies Lebanon, causing an increase in the number of Lebanese immigrants to the United States.

**1984** Abdeen Jabara wins a harassment and illegal surveillance lawsuit against the Federal Bureau of Investigation (FBI).

**1985** Alexander Michel Odeh, Western Regional Director of the American-Arab Anti-Discrimination Committee (ADC), is killed in his office in California after a bomb explodes.

**1985** The Arab American Institute (AAI) is formed to encourage the participation of Arab Americans in electoral politics.

**1986** The Immigration Reform and Control Act is passed in an effort to curb illegal immigration by prohibiting the hiring of undocumented immigrants.

**1987** Arab Americans win acknowledgment from the U.S. Supreme Court that they are protected, under existing

**James Abourezk.** *Reproduced by permission of Corbis Corporation (Bellevue).*

**A voter registration drive in Dearborn, Michigan.** *Reproduced by permission of the Arab American Institute Foundation.*

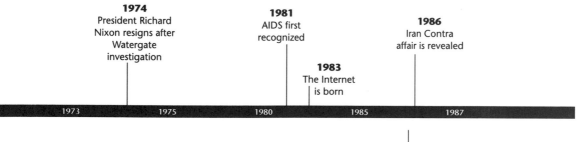

**1974** President Richard Nixon resigns after Watergate investigation

**1981** AIDS first recognized

**1986** Iran Contra affair is revealed

**1983** The Internet is born

1973        1975        1980        1985        1987

Timeline | xxiii

**Ralph Nader.** *Reproduced by permission of the Library of Congress.*

U.S. civil rights legislation, from discrimination based on ethnicity.

**1988** The Arab Network of America (ANA) is created and begins its operation as a national radio broadcaster.

**1988** Arab American senator George Mitchell becomes U.S. Senate majority leader.

**1990** Iraq invades Kuwait. The United Nations, with the full support of the United States government, implements economic sanctions against Iraq.

**1991** The U.S.-led military coalition launches the Gulf War to remove Iraq from Kuwait. The coalition defeats Saddam Hussein's forces, and many Iraqis, Kuwaitis, and Palestinians flee to the United States.

**1991** The Arab Network of America (ANA) TV is inaugurated.

**1993** Israel and the Palestine Liberation Organization (PLO) sign the Oslo Accords, a peace agreement which calls on Israel to withdraw from Palestinian territories it has occupied since 1967 in exchange for the PLO's recognition of Israel.

**1994** California voters pass Proposition 187, which denies state education, medical, and welfare services to undocumented immigrants.

**1994** Arab American Spencer Abraham is elected to the U.S. Senate.

**1996** Ralph Nader, an Arab American, runs for president of the United States as the nominee of the Green Party, a political party primarily concerned with environmental issues.

**1996** The U.S. Congress passes the Illegal Immigration Reform and Immigrant Responsibility Act of 1996 and the Antiterrorism and Effective Death Penalty Act of 1996. These laws allow secret evidence to be used against im-

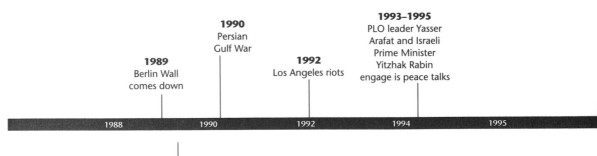

**1990**
Persian
Gulf War

**1993–1995**
PLO leader Yasser
Arafat and Israeli
Prime Minister
Yitzhak Rabin
engage is peace talks

**1989**
Berlin Wall
comes down

**1992**
Los Angeles riots

| 1988 | 1990 | 1992 | 1994 | 1995 |

migrants and foreign visitors for deportation. The law has been implemented almost exclusively against Arabs and Arab Americans.

**1996** Another U.S. governmental organization, the Federal Aviation Administration, institutes a profiling system that describes Arabs and Arab Americans as persons likely to commit acts of terrorism.

**1999** King Hussein of Jordan, the longest reigning Arab ruler, dies.

**1996**
South Africa adopts democratic constitution

**1999**
NATO intervenes in the Serb-Albanian conflict

1996    1997    1998    1999

# Words to Know

## A

**Allah:** the name for God in the Arabic language.

**Americanization:** learning the customs, language, and rules of American society and letting go of native customs and traditions.

**American-Arab Anti-Discrimination Committee (ADC):** a group started by Senator James Abourezk in 1980 to improve the image of Arab Americans in the United States, to fight racism against Arab Americans, and to reunite the Arab American community.

**Arab-Israeli conflict:** the political struggle that began with the creation of the state of Israel in 1948 on Palestinian land.

**Arabize:** when a society adopts the language and culture of the Arabs as their own.

**Ashura:** observed during the first ten days of the Muslim month of Muharram, it commemorates the assassination of the prophet Muhammad's grandson Hussein.

**Assimilate:** when a person or a group drops their own culture (such as changing their name and style of dress) and adopts the majority culture, usually referred to as the dominant or mainstream culture.

# B

**Backlash:** a reaction against a group of people due to a particular event or conflict with another group that may result in discrimination or violence.

**Baklava:** a dessert made of thin sheets of pastry layered with nuts, honey, and butter.

**B.C.E. (before the common era):** another term for B.C., which stands for "before Christ" (referring to the birth of the Christian figure Jesus Christ).

**Bedouins:** nomadic peoples who often herd livestock and trade as they move from place to place.

**Bicultural education:** programs that teach the history and culture of the students' country of origin alongside that of their new country.

**Bilingual:** fluent in two languages.

**Bilingual education:** programs that teach in the students' native languages along with the language of the country where they are living.

**Borrowing:** adapting a word from one language into another language. These borrowed words are sometimes referred to as loan words.

**Brain drain:** this occurs when many educated and highly skilled citizens of a country immigrate to another country in order to find work or better paying jobs, leaving their home country in need of educated and skilled workers.

# C

**Caliphs:** the religious and political leaders of the Muslim community after the death of Muhammad.

**Capitalism:** an economic system in which the means of production and distribution of goods and services—factories, transportation, communications—are owned by private, profit-making individuals and companies.

**C.E. (common era):** another term for A.D., which means "after death" (referring to the death of the Christian figure Jesus Christ).

**Census:** an official count of the number of people in a given population.

**Chain migration:** a continuous pattern of immigration in which once an immigrant has established himself in a new country he begins to bring other family members and friends.

**Christianity:** religion that believes Jesus Christ was the son of God. The Christian religion is based on Jesus' teachings and the teachings of the Bible.

**Civil rights:** the rights of individuals as guaranteed by laws, the Constitution, and the Bill of Rights. Such rights include the right to freedom of speech, freedom of religion, the right to vote, the right to equality before the law, and the right to engage in political activity.

**Classical Arabic:** the Arabic language that was spoken in the Arabian Peninsula at the time of Muhammad and which was used to write the Muslim holy book, the Qur'an (also spelled Koran).

**Communities:** groups of people, often living near each other, with common interests and connections.

**Country of origin:** the country in which a person is born.

**Crusaders:** European Christian armies who attempted to conquer parts of the Muslim Arab world.

**Culture:** the language, traditions, and values (beliefs about what is right and wrong) of a community or society.


# D

**Debkeh:** group folk dancing performed at weddings and community events.

**Demographics:** the study of the characteristics of human populations and the classification of them into categories such as age, education, profession, or ethnicity.

**Dialect:** a particular local version of a language that can be understood by speakers of other forms of the same language.

**Discrimination:** the unfair treatment of individuals or groups on the basis of their group identity, rather than on the basis of their personal merits. Some discrimination is the act of prejudiced individuals; some discrimination is institutionalized in laws, regulations, or policies of government agencies, corporations, or other organizations.

**Diverse:** pertaining to people, differences in national, racial, religious, and ethnic backgrounds.

**Druze:** a small branch of Islam developed in the eleventh century. The largest Druze community in the Arab world is in Lebanon.

# E

**Eastern Orthodox Christianity:** a branch of Christianity that split from Roman Catholicism in the eleventh century. It includes Antiochan, Coptic, Syrian, and Assyrian Orthodox Churches. These are sometimes referred to as the Middle Eastern, or Arab, churches.

**Economic sanctions:** an official trade boycott against a country deemed to be in defiance of international law. Sanctions can include restricting how much oil a country can export to other countries and what that country can buy from others—including food, medicine, and machinery.

**Eid:** the Arabic word for holiday.

**Eid al-Adha:** a Muslim holiday that marks the end of the Hajj, it commemorates events in the lives of the prophet (holy seer) Abraham and his family.

**Eid al-Fitr:** a Muslim holiday that marks the end of Ramadan, the month of fasting.

**English as a Second Language**: English-language instruction for non-native speakers.

**Entrepreneurship**: self-employment; having your own business.

**Ethnic group**: a group of people who speak the same language, share many cultural habits and traditions, or have a common history.

**Ethnomusicology**: the study of music of various cultures.

**Extended family**: a whole group of relatives, including husbands, wives, children, parents, grandparents, cousins, aunts, uncles, nieces, and nephews.

# F

**Federation**: a union of groups joined by an agreement or common purpose.

**Fertile Crescent**: the area along the Tigris and Euphrates Rivers in present-day Iraq.

**First language**: the language a person learns at home or speaks most fluently. A second language is usually learned at school, or outside of the home.

**First-generation immigrants**: people who were born in one country and then immigrated to another.

**Fluent**: having the language skills of a native speaker.

# G

**Gaza Strip**: a strip of land along Israel's southwest Mediterranean coast occupied by Egypt from 1948 until 1956, when Israel occupied the territory for a year. Israel pulled out in 1957, then annexed the strip again during the 1967 Six Day War. Violence between the Palestinians and Israelis continued in the region. In May 1994 the two groups signed an accord giving Gaza self rule. Israeli troops then withdrew from the region.

**Golan Heights:** an area along the border of Israel and Syria that originally belonged to Syria and was annexed by Israel in the 1967 Six Day War.

**Gulf War:** in 1990, Iraq invaded Kuwait; when Iraqi leader Saddam Hussein refused to withdraw his troops, the United Nations (UN) authorized military action. UN forces (largely American) drove the Iraqi invaders out of Kuwait in 1991.

**The Great Migration:** the period in U.S. history between 1880 and 1924 when more than twenty million immigrants entered the United States.

**Greater Syria:** a part of the Arab world under the Ottoman Empire (of the sixteenth through nineteenth centuries), that included present-day Syria, Lebanon, Jordan, Palestine, and Israel.

# H

**Hadith:** the sayings and acts of Muhammad.

**Hafla (plural haflat):** a get-together that is a cross between a concert and a party.

**Hajj:** the Muslim pilgrimage to Mecca, the birthplace of the prophet Muhammad. All Muslims are obligated to do this once in his or her lifetime if they are financially and physically capable of doing so.

**Hate crime:** a criminal offense committed against a person or property that is motivated by the offender's bias against a race, religion, or ethnic group. Such crimes include physical assault, vandalism or destruction of property, and even intimidation through threatening words or conduct that causes others to have a reasonable fear of bodily harm.

**Henna:** a dye made from henna tree leaves that is used to color hair and to decorate hands and feet.

**Hijab:** a head scarf worn by some Muslim women to cover their hair and necks.

**Holy Land:** a place of religious pilgrimage. Palestine is called the Holy Land by Jews, Christians, and Muslims.

**Hummous:** a dip made from garbanzo beans, tahini (sesame seed butter), and garlic.

# I

**Imam:** a Muslim religious leader. Imams lead the congregational prayers at noon on Fridays.

**Immigrant visas:** a document required by some governments for immigration purposes.

**Imperialistic:** having to do with a country or society that seeks to extend its control over other territories by colonizing them or dominating them economically and militarily.

**Integration:** the process by which immigrants adapt to and become part of their new society.

**Intifada:** the Palestinian uprising against the Israelis that began in the late 1980s.

**Islam:** the Muslim religion, based on belief in Muhammad as the chief and last prophet of God. Islam follows the teachings of the Qur'an (also referred to as the Koran). The word "Islam" is sometimes used to mean the worldwide Muslim community.

**Islamicize:** when a society adopts the Muslim faith as their own.

**Israel:** A Jewish state established in the Palestine region in 1948. Since its creation, neighboring Arab countries have refused to recognize Israel as a legal state (with the exception of Egypt, which recognized it in 1979). The region remains in a state of constant struggle over the territory.

# J

**Jerusalem:** one of the world's oldest cities, known to have been inhabited as early as 4000 B.C.E. The city is considered holy by Jews, Christians, and Muslims. At the start of the Arab-Israeli wars in 1948 Jerusalem was divided into the Old City and the New City. Israel's capital was the New City while the Old City was under Jordanian control. During the Six Day War of 1967, Israel annexed the Old City as well.

**Judaism:** the Jewish religion, based on the teachings of the Old Testament of the Bible and Talmud.

# K

**Karbala:** a city in southern Iraq, where Muhammad's grandson Hussein was killed.

**Kibbeh:** a meatball made from ground lamb and cracked wheat.

**Kushari:** a popular Egyptian dish, made of rice, lentils, pasta, and tomato sauce.

# L

**Language family:** a group of languages thought to have derived from a common language thousands of years ago.

**League of Arab States (Arab League):** formed in 1945, this group of Arab countries opposed the creation of Israel in the Palestinian region and used military action to try to force Israelis out of the area. The countries that make up the Arab League are: Algeria, Bahrain, Djibouti, Egypt, Iraq, Jordan, Kuwait, Lebanon, Libya, Mauritania, Morocco, Oman, Palestine, Qatar, Saudi Arabia, Somalia, Sudan, Syria, Tunisia, the Union of Arab Emirates, and Yemen. The countries of the League have agreed to work together on issues such as education, law, finance, trade, and foreign policy.

**Liberal democracy:** a society in which the citizens have some control over how the country is governed, usually by choosing their leaders through elections.

**Lingua franca:** a language used to communicate between people who speak different languages.

**Lunar calendar:** a calendar that divides the year into twelve months, each starting with the new moon. The lunar calendar year has 354 days, 11 days shorter than the Gregorian calendar used in the West.

# M

**Mahrajan (plural mahrajanat):** an outdoor festival that lasts for two or three days involving music, dance, food, and artifacts, usually attended by thousands of people.

**Mainstream culture:** the culture of the majority of the people, also referred to as the dominant culture.

**Majority:** the social or ethnic group that is most numerous and powerful within a society.

**Mandate:** a region that an outside country governs and controls.

**Mecca:** located in modern Saudi Arabia, it is the most important holy city to Muslims worldwide.

**Middle East:** term used mostly by Westerners to describe the area of southwest Asia and northeast Africa. The Middle East includes the countries of the League of Arab States plus Cyprus, Israel, part of Turkey, and Iran (which is Persian, not Arab).

**Minorities:** groups within a society that are different from the majority of people, or that have less access to political and economic power. In the United States, these include citizens of non-European background and foreign-born Americans.

**Monotheism:** the belief that there is only one God.

**Mosque:** the Muslim place of worship, similar to a church for Christians.

**Muhammad:** the prophet believed by Muslims to be the most recent and final messenger of God.

**Muslim:** A person who practices the Islamic religion (see Islam).

# N

**Nationalism:** the belief that citizens should have their own government, rather than be governed by an outside force.

**Native language:** the language spoken by the original inhabitants of an area. (A person's native language is the language he or she learned first.)

**Naturalization:** the process by which immigrants become citizens of a new country.

# O

**Ottoman Empire:** a Turkish Empire that dominated large portions of Asia Minor and southern Europe from about 1300 until the late 1500s. The Ottoman rule of Turkey ended in 1922.

# P

**Palestine:** region on the eastern shore of the Mediterranean Sea now comprised of Israel and parts of Jordan and Egypt. It is a very ancient region that was called Canaan in the Bible. Jews consider Palestine the holy land because it is the land God promised them in the Bible; it is also the holy land for Christians because it is where Jesus lived and preached; and for Muslims it is holy because they consider themselves the heirs of both Judaism and Christianity. Palestine was under Turkish Ottoman rule until 1920. After the Turks were on the losing side of World War I (1914–18), Palestine was under British control until 1948, when most of it was turned into the independent Jewish state of Israel.

**Palestinian National Council (PNC):** A legislative body that functions as a Palestinian government with citizens but no physical country.

**Palestinian Liberation Organization (PLO):** A coalition of several Palestinian organizations that acts under the supervision of the Palestine National Council (PNC).

For many years after its founding in 1964, the PLO used guerilla (suprise and undercover) war tactics to try to force Israel out of Palestine.

**Parent language:** a language from which two or more later languages evolved.

**Peddlers:** people who sell household goods door-to-door in areas not well-served by stores.

**Prejudice:** unjustified prejudgments about others on the basis of their group identity. This usually refers to unreasonable negative opinions and feelings about other groups.

**Profiling:** a system used by airports to help employees choose which passengers to single out for questioning and searches. It involves looking for certain characteristics that are thought to be more likely to identify a potentially problematic passenger. People of Arab descent have frequently been singled out as potential terrorists.

**Pull factors:** things that draw people from their homeland to another land, such as business opportunities, schooling, and the presence of family members who immigrated previously.

**Push factors:** things that force people to leave their homeland, such as economic depressions, wars, famine, or natural catastrophes.

# Q

**Quotas:** pertaining to immigration, limits that are placed on the number of immigrants from a particular country who come to live in another country.

**Qur'an:** also spelled Koran; the holy book for Muslims.

# R

**Ramadan:** the ninth lunar month during which Muslims fast from sunrise to sunset.

**Refugees:** people who leave their home countries due to wars and other hardships and seek refuge elsewhere.

**Remittances:** the money immigrants send to their home countries to support their families.

# S

**Salah:** the Arabic word for prayer.

**Second language acquisition:** learning to speak a second language.

**Second- and third-generation immigrants:** people who are born in one country but whose parents or grandparents were born in another country and immigrated to the country of the child's birth.

**Secular nationalism:** the belief that an independent country should be governed by nonreligious ideals, laws, and institutions.

**Secular:** nonreligious.

**Shahada:** the basic declaration of faith for Muslims that says, "There is no god but God, and Muhammad is his messenger." It is one of the five pillars of Islam.

**Shari'a:** the code of Islamic law.

**Sheik:** the leader of a family, village, or tribe.

**Shi'a:** a branch of Islam. The Shi'a have a significant following in Lebanon and southern Iraq. The majority of the people in the Middle Eastern (but non-Arab) country of Iran are Shi'a.

**Six Day War:** a conflict that started between Egypt and Israel on June 5, 1967, and lasted until June 10, 1967. Egypt's leader Gamal Abdal Nasser (1918-1970) blocked Israeli ships from passing through the Gulf of Aqaba (Israel's major access to trade with other countries) and began massing troops on the Israeli border. Concerned that it was about to be attacked, Israel moved first and invaded Egypt, taking possession of the Gaza Strip and the Sinai Peninsula as well as the Golan Heights of Syria and part of Jordan.

**Social justice:** fair and equal treatment of all groups in a society by others, and equal access to a reasonable standard of living and lifestyle.

**Socialism:** an economic system in which people of a country, through the government, own the means of production and distribution of goods and services—including factories, transportation, and communications.

**Stereotype:** an oversimplified and misleading image or idea about a group of people—including racial, ethnic, cultural, and religious groups. Stereotypes usually portray people in a negative and distorted way.

**Suez War:** in 1956 Egypt took control of the Suez Canal and was consequently invaded by Israel, Britain, and France.

**Sunni:** a branch of Islam. The majority of Muslims worldwide are Sunni Muslims.

# T

**Tabbouleh:** a salad of chopped parsley and tomato mixed with cracked wheat.

**Terrorist:** a person who uses violence or threats to accomplish goals, which are usually political.

# U

**U.S. Census Bureau:** the federal office responsible for counting the number of people living in the United States.

# W

**West Bank:** an area formerly known as Judea and Samaria, the West Bank of the Jordan River was occupied by Jordan from 1948 until 1967, when it was captured by Israel. It contains several important cities, including Bethlehem and the Old City of Jerusalem.

# Z

**Zionist:** A person who supports the existence of Israel as a Jewish nation in Palestine.

# Research and Activity Ideas

The following list of research and activity ideas is intended to offer suggestions for complementing social studies and history curricula, to trigger additional ideas for enhancing learning, and to suggest cross-disciplinary projects for library and classroom use.

**Arab-Israeli Conflict:** Study the history of the Arab-Israeli conflict and the current controversy surrounding the issue. Then form two teams—each taking a different side in the controversy—and debate the issues.

**Arab Music:** Choose one of the following musicians: Hassan Hakmoun, Hamza El Din, Ali Jihad Racy, or Simon Shaheen. Research his background and the type of music he performs. Obtain a copy of his tape or CD from your local library or music store and list the differences heard between his music and the music you hear on the radio.

**Artist's Book:** Arab American artist Etel Adnan writes poetry on accordian-like books that unfold to stretch twenty to thirty feet (see page 236). Try making your own artist's book. Take the longest paper you can find or tape several papers together to make a long strip. Use heavy paper and fold the strip like an accordian. Write your favorite poem or story on the paper then illustrate it using watercolor, color pencils, or another medium.

**Islamic Schools:** Go to your local or school library and research the several types of Islamic schools that have existed over time, both in the United States and the Arab world. Then select a type of Islamic school and set up a classroom. Choose one person to play the teacher, and three to five people to play the students. Discuss the similarities and differences between Islamic schools and your school.

**Life of a Politician:** Research the life of a well-known politician or public servant of Arabic descent. Find out what his or her major contributions to public service have been and what role the individual's ethnic background played in his or her career and political views.

**Map Identifications:** On a map of the Middle East, pinpoint the important religious cities, government centers, places of key battles, and rivers in the Arab world. For each site create a notecard that explains why these places are important and what happened in each location.

**Model Arab League:** Divide into small groups with each group selecting an Arab state to represent. Assign a topic or issue, for example, the Gulf War or the civil troubles in Lebanon. Each group will then prepare reports and presentations on what positions their state would most likely take on a given issue and why. After all the states have presented their cases, the entire group will debate the issue and attempt to come to some consensus or agreement over possible courses of action or statements of positions.

**Opening a Business:** Form a group and imagine each person is a part of your extended family and that together you're opening a business. Choose who will play each role (grandma, grandpa, aunt, cousin, etc.) Write a business plan describing what kind of business it will be, how you and your family will cover the costs of the building, operating expenses, etc., and what each family member's duty will be. Be sure to include the positive and negative aspects of having a family-owned business.

**Personal History:** Interview somebody who has immigrated to the United States (either from an Arab country, or from another country). To prepare for the interview, create a list of questions that arise from your research on what it was like to live in his or her home country (food, dress, schools, etc.).

**Stereotypes:** What are some of the stereotypes of Arabs? Give examples of stereotypes in films. Explain why stereotypes are harmful and offer ideas for what can be done to eliminate or counteract stereotypes.

**Traditional Arts:** Pick one of the Arab American traditional arts: henna, embroidery, or calligraphy. Explore its origins and find out if it is still widely practiced today. Present your discoveries; include visual aids, or invite an expert in to give a demonstration to your class.

**Volunteer:** Contact an Arab American organization and either offer to volunteer a few hours after school to help with a community service activity, or attend an event sponsored by that organization.

# ARAB AMERICAN ENCYCLOPEDIA

# Who Are the Arab Americans?

The United States of America is one of the most diverse nations on earth. Other than Native Americans (American Indians), every American can trace his or her background to some other nation or country. While Europeans were the first people to settle in North America, other groups followed, including people from the Arab world.

## The Arab world

The Arab world refers to the twenty-one Arab countries that cover vast territories extending from the African shores of the Atlantic Ocean to the Arab/Persian Gulf in Asia. These countries are members of the League of Arab States, also known as the Arab League. It was founded in 1945 to strengthen relationships, encourage cooperation, and mediate conflicts among its members.

The Arab world is the home of 260 million people. Arabic is the native language of the overwhelming majority (92 percent), and is a significant unifying force among the

## The Countries of the Arab World

The Arab countries in Africa include:

- Mauritania
- Morocco
- Algeria
- Tunisia
- Libya
- Egypt
- Sudan
- Somalia
- Djibouti

The Arab countries in Asia include:

- Syria
- Lebanon
- Iraq
- Jordan
- Palestine
- Saudi Arabia
- Bahrain
- Kuwait
- Oman
- Qatar
- The United Arab Emirates
- Yemen

Arab people. In addition to the Arabic language, Arabs have a shared history and cultural heritage that has given rise to their collective cultural, ethnic, and national Arab identity.

Yet, the Arab world is a diverse area with numerous religious and ethnic groups. The majority of Arabs are Muslims, but many Arabs are Christians, and a smaller number are Jews. The Arab world is also home to non-Arab ethnic groups, including the Chaldeans, Assyrians, Kurds, Berbers, and Armenians.

## Who are the Arab Americans?

Arab Americans are among the many ethnic groups that make up the population of the United States. They trace their ancestry (roots) to an Arab country such as Lebanon, Syria, Palestine, Yemen, Egypt, or Morocco.

Arabs have been coming to the United States since the late 1800s. Like other immigrants, they were attracted by economic and educational opportunities available in America. Since the 1970s the number of Arab Americans has increased rapidly due to changes in the U.S. immigration laws and to wars or economic hardships in many Arab countries. Arab Americans are one of the fastest growing minorities in the United States. Although statistics about their numbers vary, it is estimated that in 1995 there were three million Arab Americans. Some demographers (people who study populations) estimate that Arab Americans will number close to five million in the year 2000.

The first Arab immigrants were a relatively homogeneous group of people (similar to each other). They were mostly Christians from Syria and Lebanon. Many of them came from rural areas and had a limited amount of formal education. Palestinians, Jordanians, Yemeni, Iraqis, Egyptians, and people from other Arab countries followed. The more recent Arab immigrants, especially those who have arrived since the 1970s, tend to be more diverse in terms of their country of origin, religious background, and educational achievements (see chapter 4).

Arab Americans are found in almost every state, although they tend to cluster in a few major cities like New York, Chicago, Detroit, Los Angeles, San Francisco, and Boston. Some of these cities have neighborhoods with large concentrations of Arab Americans and have Arabic restaurants, grocery stores, and other businesses. The largest such Arab American neighborhood is found in Dearborn, Michigan.

Today Arab Americans are an extremely diverse group of people in every way imaginable. Approximately 50 percent are Christian and 50 percent are Muslim. Some Arab Americans trace their backgrounds to African countries, while others come from Asian countries. Some are born in the United States with American-born parents and grandparents and their knowledge of Arabic language is rather limited. Others are recent immigrants who are fluent in Arabic but speak little English. Arab Americans are also very diverse in terms of jobs and income. Some are professionals, like doctors and lawyers, while others work in factories or on farms and have limited incomes. Many Arab Americans own their own businesses. Some Arab American women stay home to raise their children and take care of their families, while others can be found in all kinds of professions.

## Fact Focus

- Arab Americans can trace their roots to the twenty-one countries of the Arab world. Twelve of these countries are in Asia and nine are in Africa.

- Ethnic and cultural diversity are becoming much more accepted in the United States. Today, many Arab Americans find it easier to claim their identity and cultural heritage than did their parents or grandparents.

- Athough Arab Americans are found in every state, the majority of them tend to live in large cities like New York, Detroit, and Los Angeles.

- The largest Arab American neighborhood is in Dearborn, Michigan.

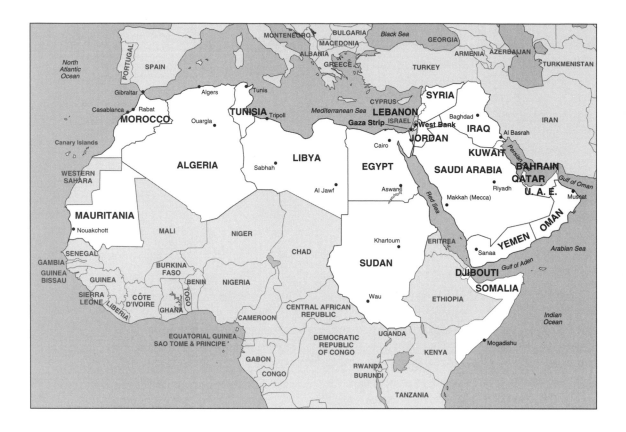

Map of the Arab countries. The Gaza Strip and parts of the West Bank are currently under Palestinian control. The final status of the borders, the final status of Jerusalem, and the future of Palestinian refugees are still under Palestinian-Israeli negotiation.

# Arab American identity

Despite their diversity, Arab Americans have much in common. They feel bound by a shared history, values, and culture. They trace their roots to the same region of the world. They speak Arabic—or their parents and grandparents did.

A person's identity is rather complex, and every person has multiple identities. Our gender (male or female), religion, ethnicity, nationality, political affiliation, and place of residence are all important ways in which we identify ourselves. A person can be a female, Muslim, Syrian American, Republican, and a New Yorker all at once. Which part of our identity is the most important varies from one person to another and changes with time and circumstances. In times of war, nationality may become the most important, like being Serbian or American. During an election, our political affiliation may become more important, such as being Republican, Democrat, or Independent.

Arab Americans are no different. While the majority of people who come from an Arab country identify themselves as Arab American, some also identify themselves in terms of their country of origin, such as Syrian American or Yemeni American, or in terms of their religion, such as Muslim American or Jewish American. On the other hand, some who trace their ancestry to an ethnic minority in the Arab world, such as the Chaldeans from Iraq, might identify themselves as Chaldean American or Iraqi American, rather than as Arab American.

Like many other ethnic groups in the United States, many second- and third-generation Arab Americans—people born in the United States whose parents or grandparents came as immigrants—have married outside their ethnic group and identify themselves as Americans. Although they might know a few Arabic words and eat some Arabic foods, they mostly identify with mainstream American culture rather than Arab American culture.

## Preserving Arab American identity

Like other ethnic groups, Arab Americans try to preserve their ethnic identity and culture. But for many, especially the earlier immigrants, maintaining Arab culture has not always been an easy or simple process.

Because northern Europeans were the first to settle in the United States, their culture became the dominant culture, often referred to as the mainstream culture. When Arab immigrants started coming to the United States in the late 1800s, they were a very small minority, and settled mostly in Boston and New York. While the first-generation immigrants (those who came from an Arab country) lived in their own ethnic enclaves (neighborhoods), pretty much isolated from the larger

Six boys at a street fair in Dearborn, Michigan. The largest Arab American neighborhood is found in Dearborn. *Reproduced by permission of Millard Berry.*

society, their children felt the pressure to assimilate (adopt the mainstream culture). At that time it was assumed that to be considered a loyal American a person should adopt the dominant culture. Many immigrants, including Arab Americans, accomplished this by changing their name and style of dress and speaking their native language only within the walls of their homes. Others, however, struggled to preserve their identity and culture by building institutions (including social clubs, churches, and mosques), establishing Arabic newspapers and radio shows, and teaching their children Arabic.

More recent immigrants from the Arab world who want to maintain their cultural identity have an easier time doing that. These new immigrants generally come to cities where there are already established Arab American communities. Also, they tend to have stronger ties with their country of origin. Many of the second- and third-generation Arab Americans (the children of the earlier immigrants), whose parents felt pressure to assimilate, are reclaiming their Arab American heritage. This is reflected in their art, literature, and theater and in the many national institutions they have built to address the needs and concerns of Arab Americans. The fact that ethnic and cultural diversity are becoming much more accepted in the United States has helped Arab Americans to preserve their ethnic identity and to be proud of their rich cultural heritage.

## For More Information

Abraham, Nabeel. "Arab Americans." In *Gale Encyclopedia of Multicultural America,* Vol. 1. Detroit: Gale Research, 1999.

Abraham, Nabeel, and Andrew Shryock, eds. *Arab Detroit: From Margin to Main Stream.* Detroit: Wayne State University Press, in press.

Abraham, Sameer, and Nabeel Abraham, eds. *Arabs in the New World: Studies on Arab-American Communities.* Detroit: Wayne State University Press, 1983.

Abu-Laban, Baha, and Michael Suleiman, eds. *Arab Americans: Continuity and Change.* Belmont, MA: Association of Arab-American University Graduates, 1989.

"The Arab Immigrant." *Aramco World Magazine,* September/October 1986.

Aswad, Barbara, ed. *Arabic Speaking Communities in American Cities.* Staten Island, NY: Center for Migration Studies, 1974.

Cole, Donald. *Immigrant City: Lawrence, Massachusetts, 1845-1921.* Chapel Hill: University of North Carolina Press, 1963.

Conklin, Nancy Faires, and Nora Faires. "Colored and Catholic: The Lebanese in Birmingham, Alabama." In *Crossing the Waters: Arabic-Speaking Immigrants to the United States before 1940,* edited by Eric Hooglund. Washington, D.C.: Smithsonian Institution Press, 1987.

 **Words to Know**

- **Assimilate:** when a person or a group drops their own culture (such as changing their name and style of dress) and adopts the majority culture, usually referred to as the dominant or mainstream culture.

- **Demographics:** the study of the characteristics of human populations and the classification of them into categories such as age, education, profession, or ethnicity.

- **Diverse:** refers to groups of people that are of different national, racial, religious, and ethnic backgrounds.

- **Ethnic group:** a group of people who speak the same language, share many cultural habits and traditions, or have a common history.

- **First-generation immigrants:** people who were born in one country and then immigrated to another.

- **Homogeneous:** refers to groups of people that are of similar national, racial, religious, and ethnic backgrounds.

- **Mainstream culture:** the culture of the majority of the people, also referred to as the dominant culture.

- **Second- and third-generation immigrants:** people who are born in one country but whose parents or grandparents were born in another country and immigrated to the the country of the child's birth.

Haiek, Joseph R. *Arab-American Almanac.* 4th ed. Glendale, CA: News Circle Publishing House, 1992.

Harik, Elsa Marston. *The Lebanese in America.* Minneapolis: Lerner Publication Company, 1987.

Hooglund, Eric, ed. *Crossing the Waters: Arabic-Speaking Immigrants to the United States before 1940.* Washington, D.C.: Smithsonian Institution Press, 1987.

Hooglund, Eric, ed. *Taking Root: Arab-American Community Studies.* Vol. 2. Washington, D.C.: American-Arab Anti-Discrimination Committee, 1985.

Naff, Alixa. *The Arab Americans.* New York: Chelsea House Publications, 1988.

Naff, Alixa. *Becoming American: The Early Arab Immigrant Experience.* Carbondale: Southern Illinois University Press, 1985.

Shakir, Evelyn. *Bint Arab: Arab and Arab American Women in the United States.* Westport, CT: Praeger, 1997.

Suleiman, Michael, ed. *Arabs in America: Building a New Future.* Philadelphia: Temple University Press, in press.

Zogby, James, ed., and Pat Aufderheide and Anne S. Mooney, asst. eds. *Taking Root Bearing Fruit: The Arab American Experience.* Washington, D.C.: American-Arab Anti-Discrimination Committee,, 1984.

*Anan Ameri is the Cultural Arts Director of the Arab Community Center for Economic and Social Services (ACCESS). She received her B.A. from the Jordanian University in Amman, Jordan, her M.A. from Cairo University in Egypt, and her Ph.D. in Sociology from Wayne State University in Detroit, Michigan.*

# Early History

## 2

## What is the Arab world?

The Arab world covers a vast territory that includes much of northern and eastern Africa and western Asia. This region, along with Turkey and Iran, is commonly known as the Middle East, although Arabs don't refer to themselves as Middle Easterners. There are twenty-one Arab nations in the world today (see chapter 1).

Arabs, as a group, often speak the same language, share many cultural habits and traditions, and have a common history. For this reason they are thought of as an ethnic group. But the Arab world is ethnically diverse and many ethnic groups besides Arabs live in Arab nations. Kurds live in present-day Turkey, Iran, and Iraq; Chaldeans live in northern Iraq; Berbers reside in much of North Africa; and Armenians are scattered throughout many eastern Mediterranean nations. These four ethnic groups each have their own language. Kurds and Berbers are Muslims, while Armenians and Chaldeans are Christians. All four are culturally similar to the Arabs and most speak Arabic in addition to their own language.

The streets of Cairo, one of the largest cities in the world, are always congested with vehicle and pedestrian traffic. *Reproduced by permission of Corey Langley.*

Although the neighboring nations of Turkey and Iran share similar histories and cultures with the Arab world, the majority of their citizens are not Arabs, nor do they speak Arabic. In Israel, a predominantly Jewish state, Hebrew is the national language, but about 20 percent of Israeli citizens are Palestinian Arabs.

Traditionally, some Arabs have been tribal nomads, or Bedouins (pronounced BED-O-wins), who travel with their herds of camels, goats, and sheep from oasis to oasis. (An oasis is a fertile area with water surrounded by desert.) Most rural Arabs are farmers who live along fertile rivers or coastal areas. Sixty percent of the population of the Arab world, however, now live in cities. As a crossroad between east and west, the Arab world has long been a center for trade, with many cities or commercial urban centers. Cities like Damascus in Syria and Jericho in Palestine are among the oldest continuously inhabited cities in the world, and Cairo, Egypt, is one of the largest cities in the world.

The land in the Arab world is as geographically diverse as it is in the United States. Large portions are predominantly arid (dry), including the vast Sahara and Arabian deserts. Mountain ranges cut across many Arab states, including Morocco, Lebanon, and Syria, as well as the southern Arabian Peninsula. The coastal areas are more fertile, and many Arab states enjoy a Mediterranean climate with warm, dry summers and rainy winters. The fertile areas along two major river systems, the Nile and the Tigris and Euphrates, have been centers of civilizations since ancient times.

## Pre-Islamic history

Many of the world's oldest civilizations evolved in the Arab world. From 7000 B.C.E. (before the common era, or "before Christ") the area known as the Fertile Crescent—along the Tigris and Euphrates Rivers in present-day Iraq—gave rise to many powerful empires. The Babylonian Empire lasted more than four centuries and by 1750 B.C.E. had created one of the first legal systems with written laws (the Hammurabi Code). The Nile River was the center for the empires of the pharaohs (Egyptian kings), the pyramids of ancient Egypt, and the Kushites in the Sudan.

In Tunisia and Lebanon, the Carthaginian and Phoenician Empires (1000 B.C.E.–700 B.C.E.) were centers for flourishing civilizations based on trade and commerce. The Phoenicians created one of the first written alphabets. These empires fell to the Greek Empire by 700 B.C.E. Eventually, North Africa and the entire eastern Mediterranean were conquered and incorporated into the Roman Empire.

In the Arabian Peninsula, the cities of Mecca and Medina grew rich from the trade in very expensive and desir-

 **Fact Focus**

- The Arab world stretches from Morocco in North Africa to the Persian (Arab) Gulf in western Asia.

- Many early civilizations emerged in the Arab world and a number of the world's oldest cities are found there.

- Three of the world's major religions—Judaism, Christianity, and Islam—originated in the Arab world.

- The Umayyad and Abbasid Caliphates were major empires in the Arab world from 650 to 950. During this "golden age," the Arab world was the center of a vibrant cultural, artistic, and scientifically advanced civilization.

- In the Battle of Yarmuk in 637, Arab women carrying tent poles led charges against the Byzantine army.

abie fragrant incenses and perfumes. Mecca was also a holy spot to which Bedouin tribes made pilgrimages, or travels, to worship at religious sites.

Throughout much of the Arabian Peninsula, and the ancient world in general, polygamy (having more than one wife) was relatively common among tribal nomads and the wealthy. Although Islamic law allowed the practice of polygamy, it also granted legal rights to women many centuries before similar rights were granted in Christian societies. In practice, most Muslims had only one wife and monogamy (having only one wife) has been the norm throughout most of the Arab world.

# Arab/Islamic empires

According to Muslim faith, by 610 C.E. (common era, also called A.D.) the prophet Muhammad, a merchant in the city of Mecca, began to receive revelations from *Allah*. (Allah is the word for God in Arabic.) These revelations were eventually written down in the *Qur'an* (also written Koran; Muslim holy book) and became the foundation for Islam, one of the major world religions (see Chapter 7). Within a few decades, the majority of the Arabs in the Arabian Peninsula had converted to Islam. After Muhammad's death in 632, his followers gathered together to select a Caliph (the religious and political leader of the Muslim community) to rule. The first four Caliphs were dynamic, energetic rulers who ruled over a growing Arab/Islamic Empire. The fifth Caliph came from the wealthy and powerful Umayyad family and he moved the capital from Mecca to Damascus in present-day Syria. His family continued to rule until they were overthrown in 750.

Within one hundred years the Arab/Islamic Empire spread westward from Arabia to North Africa, into the Iberian Peninsula (present-day Spain and Portugal), and for a short time into France. At the same time, it spread eastward all the way to the Indus River (present-day Pakistan). As the Arab armies moved northward out of Arabia, they moved into territory held by the Byzantine Empire, a remnant of the old Roman Empire. At the Battle of Yarmuk (in present-day Syria) in 637, the Arabs decisively defeated the Byzantine forces. These early Arab armies traveled with their entire families and

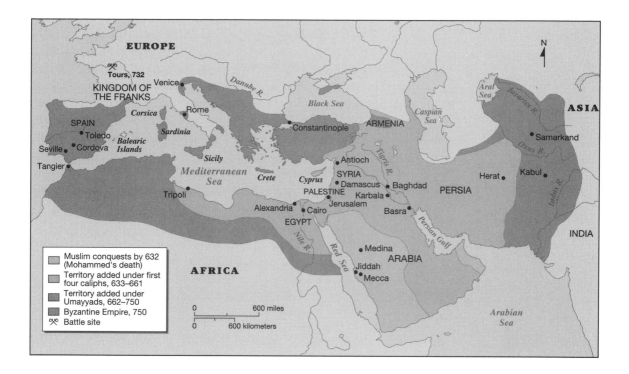

women took part in battles. During the Battle of Yarmuk, Arab women led charges against the Byzantine army by carrying long, pointed tent poles.

Although conquered peoples in most earlier empires had been forced to convert to the religions and practices of the ruling power, the Arabs did not force people to convert to Islam. Nor were the conquered peoples forced to assimilate or adopt Arab culture. Under Islamic law, "People of the Book" (Jews and Christians) could not be forced to convert. They also did not serve in the military, but they did have to pay an additional tax. However, the taxes levied by the new Arab/Islamic Empire were often lower than those under previous rulers.

As a result of this generally kind treatment, and the benefits in trade, political power, and status that could be gained from belonging to the Muslim community, most people from North Africa who came to live on the Indus River gradually converted to Islam. Over time, Arabic became the dominant language of all the people within the empire. The entire territory from North Africa to the Arab/Persian Gulf was gradually Arabized (adopting the Arabic language and culture) and Islamicized (adopting the Muslim religion), although some groups chose to keep their own language and religion.

From 650 to 750 the vast Arab/Islamic Empire was ruled by the Umayyad Caliphate. Damascus, the capital of the Umayyad empire, soon became a major commercial and cultural center. By 750 the Umayyad dynasty was overthrown by the Abbasid Caliphs, named after Abbas, the first Caliph in this dynasty or line of rulers. The Abbasids built a new, lavish capital in Baghdad. Known as the City of Peace, Baghdad became the fabled city in the novel *Tales of the Arabian Nights*. The Abbasid Empire reached the peak of its power under Caliph Harun al-Rashid in the late 700s. At the same time, the Umayyads established rich, glorious cities in Cordoba and Granada in Spain. Known as the Moorish Empire in the West, the Umayyads ruled much of Spain until 1492, when they were removed during the Christian reconquest.

## The Arab/Islamic golden age

During the so-called Golden Age of Islam, the Caliphs in Damascus and Baghdad encouraged practice in the arts, education, literature, and science. Arab scholars became world famous for their work in the sciences, particularly astronomy and geometry, and in medicine. The major contributions of Arab scholars included the use of the zero, the identification and naming of many star constellations, and advances in the fields of navigation, optics (the science that deals with light), and medical care.

Arabs were also important in saving and translating Greek works for the use of future generations. Poetry was especially popular; Arab rulers were keen supporters, or patrons, of court poets, musicians, and artists. Because the depiction of human bodies was discouraged by Islam, Muslim artists were known for their use of decorative geometric patterns and Arabesques (ornate designs of intertwined vines, leaves, and flowers). Calligraphy, finely designed ornamental writing, was used to decorate many buildings, books, and glass or ceramic wares.

Umayyad and Abbasid Caliphs were also enthusiastic builders. They financed the construction of the vast Umayyad mosque in Damascus, the Dome of the Rock and al-Aqsa

mosques in Jerusalem, and the Ibn Tulun mosque in Cairo, among many others. The Alhambra, or "Red Castle," in Spain is one of the most elaborate and well-preserved court palaces that still stands today. They also built huge hospitals, soup kitchen complexes (to feed the needy), and *suqs* (markets with many stalls selling different things).

**Palestinian woman pray outside Jerusalem's Dome of the Rock.** *Reproduced by permission of Corbis Corporation (Bellevue).*

## Decline of Arab empires

Like most vast, complex empires, the Arab empires were weakened by internal disputes and external enemies. Local rulers frequently broke away from the main or centralized government to establish their own independent political units. By 950, the Caliphs in Baghdad had lost control over North Africa, Egypt, and much of western Asia.

The political weakness of the Arab world in the 1090s enabled Christian Crusaders (armies that invaded in the

**Salahed-Din was a successful leader of the Muslim armies against European Christians during the first Crusades.**

*Reproduced by permission of Corbis Corporation (Bellevue).*

name of Christianity) from Europe to conquer Jerusalem and the territory along the eastern Mediterranean. The Crusaders sought to regain control of Christian holy places, especially the city of Jerusalem. While some soldiers were sincere Christians, many others joined the Crusades for adventure and the possibility of becoming wealthy from conquest and taking goods from conquered peoples. But by 1187, unified Arab/Muslim forces under Salahed-Din (Saladin) retook Jerusalem and began to push the Crusaders out of the Arab world. The last Crusader kingdom fell in 1291.

Impressed by the richness of Arab/Islamic culture and lifestyles, Christian Crusaders returned to Europe with new foods, styles of dress, music, and manufactured goods. This contributed to a growing demand in Europe for goods, particularly textiles (woven cloth materials) and spices, from the Arab world. Italian city-states established direct commercial ties with the Arab world and grew rich from the east-west trade. This wealth helped to provide the financial support for a major growth in artistic and cultural activities in Europe. This era of dynamic creativity in the arts, architecture, literature, and music is known as the Renaissance.

In the 1300s, much of the Arab world, particularly Baghdad, was devastated by the Mongols (nomadic armies from central Russia). The Mongols were known as expert horseback riders and as cruel and often extremely violent conquerors. The Mongol leader Timurlane conquered all of Persia and Iraq in the late 1300s. Although he was a Muslim, Timurlane, who was known for his ruthless treatment of conquered peoples, was viewed as the "scourge of God" (feared and hated conqueror) by Muslims and Christians. After his death, Timurlane's kingdom immediately collapsed and local leaders reasserted their authority.

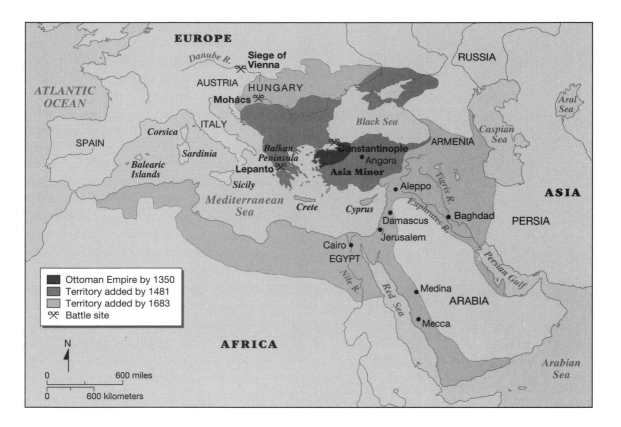

The map legend reads:

- Ottoman Empire by 1350
- Territory added by 1481
- Territory added by 1683
- ✄ Battle site

# Expansion of the Ottoman Empire

Meanwhile, an ethnic Turkish/Muslim dynasty emerged in the Anatolian Peninsula (present-day Turkey). Founded by Osman, the Ottoman Empire (a mispronunciation of the name Osman) conquered all of Anatolia, the Balkans of south-central Europe, and by 1517, the Arab provinces. The Ottomans ruled the Arab world (except for Morocco, which it never conquered) from the 1500s to the twentieth century. Arabs constituted the largest ethnic group within the Ottoman Empire, outnumbering all other ethnic groups, including the Turks.

The Ottomans also established direct control throughout the Balkans and twice reached the gates of Vienna, deep in European territory in present-day Austria. Consequently, the exchanges between the Ottoman Empire and the West (Christian western Europeans) were often hostile, although trade continued to flourish when the two sides were at war.

The Ottoman Empire, showing territories added up to 1683.

The Ottoman government, like that of most huge, diverse empires, was highly centralized—meaning that most of the political power was held by the central government. The leader of the empire, the sultan, ruled from the capital of Constantinople (later known as Istanbul). The empire was divided into provinces, each with its own governor, who was appointed by the sultan. Territories that were far from the center of power in Turkey, however, enjoyed considerable local autonomy (freedom). The Arab territories of Algeria, Sudan, and Kuwait were often ruled on a day-to-day basis by local rulers with little outside interference from the Ottomans.

Islam was one of the major forces holding this diverse empire together. Because the empire both defended and protected the Muslims, the Ottomans believed the empire was "the sword and guardian of Islam." Arabs and other ethnic groups within the empire enjoyed a great deal of upward mobility and often reached high positions within the government (only the sultanate was reserved for the sons from the family of Osman). Until its long decline beginning in the 1700s, the Ottoman Empire was, in many ways, the continuation of the past glorious empires during the Golden Age of Islam. When the empire was strong and the sultans were dynamic leaders, the Arabs and others within the empire often prospered.

Under the ruler Suleiman the Magnificent in the mid-1500s, the Ottoman Empire reached the peak of its power. During this time the Turkish Ottomans incorporated many earlier Arab artistic styles into their buildings, ceramics, textiles, and literature. Many Ottoman mosques and monumen-

**Suleiman the Magnificent.**
*Reproduced by permission of Corbis Corporation (Bellevue).*

tal structures are still to be found in modern Arab cities such as Cairo.

As the Ottoman Empire began to decline in the 1700s, corruption and economic depression caused hardships throughout the empire, including the Arab provinces, and the Ottoman Empire became known as the "Sick Man of Europe." During this time Great Britain and France became increasingly imperialistic (seeking control of territory, resources, and people outside their own borders) and both began to interfere politically, economically, and sometimes militarily in Arab territories on the edges of the Ottoman Empire. By the mid-1800s Arabs attempted to reassert their own identity and began to consider ways to break away from Ottoman control. In spite of these pressures, the Ottoman Empire survived and retained control over most of the Arab world until World War I (1914-18).

# For More Information

as-Saffar, Muhammad. *Disorienting Encounters: Travels of a Moroccan Scholar in France in 1843-1846: The Voyage of Muhammad as-Saffar,* edited and translated by Susan Gilson Miller. Berkeley: University of California Press, 1992.

Fisher, Sydney Nettleton, and William Ochsenwald. *The Middle East: A History.* 5th ed. Vol. 1. New York: McGraw-Hill, 1997.

Maalouf, Amin. *The Crusades through Arab Eyes,* translated by Jon Rothschild. New York: Schocken Books, 1989.

Maalouf, Amin. *Leo Africanus,* translated by Peter Sluglett. New York: New Amsterdam Books, 1992.

Shabbas, Audrey, and Ayad Al-Qazzaz, eds. *Arab World Notebook.* Berkeley, CA: Najda (Women Concerned About the Middle East), 1989.

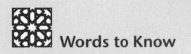 **Words to Know**

- **Arabize:** when a society adopts the language and culture of the Arabs as their own.

- **B.C.E. (before the common era):** another term for B.C., which stands for "before Christ" (referring to the birth of the Christian figure Jesus Christ).

- **Bedouins:** nomadic peoples who often herd livestock and trade as they move from place to place.

- **Caliphs:** the religious and political leaders of the Muslim community after the death of Muhammad.

- **C.E. (common era):** another term for A.D., which means "after death" (referring to the death of the Christian figure Jesus Christ).

- **Crusaders:** European Christian armies who attempted to conquer parts of the Muslim Arab world.

- **Fertile Crescent:** the area along the Tigris and Euphrates Rivers in present-day Iraq.

- **Islamicize:** when a society adopts the Muslim faith as their own.

- **Oasis:** a fertile area with water surrounded by desert.

- **Qur'an:** also spelled Koran; the holy book for Muslims.

Wibke, Walther. *Women in Islam*. Princeton: M. Wiener Publishers, 1993.

*Janice Terry is a professor of Middle Eastern History at Eastern Michigan University. She holds an M.A. in Arab Studies from the American University of Beruit and a Ph.D. in Oriental and African Studies from the University of London.*

# Modern History

**3**

## The Arab world in the 1800s

The Ottoman Empire, which was based in Constantinople (present-day Istanbul, Turkey) and controlled by ethnic Turks, ruled the Arab world from the early 1500s to the early 1900s. By the 1850s, the once glorious and powerful empire was in a very weak state. Indeed, it was known in the West as the "Sick Man of Europe." As the empire declined, the Arab people suffered from poverty and from the inefficiency and corruption of the Ottoman government. At the same time more powerful Western nations, such as France and Great Britain, were seeking to militarily and economically use other countries for their own benefit. They took advantage of the weak Ottoman Empire by taking control of Arab territory in Africa and the Middle East.

## European imperialism

Despite Algerian resistance, the more militarily powerful French conquered Algeria in 1830. In 1881 the French expanded into neighboring Tunisia and in 1912 added Mo-

**French troops hunting Algerian rebels, c. 1956.**

*Reproduced by permission of Corbis Corporation (Bellevue).*

rocco to their empire. Tunisia and Morocco would not become independent until the 1950s, and Algeria had to fight a bloody war before achieving independence in 1962. In 1882 Great Britain invaded Egypt and later occupied the Sudan. The British wanted to control Egypt because of the Suez Canal—a vital link for communication and transportation within the huge empire. Great Britain also took direct control over Aden (South Yemen). During the nineteenth century, the British signed alliances, or treaties of friendship, with local rulers around the Arabian Peninsula in order to control the sea lanes and key ports in the region.

Although the Ottoman Empire tried to reform its government and military, it was powerless to stop the European nations from taking the Arab territories. The reforms the Ottomans enacted also failed to improve the economic and political conditions in the Arab world. A few cities in the Arab world prospered as commercial and trading centers, but the majority of Arabs remained poor peasants who worked as tenant farmers on land owned by feudal lords.

## Christian missionaries

In the 1800s, Christian missionaries from Europe and the United States began to establish schools, hospitals, and churches in Arab territories. They enjoyed close contact with Christian Arabs, particularly in Lebanon and Palestine. Although not many Muslims converted to Christianity, many wealthy Arabs and those living in urban areas were influenced by Western ideas and technology. Universities such as the American University of Beirut provided Western educators and exposed a new generation of the Arab elite (the wealthy) to the political ideals of liberal democracy and secular nationalism. Liberal democracy is the idea that citizens should have a say—usually through voting—in how their country is governed, and secular nationalism suggests that countries be self-governed (nationalism) by non-religious (secular) ideals, laws, and institutions.

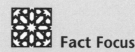 **Fact Focus**

- As the Ottoman Empire declined, Arab desires for national independence increased.

- In the 1800s, European nations took over a number of Arab territories. France took over Algeria and Tunisia, while Great Britain took over Palestine, Egypt, the Sudan, and the territory along the coastal area of the Arabian Peninsula.

- From the mid-1940s to the late 1980s, the United States and the Soviet Union, two superpowers, sought to dominate the Arab world. The Arab world is important because of its strategic geographic location between the East and West and because it controls the largest oil reserves in the world.

- The Arab-Israeli conflict led to five major wars; the struggle for Palestinian self-determination remains a major issue.

## Arab nationalism

By the 1850s, Arab nationalist leaders, who often came from Greater Syria (present-day Syria, Lebanon, Jordan, Palestine, and Israel), began to organize against both Ottoman and Western domination. Arab nationalists wanted one unified, independent Arab nation. They also wanted this nation to be secular (not based on religion) and democratic (in which people elect their own leaders). Some other ethnic groups in the Ottoman Empire, including the Armenians and Kurds, also grew more nationalistic. In 1914 the Ottoman government joined World War I on the side of the Central Powers (Germany and Austria-Hungary) against the Allies (Great Britain, France, Russia, and, ultimately, the United States). The Arabs, however, sided with the Allies with the hope that if they fought against the Ottoman Empire the Allies would grant them independence once the war was over.

# World War I and the changing Arab world

World War I (1914-18) was a major turning point in Arab history. During this period, the British signed three conflicting agreements about what to do with the Arab territories of the Ottoman Empire once the war was over.

### British-Arab agreement

The first agreement, the Sherif Husayn-McMahon Correspondence (1915-16), was between the Arabs and the British. In a secret exchange of letters, the British agreed to support an Arab revolt led by the Arab nationalist Sherif Husayn, a religious and political leader in the holy city of Mecca. The British hoped that the Arab revolt would weaken the Ottoman Empire's war effort, thereby helping their own.

In exchange for their alliance with the British during the war, the Arabs were to be granted an independent Arab nation when the war was over. The Arab nation was to include territory that everyone, including the British, agreed had a majority Arab population. This included the present-day nations of Syria, Jordan, Saudi Arabia, Palestine, and Israel. Because the British wanted Iraq—where the land was rich with petroleum—and France wanted Lebanon, these countries were not included in the proposed Arab state.

In 1916 the Arabs rose up in an armed revolt against the Ottoman Empire. Believing that they were to become independent when the war was over, the Arabs fought with the British on the side of the Allies for the remainder of the war.

### British-French agreement

At the same time they made the agreement with the Arabs, the British made another secret arrangement. The second agreement, the Sakes Picot Agreement of 1916, was between the British and the French. Under this agreement, Turkey, the heartland of the Ottoman Empire, was to be divided (partitioned) among the winning Allies. Further, the Arab world was to be divided between the British and the French. France was to get direct control (mandates) over Syria and Lebanon, and Britain was to control Iraq, Jordan, and Palestine. Britain was also to receive a "sphere of influence" over present-day Saudi Arabia. Britain didn't request total control over Saudi Arabia because in 1916 no one knew that the territory contained vast resources of petroleum.

## Balfour Declaration

To complicate matters further, the British made a third agreement. This agreement was between the British and the Zionists, or Jewish nationalists, who actively sought to establish a Jewish state (Israel) in Palestine, a part of their holy land, since the late 1800s. In 1917 the British issued the public Balfour Declaration. Named after the sitting British foreign secretary, Lord Balfour, the Balfour Declaration stated that "His Majesty's Government views with favor the establishment of a Jewish homeland in Palestine." Although the wording in the declaration was vague, the statement did seem to promise British support for the Zionists to establish a Jewish state in Palestine.

The Balfour Declaration also stressed that Zionist efforts should not prejudice the existing rights of Jews elsewhere or the "civil and religious" rights of the non-Jewish population in Palestine. Under this declaration, the Palestinian Arabs, then 90 percent of the population in Palestine, were not named; neither were they consulted about the statement before its publication. Not surprisingly, the Palestinians and other Arabs opposed the Balfour Declaration.

These three contradictory agreements provoked many conflicts that remain unresolved at the end of the twentieth century. Under the terms of these three agreements, parts of Arab territory were promised to three different groups: the Arabs, the French and the British, and the Zionists (Jewish nationalists).

## The Arab world after World War I

After World War I, the victorious Allies held an international conference in Paris in 1919 to decide what to do in the aftermath of the war. Woodrow Wilson, president of the United States, publicly stated his support for the self-determination (national independence) of all the peoples of the world. As a result, nationalists from all over the world, including Sherif Husayn's son, Prince Feisal, came to Paris to argue for national independence. In spite of British, French, and Zionist opposition, the Arabs hoped Woodrow Wilson and the United States would help them gain national independence.

To decide what should be done with the Arab territories of the Ottoman Empire, Wilson wanted an international commission to travel to the Middle East to find out what the people wanted. The British, French, and Zionists opposed such a commission because they wanted to dominate the region and they knew that the Arabs wanted independence. As a result, they refused to participate in the commission. Wilson then appointed an American taskforce, the King-Crane Commission, to ask the Arabs what they wanted. In their fact-finding tour, the King-Crane Commission found that the majority of the Arabs wanted independence, but by the time the King-Crane Commission delivered its report, the British and French had already decided to divide the Arab territory. Thus, the Sakes Picot Agreement was implemented—France received mandates over Syria and Lebanon, and Britain received mandates over Iraq, Jordan, and Palestine.

The Arabs were not granted independence and their territory was divided into separate nations under the control of France and Britain. Although the Zionists did not immediately get an independent Jewish state, the British did allow more Jews to settle in Palestine and often favored the Zionists politically.

# Arab opposition to foreign control

From the 1920s to the 1940s, Arabs continued to struggle—militarily, politically, and economically—against imperial domination. The French and the British repeatedly had to use military force to defeat Arab nationalist movements.

## Syria and Lebanon

The Syrians never accepted French control and fought against it until they became independent after World War II, in 1946. In Lebanon, the French established a confessional system of government in which political power was divided along religious lines. This system favored the Christian Maronites, who had historical connections to the French. The confessional system contributed to a long civil war from the mid-1970s to the mid-1980s. It also caused many of the problems that continue to plague Lebanon into the twenty-first century. To escape the violence and to find jobs, many Lebanese immigrated to the United States and other western nations.

## Egypt

A full-scale revolution against British control erupted in Egypt in 1919. Faced with massive strikes, boycotts, and demonstrations—many of them led by women—the British put in place a constitution that provided for an Egyptian king to rule along with a democratically elected Parliament (British rule). The British, however, continued to interfere directly in Egyptian politics whenever they felt their interests were threatened. The Egyptian monarchy continued to rule, with indirect British control, until it was overthrown in a revolution led by Gamal Abdal Nasser in 1952.

## Iraq

After using military force to subdue local opposition, the British installed Feisal (Sherif Husayn's son) as king of an inde-

**Gamal Abdal Nasser (1918-1970).** *Reproduced by permission of the United Nations.*

pendent Iraq. Britain retained indirect control of Iraq through a series of treaties that allowed it to intervene militarily whenever its interests were threatened. That indirect control continued until the monarchy was overthrown in a military-led revolution in 1958.

### Jordan

In Jordan, the British chose Abdullah, Sherif Husayn's eldest son and Feisal's brother, to become king. His family, the Hashemites, continues to rule Jordan into the twenty-first century.

### Palestine

Great Britain kept direct control over Palestine, where it had major strategic and political interests. Until the end of World War II, Britain tried to balance the conflicting nationalist demands of the Zionists for a Jewish state and the Palestinian demands for an Arab state. As the Jewish population in Palestine increased during the 1930s, the conflicts between the Zionists and Palestinians grew.

## The Arab-Israeli conflict

After World War II, neither the British nor the French were strong enough militarily or economically to hold onto their empires, and the Arabs gradually gained their independence. In 1947, the British turned the problem of Palestine over to the newly formed United Nations. The United Nations, a newly formed international organization devoted to keeping peace and fostering cooperation among nations, recommended that Palestine be divided into a Jewish state and an Arab state. Under the United Nations plan, about 50 percent of Palestine, including the most fertile land, was allotted to the Zionists, who at the time only made up about one-third of the population and only owned about 20 percent of the land. The other half of Palestine was to go to the Palestinian Arabs, who owned most of the land. The Palestinians and other Arabs opposed this division. When the Zionists declared the independent state of Israel in 1948, war immediately broke out.

The Israelis won the 1948 war and added more territory under their control; over 800,000 Palestinians lost their homes and livelihoods. Many escaped and became refugees in surrounding Arab nations.

The Arab-Israeli conflict resulted in major wars in 1956, 1967, 1973, and 1982. The Israelis won these wars. In 1967 Israel occupied all of historic Palestine and parts of Egyptian and Syrian territory as well. These conflicts and upheavals forced many Arabs to immigrate to the United States or other nations around the world in search of jobs and more peaceful places in which to raise their families.

None of these wars led to peace or to a resolution of Palestinian demands for self-determination. Even peace treaties between Israel, Egypt, and Jordan—and some agreements with the Palestinians—have failed to resolve the issue of Palestinian rights. As long as the Palestinians remain displaced and without a state of their own, the conflict and violence seem likely to continue.

# The Cold War and the Arab world

The Cold War, lasting from the mid-1940s to the late 1980s, was a period of heightened tensions between the United States and its allies and the Soviet Union and its allies. During this time the Arab world became a focus of the rivalry between these two, both of whom wanted to dominate this strategic region due to its vital oil reserves. Most Arabs, however, did not want to be dominated by either superpower, and continued to struggle for real independence. Secular Arab nationalism peaked under the leadership of Gamal Abdal Nasser, the leader of Egypt, in the 1950s and 1960s. Nasser attempted, but failed, to stay neutral in the Cold War. Although he did not grant full democratic rights to Egyptian citizens, Nasser supported education, women's rights, and several social welfare programs.

Over 800,000 Palestinians lost their homes and livelihoods as a result of the Arab-Israeli conflict. These Arab refugees, unable to find shelter in houses or tents, were forced to establish dwellings in the open air. *Reproduced by permission of Corbis Corporation (Bellevue).*

During the Cold War, some Arab states, including Egypt, Iraq, and Syria, adopted socialism as a means toward economic development. Socialism is an economic system in which people of a country, through the government, own the means of production and distribution of goods and services—including factories, transportation, and communications. The socialist Arab nations tended to support the Soviet Union. Other Arab states, however, particularly Saudi Arabia and Jordan, developed close ties to the United States. These states tended to favor capitalist economic systems, which are based on private rather than public ownership of the means of production and distribution.

## Oil boom and economic wealth

Although the commercial production of oil was well under way in the Arab/Persian Gulf region as early as the 1930s, it was the oil boom of the 1970s that made some oil-producing Arab states very rich. Libya, Saudi Arabia, and Kuwait began to have some of the highest per capita (per person) incomes in the world. The oil-rich nations used their petro-dollars (oil revenues) to build modern cities with advanced communication systems, roads, hospitals, and schools. Kuwait and other wealthy Arab states had complete welfare systems for all their citizens, providing free schooling and health care as well as low-cost loans for housing and new businesses.

Most of the oil-rich nations, however, had very small populations in the 1970s. At the time, the majority of Arabs lived in nations such as Egypt, Syria, and Yemen, which have little or no oil and few other natural resources. Consequently, most Arab nations remained poor. In Yemen, the poorest Arab country, civil wars and political instability led to violence and increased poverty. In search of jobs and safe homes for their families, many Yemenis immigrated to the United States.

The wealth of the Arab world remains unequally distributed. A small percentage of people live very well, while the vast majority struggle to survive economically. The great imbalance between the number of rich and poor people continues to be a source of political strife and dissatisfaction.

# Iraq and the Arab/Persian Gulf

With its vast oil reserves and strategic location, the Arab/Persian Gulf is important to the United States and the rest of the Western world. When the conservative, pro-West monarchy of the shah in Iran was overthrown in an Islamic-led revolution in 1979, many rulers in neighboring Arab states feared that Islamic revolutions might take place in their own countries.

Iraq, with the support of other Arab and Western countries, tried to limit the power of Iran's new government through war. For eight years during the 1980s the Iran-Iraq war dragged on. Neither side won this war, but both suffered enormous human and economic losses. After this war, Saddam Hussein, the dictator of Iraq, attempted to regain economic and political advantage by invading neighboring Kuwait in August 1990. This aggression resulted in a United States-led coalition, which included Arab and Western na-

Arial view of an oil drilling rig in the Saybah field in Saudi Arabia. The oil boom of the 1970s made this oil-producing state very rich.
*Reproduced by permission of Corbis Corporation (Bellevue).*

tions, to free Kuwait and remove Saddam Hussein from power. To do this, the United States and its coalition used military force and economic sanctions (cutting off trade) against Iraq. It was known as the Gulf War.

The Gulf War of 1991 was a military success for the allied coalition, yet the political and military future of the Arab world remains uncertain. After years of devastating economic sanctions and the deaths of approximately one million Iraqis—mostly women and children—Saddam Hussein remains firmly in power. As a result of these wars, more Arabs were forced to flee their homes. Many Iraqis became refugees in other Arab nations, or fled to Western nations, including the United States.

## Democracy versus dictatorship

The wars of the 1960s, 1970s, and 1980s did not lead to democracy. Most Arab regimes remained dictatorships.

Some, such as Iraq and Syria, were military dictatorships, or one-party states, while others, such as Saudi Arabia and the United Arab Emirates, were ruled by authoritarian kings. Although Jordan, Yemen, Lebanon, Kuwait, and the Palestinians moved toward democracy, most Arabs were denied full democratic rights by their governments.

*An Iraqi tank, destroyed in the Gulf War, rests near a series of oil well fires in northern Kuwait. Reproduced by permission of AP/Wide World Photos.*

## Islamist movements

The failure of rulers and politicians to establish democratic governments led many Arabs—and others around the world—to turn to religion as a possible solution to their problems. In the 1980s many Islamist movements, demanding rule by Muslim religious law (the *Shari'a*), emerged in Algeria, Egypt, Sudan, the Gulf states, and other Arab countries. When existing rulers refused to open up the political systems to more popular participation, some Islamists turned to violence to achieve their goals. This led to wars in Algeria and increased violence in the Sudan and other Arab nations.

Throughout the twentieth century, the Arab world has been a region of conflict and rapid change. Although strides have been made in education and solving social problems, many Arabs remain economically poor and without political power. As a result, the Arab world is likely to remain a region of change and uncertainty.

## For More Information

David, Ron. *Arabs & Israel for Beginners.* New York: Writers and Readers, 1993.

Hiro, Dilip. *Dictionary of the Middle East.* New York: St. Martins Press, 1996.

Shabbas, Audrey, and Ayad Al-Qazzaz, eds. *Arab World Notebook.* Berkeley, CA: Najda (Women Concerned About the Middle East), 1989.

Smith, Charles D. *Palestine and the Arab-Israeli Conflict.* New York: St. Martins Press, 1995.

*Janice Terry is a professor of Middle Eastern History at Eastern Michigan University. She holds an M.A. in Arab Studies from the American University of Beruit and a Ph.D. in Oriental and African Studies from the University of London.*

# Immigration to the United States

## 4

## Arabs in the Great Migration

**M**any people think Arabs are new to the United States, while in fact Arabs have been coming to the United States for hundreds of years. There are reports that Arabs came to the Americas with the Spanish explorers in the fifteenth century. In the late 1700s, Arabs from Morocco, a North African country, were discussed by the South Carolina House of Representatives when it decided that Moroccan Arabs living in the state should be treated according to the laws for white people, not the laws for blacks from Africa. Arab traders were well represented at the 1876 Philadelphia Centennial Exposition and the 1893 Chicago Colombian Exposition. The first Arabic-language newspaper in the United States started publishing in 1892. By 1895, there were three Arab churches in New York, and many more spread across the nation over the next twenty years. The first Arab mosque was built in Highland Park, Michigan, in 1923.

Arab immigrants were a significant part of the Great Migration, the period in U.S. history between 1880 and 1924, when more than 20 million immigrants entered the United

More than 20 million immigrants entered the United States during the Great Migration (1880-1924). *Reproduced by permission of Corbis Corporation (Bellevue).*

States. Most of these immigrants came from southern and eastern Europe, but more than 95,000 Arabs came to the United States from Greater Syria alone. Greater Syria includes present-day Syria, Lebanon, Jordan, Palestine, and Israel. Smaller numbers of Arabs came from Yemen, Iraq, Morocco, and Egypt during this time. By 1924, there were about 200,000 Arabs living in the United States.

Like other immigrants of this period, many Arab immigrants re-settled in cities of the northeastern and midwestern United States, such as New York, Boston, Detroit, Chicago, and Cleveland. But unlike other immigrant groups of this time, Arab immigrants could also be found in every state in the nation, as well as in small towns and communities where no other Arab families lived. This is because many Arab immigrants went into business as peddlers—persons who sold household goods door-to-door in small or rural areas not well served by stores.

In the early part of this large migration of Arabs most of those who came to the United States were young men looking for work. However, between 1899 and 1910, many Arab immigrants from Greater Syria decided to bring their families to the United States to start a new life, and as a result 32 percent of Arab immigrants from Greater Syria were female—a much larger percentage of females than that of the many other groups coming at this time. By 1919, nearly half of the immigrants from Greater Syria were female.

As the number of immigrants who came to the United States during the Great Migration grew, resistance to them grew among Americans born in the United States. Nativist movements (groups of people working to end immigration to the United States) claimed the immigrants were un-American, had cultures that did not fit with American culture, were more likely to be criminal and poor, and did not understand the American political system. These movements grew in strength, and a series of laws passed by the U.S. Congress in 1917, 1921, and 1924 caused immigration from all countries except those in northern and western Europe to slow down to a trickle. Arabs, Italians, Poles, Greeks, Slovaks, Eastern European Jews, and many others were no longer welcomed. Asians were completely forbidden to enter the country. The Great Migration had ended and a period like it in U.S. history would not begin again until 1965.

There are notable differences among the Arab immigrants who came to the United States during the Great Migration. Some groups started family migrations and planned to

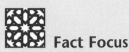 **Fact Focus**

- The first Arabs are thought to have come to the United States with the Spanish explorers in the fifteenth century.

- By 1919 half of the Arabs immigrating to the United States from Greater Syria were female.

- More than 20 million immigrants entered the United States during the Great Migration—from 1880 to 1924.

- Ninety percent of the Syrians and Lebanese who came during the Great Migration were Christians.

- Between 1965 and 1992 the six Arab countries from which the most immigrants came were Lebanon, Jordan/Palestine, Egypt, Iraq, Syria, and Yemen.

- Major events that have promoted Arab immigration to the United States in recent decades include the Arab-Israeli wars, the Israeli occupation of southern Lebanon, the Gulf War, and the loss of jobs in the oil-rich Arab Gulf states.

stay in the United States. Others were mostly composed of men seeking work who planned to return home after a while. Some groups clustered in certain cities, while others were equally likely to move anywhere in the United States. While the most common occupation of early Arab immigrants was in retail sales—where they worked as peddlers or shopkeepers—others were manufacturers of linens and clothing, wholesalers, and factory workers. Women also worked in many of these occupations.

## Syrians and Lebanese

Syrians and Lebanese were the largest group of Arab immigrants coming to the United States during the Great Migration. They were at least 80 percent of all Arab immigrants. While Syria and Lebanon have Muslim, Christian, and Druze religious communities, about 90 percent of the early Syrian and Lebanese immigrants were Christian. Most of them came from the area known at that time as Mt. Lebanon, now part of the country of Lebanon. Most of them came to the United States to make money and, at least in the beginning, planned to save this money, send it back home, and return home themselves someday. Interviews conducted with these early immigrants showed that most of them were neither fleeing starvation nor persecution. They were simply looking for a better life for themselves and their families. As word spread throughout Syria and Lebanon about how successful these immigrants were at making money in the United States more left for America.

In the United States, Syrian and Lebanese immigrants were mostly engaged in retail trades. This occupation was strengthened by Syrian and Lebanese successes in the manufacturing and importing of silk, lace, linen, and clothing. Syrian and Lebanese peddlers could establish themselves anywhere in the United States and sell these goods door-to-door, at better prices than most stores, and to people in the countryside who had little access to stores. Other Syrian and Lebanese immigrants opened grocery stores in large cities and in small towns. Both women and men worked in these businesses and some say women peddlers were more successful than men, since most of their customers were women.

A smaller number of Syrians and Lebanese worked in industry. In New England, some Syrians and Lebanese worked in clothing mills and silk factories. In Pittsburgh, Cleveland, and Detroit, some Syrians worked in iron shops and automobile factories, attracted by high wartime wages. In other parts of the United States, Syrians and Lebanese worked in coal mining, the oil industry, and as farmers. But selling goods was the occupation of most early Syrian and Lebanese immigrants in the United States.

Because of the type of work they did, Syrian and Lebanese immigrants could be found all over the United States. Because they were successful, many decided to bring their families to the United States and stay permanently. This was less likely to happen among Syrians and Lebanese of the Muslim and Druze faiths, who felt that their families would be better off living among people who shared their religion. As a result, most of the Muslim and Druze immigrants were men who lived in the United States without their families.

Opening of a Syrian-owned grocery store in 1916 in Detroit, Michigan. Many Syrian immigrants opened grocery stores in large cities.
*Reproduced by permission of the collection of Warren David.*

## Palestinians

Palestinians were the second largest group of Arab immigrants during the Great Migration. They made up about 10 percent of all Arab immigrants who came during this time. Like the Syrians and Lebanese, most Palestinians were Christians who came to the United States seeking a better economic life. Also like the Syrians and Lebanese, most Palestinians worked in peddling and retail trade. They bought goods to sell from Palestinian wholesalers who were connected by business networks to Syrian and Lebanese importers and manufacturers.

In this early period, Palestinians tended to settle and work in East Coast and Midwestern cities. They often sold goods in the newly emerging black communities of the North. Sometimes they traveled out of the city to sell goods in other nearby towns, but they usually returned to their urban home. As a result of this business pattern, Palestinians were more likely to be found concentrated in cities than the Syrians and Lebanese.

As word of their successes in retail trade reached their homeland, more Palestinians came to the United States. Like the Syrians and Lebanese, Palestinian Christians were more likely than Palestinian Muslims to bring their families to live permanently in the United States.

## Yemenis

Yemenis were a small part of the early Arab migration. Living in a country with a very long coastline on the Indian Ocean and the Red Sea, Yemenis have for hundreds of years traveled and settled in nearly every country of the world arriving in these places largely by ship.

Early Yemeni immigrants were men who arrived on ships, looking to improve their economic status, often not knowing that the United States was their destination. Once in the United States, the early Yemeni immigrants became workers who took on very strenuous jobs that required mostly manual labor. Yemeni immigrants were mostly found in one of two types of occupations—farm workers in California's San Joaquin Valley or laborers in the automobile factories and iron foundries of Detroit, Michigan; Buffalo, New York; and Canton, Ohio. Because of their intention to return to Yemen after saving money in the United States, few early Yemenis brought their families to the United States.

## Chaldeans and Assyrians

Chaldeans and Assyrians are Aramaic-speaking Christian communities whose origins lie in northern Iraq, southeastern Turkey, and northwestern Iran. Most of them believe they have a unique ethnic identity, which is not Arab. Since nearly all of the Chaldeans and some of the Assyrians who immigrated to the United States in this early period were from Iraq, we include them in this chapter.

Most of the Chaldeans came from the village of Telkaif in northern, modern-day Iraq. Many of the Assyrians were originally from Turkey, but fled persecution and went to Iran around the time of World War I (1914-18). Other Assyrians came from Iranian villages, and some came from Iraq. Chicago became the main destination for Assyrian immigrants while Chaldeans favored Detroit. Both of these communities started as all-male communities, but eventually some members of each of these communities decided to permanently settle in the United States and brought their families over.

Compared to the number of Syrian and Lebanese immigrants who arrived in the United States during the Great Migration, the early Chaldean and Assyrian communities were quite small, with about thirty families each and a much larger number of unaccompanied men. Occupationally, Assyrians in Chicago and Chaldeans in Detroit took very different paths. Like Syrian, Lebanese, and Palestinian immigrants of the time, the early Chaldean immigrants who lived in Detroit worked in retail trade. Assyrians in Chicago, on the other hand, were more likely to be laborers, working as masons, carpenters, painters, tailors, cooks, waiters, hotel staff, and factory workers.

# Immigration slows down: 1925-65

In the years between 1924—the end of the Great Migration—and 1965, when the U.S. Congress changed the rules for immigration, immigration to the United States from Arab countries was quite small. In fact, immigration from all countries was small when compared to the period before 1925 and after 1965. The 1924 Johnson–Reed Quota Act gave a quota, or numerical limit, on immigrants to each country in the world except countries in northern and western Europe and in Asia. Countries in northern and western Europe had no limits and immigrants from Asian countries were banned.

Each Arab country received the minimum quota of one hundred new immigrants per year. Only the wives and dependent children of United States citizens could come to the United States without being blocked by these quotas. In addition to the quotas, the Great Depression of the 1930s (a period of U.S. history in which the economy declined sharply and many people could not find jobs) and World War II (1939-45) in the early 1940s discouraged people from immigrating to the United States.

After World War II, many Arab immigrants who were United States citizens sponsored their families to immigrate to the United States. Other Arab immigrants, usually the relatives of earlier immigrants, came under quotas. Still others, like immigrants from Jordan, started a new migration to the United States. Some Arabs came to the United States to advance their education on student visas, which required them to return home once they completed their education. Many of them stayed in the United States after marriage to an American citizen or because they found an employer who would sponsor them to stay.

## Palestinian immigration: 1925-65

The single most significant change in Arab migration during the period from 1925 to 1965 began in 1936, when for the first time the number of Palestinian immigrants to the United States exceeded the number of Syrian and Lebanese immigrants. Troubles were already beginning in Palestine as the British Mandatory Government, a British government imposed on Palestine after World War I, supported the creation of a Jewish homeland in Palestine and assisted large numbers of Jewish immigrants to re-settle in Palestine. Arabs were banned from lands purchased by Jews, and Arab products and businesses were boycotted by the growing Zionist movement in Palestine. The Zionist movement called for the creation of a Jewish state in Palestine. Palestinians felt their lands, rights, and livelihoods were slowly being taken away from them by a foreign government and a foreign people. In 1936, Palestinians went on a six-month national strike to protest these actions. In 1948, the State of Israel was declared and over 800,000 Palestinians became refugees, most of them fleeing to neighboring countries. A majority of these Palestinians, and their children and grandchildren, are still refugees today.

In 1953, the U.S. Congress passed the Refugee Relief Act, the first American immigration law to specifically mention refugees as a specific type of immigrant. Under this law, 2,000 Palestinian refugees were to be admitted to the United States. The law was extended in 1957, and another 985 Palestinians were admitted to the United States as refugees between 1958 and 1963.

# Arab immigration since 1965

In 1965, the U.S. Congress passed a new immigration act that dramatically changed the size and type of immigration to the United States. The two most important changes brought about by this law were the removal of regional immigration bans and the removal of quotas that varied by country. No longer would persons from certain countries be favored over others, and there were no countries from which immigrants would not be accepted.

More than 400,000 Arab immigrants came to the United States between 1965 and 1992. If we look only at the six Arab countries sending the most immigrants to the United States—Lebanon, Jordan/Palestine, Egypt, Iraq, Syria, and Yemen—the total for this period is 360,000 people. The remaining Arab immigrants were a combination of Moroccans, Libyans, Bahrainis, Omanis, Sudanese, Tunisians, Saudi Arabians, Algerians, and a handful of immigrants from other Arab countries.

This new immigration law is considered part of the 1960s' Civil Rights Movement because its main effect was to remove the racial and ethnic discrimination in the United States immigration law that was put in place by the country quotas of the 1920s. (The Civil Rights Movement of the 1960s sought to tear down barriers—social, economic, and political, that separated less-advantaged groups, most prominently African Americans, from mainstream white America.)

Since this law went into effect, the racial, ethnic, and religious make up of the U.S. population changed significantly, as has the number of immigrants coming to the United States. During the 1970s, 4.8 million legal immigrants entered the United States; about the same number entered between 1990 and 1994. By the year 2000, post-1965 immigration to the United States will reach the same level as the Great Migration at the beginning of the twentieth century.

The 1965 law and later amendments placed a 20,000-person-per-year limit on each country and an annual global ceiling—or yearly maximum total—of 290,000 new immigrants. Parents, spouses, and unmarried children of U.S. citizens could enter without being counted against these limits. Relatives of U.S. citizens would be favored to re-

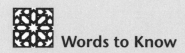

## Words to Know

- **The Great Migration:** the period in U.S. history between 1880 and 1924 when more than 20 million immigrants entered the United States.

- **Greater Syria:** a part of the Arab world under the Ottoman Empire (the sixteenth century through the nineteenth century) that included present-day Syria, Lebanon, Jordan, Palestine, and Israel.

- **Economic sanctions:** an official trade boycott against a country deemed to be in defiance of international law. Sanctions on can include severely restricting how much oil a country can export to other countries and what that country can buy from others—including food, medicine, and machinery.

- **Intifada:** the Palestinian uprising against the Israelis that began in the late 1980s.

- **Immigrant visas:** a document required by some governments for immigration purposes.

- **Peddlers:** people who sell household goods door-to-door in areas not well-served by stores.

- **Push factors:** things that force people to leave their homeland, such as economic depressions, wars, famine, or natural catastrophes.

- **Quotas:** pertaining to immigration, limits that are placed on the number of immigrants from a particular country who come to live in another country.

- **Refugees:** people who leave their home countries due to wars and other hardships and seek refuge elsewhere.

- **Remittances:** the money immigrants send to their home countries to support their families.

ceive immigrant visas. The new law also established preferred groups of immigrants based on skills they could bring to the United States.

The Arab immigrants who have come to the United States since 1965 are largely from the same countries as the Arab immigrants who came during the Great Migration, with a few exceptions. One exception is the very large number of Egyptians who have immigrated to the United States since 1965, whereas very few Egyptians came in earlier years. Another exception is Jordanians. The numbers for Jordanians are deceptive because about 80 percent of the Jordanian immigrants are actually Palestinians. Palestinians have not been counted as Palestinians by the U.S. government since the majority of the Palestinians are refugees and carry no passports, or carry passports from other countries.

The majority of Palestinian immigrants enter the United States on Jordanian passports (see pages 48-49 for a full explanation). Palestinians are also mixed among immigrants entering from Israel, Lebanon, Syria, and other Arab countries. This is because after they were dispersed from their homeland in 1948, when Israel was created out of Palestinian lands, and as a result of later migrations, they have been living in exile in many Arab countries. It is difficult to count how many Palestinians are coming to the United States. If we look at the number of Jordanian immigrants coming, it can be assumed that about 80 percent of them are Palestinians. An unknown number of Palestinians are also coming from other countries.

A majority of the post-1965 Arab immigrants are families. Some are very highly educated and work as professionals, but many others are less educated. Some come to the United States primarily for an education; others come to give their children better educational opportunities. Almost all are looking for a better economic life, but some are also escaping war and human rights abuses. A smaller number are men who work to support their families back home. These men live cheaply by sharing housing with other men, send the money they save back to their families, and go home for periodic visits. The money immigrants send to their home countries to support their families is called remittances.

Since United States immigration law encourages family migration it is likely that, in time, all of these immigrants will be joined by other family members and that their extended families will be partly re-created in the United States. The new Arab immigrants build on the foundations of earlier Arab immigrants and have expanded the size, diversity, and geographic locations of Arab communities in the United States. In general, Arab immigrants are found in three major occupational groupings: highly educated professionals, such as doctors and engineers; independent businesspersons, particularly shopkeepers; and factory workers, especially in auto-related industries.

The most significant change in the overall picture of Arab immigrants who have come to the United States since 1965 is that a much larger percentage, perhaps 60 percent, are Muslims. In earlier days, more than 80 percent were Christians. Although Muslims were part of the early Arab migration, few of them chose to bring their families over. This pattern has changed. As a result of Arab Muslim migration, as well as family migrations from many other parts of the Islamic world, Islam is now the second largest religion in the United States.

The U.S. government groups immigrants according to their country of birth. However, this may not accurately indicate nationality or ethnic group, especially in the case of Palestinians (who are largely counted as Jordanians) and Assyrians and Chaldeans (who are largely counted as Iraqis).

## Lebanese

Lebanon has sent more Arab immigrants to the United States since 1965 than any other Arab country. Between 1965 and 1992 there were 91,460 immigrants from Lebanon. This reflects a continuation of the early days of Arab immigration to the United States, when Lebanese immigration, especially among Christian Lebanese, was dominant. As noted above, U.S. immigration law encourages family migration, so people from countries in which a large number of immigrants are now American citizens have an advantage in obtaining immigrant visas. An immigrant visa is a document required by the U.S. government for immigration purposes. It is applied for, approved, and issued at a U.S. consulate in the immigrant's home country. In addition, recent Lebanese immigration is also heavily composed of newly immigrating families (persons unrelated to earlier immigrants), and many are Muslims.

Lebanese immigration to the United States rose dramatically in 1976, hit a peak in 1977, and started decreasing after that. It began increasing again in 1983, and has not slowed since. Two major events occurred that help explain the peaks. In 1975 a civil war began in Lebanon. People tend to flee war zones, and if they have the opportunity to go somewhere else safe, they will. Many of these Lebanese opted to come to the United States because they had relatives already there. Others were immigrants starting a new family migration. Still others came to the United States as refugees. In 1978 and 1979, the United States government admitted 1,000 Lebanese immigrants as refugees.

In 1982, the Israeli army invaded Lebanon, engaging in a long bombing campaign of Lebanese cities and towns, including the capital of Beirut. The army collaborated with a Lebanese group in a massacre of Palestinian refugees, and then left its army in the southern third of Lebanon as an occupying force. In 1999, the Israeli army still remains in Lebanon and continues to engage in frequent bombings of the southern region, a predominantly Muslim area. Already contending with serious fighting between different groups of Lebanese and Palestinians, Lebanon was seriously destabilized by the 1982 war and by the continuing Israeli occupation and bombings. These conditions help explain the growth of Lebanese immigration since 1983. Hundreds of thousands of Palestinian refugees live in Lebanon and some of the U.S. Lebanese immigrants are actually Palestinians.

## Palestinians and Jordanians

Palestinians and Jordanians are the second largest group of Arab immigrants to come to the United States since 1965. From 1965 to 1992 the number of Jordanians and Palestinians entering the United States carrying Jordanian passports was 80,921. Probably about 65,000 of these immigrants were originally Palestinian. As explained earlier, there are an unknown number of Palestinians that come from countries other than Jordan.

Rather than having noticeably large peaks in migration at certain times, Palestinian and Jordanian migration has been rather stable since 1965, with small changes (numbering in the hundreds) from year to year, although after 1988 their migration started a steady rise. This rise is probably due to a combination of factors: the Palestinian Intifada—or uprising—in the West Bank and Gaza (see below), the devaluation of the Jordanian currency/dollar (called the *dinar*), and decreasing opportunities for well-paying jobs in the oil-rich Arab Gulf countries. For Palestinians, these jobs were especially important because they helped men send remittances to their families living under Israeli occupation in Jerusalem, the West Bank, and Gaza.

A majority of the Palestinian immigrants of the 1965-92 period are relatives of the early Palestinian immigrants—Palestinian Christians and Muslims from Jerusalem and the West Bank. The West Bank is a part of what used to be Palestine, named for its location on the West Bank of the Jordan River. Between 1948 and 1967 it was under Jordanian rule, which is the reason most of these Palestinians carry Jordanian passports. The West Bank has been under Israeli military occupation since 1967, when Jordon lost it in a war with Israel. The Intifada, the Palestinian uprising against the Israelis who occupied their land, has been ongoing since the late 1980s.

In addition to these Palestinian immigrants, an increasing number of Palestinian immigrants are from areas that did not send immigrants in the early days. These immigrants are mostly the relatives of Palestinians who came to the United States in the 1970s and 1980s to study, then changed their status to immigrant and brought their families over. The increase in this type of Palestinian immigration is directly related to the loss of jobs in the oil-rich Arab Gulf countries. It is because of the oil industry jobs in the Arab Gulf that Palestinians sought an education in the United States. When the jobs became unavailable, however, Palestinians had little option but to stay and work in the United States. Returning home was virtually impossible due to Israeli restrictions on Palestinian residency and work.

One might expect Palestinian immigration to be even higher than it is, given the harshness of the Israeli occupation on human rights and economic levels. But counterbalancing this push factor (a push factor is a reason for people to leave their country) has been a Palestinian determination to stay on their land so it will not be confiscated by the Israeli government. Additionally, jobs in the Arab Gulf countries—when they were available—paid better than jobs in the United States. Finally, since a majority of Palestinian immigrants come as family members of U.S. citizens, they have to wait long periods before their visas allowing the to enter are available. This is true for all immigrants who are not the parents or young children of American citizens, but who come as other relatives of citizens. There is a severe global backlog in approving these visa applications—for some countries the wait is eighteen years.

Jordanians did not begin migrating to the United States until the 1950s. Most of the Jordanians in the United States are Christians, although this is changing as more Jordanian Muslims immigrate to the United States. Jordanian migration is largely a family migration.

## Egyptians

Egyptians are the third largest group of Arab immigrants to come to the United States since 1965. From 1965 to 1992 the number of immigrants from Egypt entering the United States totaled 80,884. Unlike other large Arab immigrant groups, Egyptians did not begin to migrate in significant numbers until the 1950s. The number of Egyptian immigrants in the United States began increasing significantly in 1967, skyrocketed in 1970, slowly decreased after that, and remained at a rate of 2,200 to 3,200 per year until 1991, when it increased rapidly again.

A pivotal 1967 event in Egypt was the Arab-Israeli war and the loss to Israel of a significant amount of Egyptian land. Egyptian people felt humiliation and defeat. Then, in 1970 Gamal Abdal Nasser, the popular president of Egypt, died. Egyptian spirits declined again. Many Egyptians who thought they could find a better life elsewhere left their homeland.

Egyptian immigrants tend to be highly educated professionals, including doctors, dentists, lawyers, scientists, and professors. Most of them bring their families. A large number are Coptic Christians (following an ancient Egyptian rite), some are Protestants, and many others are Muslims. Unlike other Arab immigrants, a very large percentage of Egyptians have entered the United States as professionals whose services are needed in the United States. That is, they are given immigrant visas because of their special skills, not their relationship to an American citizen. The rise in immigration in 1991 is probably due to the Gulf War. Many Egyptians were working as professionals in the Arab Gulf countries affected by this war.

## Iraqis/Chaldeans/Assyrians

Iraqis, including Arabs, Chaldeans, and Assyrians, are the fourth largest group of immigrants from the Arab world that have come to the United States since 1965. The number of immigrants from Iraq from 1965 to 1992 is 52,913. Assyrians and Chaldeans are mostly the relatives of earlier immigrants, while the Arabs, so-called to distinguish them from these groups, are part of a more recent migration of highly educated Muslims and their families and post-Gulf War (1990–91) refugees. As in earlier days, Chaldeans tend to settle in Detroit, Assyrians in Chicago, and some members of both communities in California.

Iraqi migration to the United States was relatively low and stable until 1974. In 1976 it peaked, then began falling, but not to the low levels it had been at before 1974. In the mid-1980s it fell again to low levels, rising again in 1992. Some of these patterns do not have an apparent explanation,

**An Iraqi refugee plays finger games with his nephew. Iraqis are part of the newest wave of immigration to Detroit.** *Reproduced by permission of Millard Berry.*

although between 1975 and 1976 about 1,000 Iraq-born Assyrians living in Lebanon were admitted to the United States as refugees from the Lebanese civil war; another 1,500 Assyrians came to Chicago as refugees between 1983 and 1992.

Immigration from Iraq was low in the mid-to-late 1980s, when Iraq was engaged in a war with Iran and attacks on Kurdish villages there. The Iraqi oil-based economy was very good during these years and the country was flourishing with development. Iraqi immigrants of the time said their economic life was better in Iraq than in the United States. It is also possible that the wartime conscription (drafting) of soldiers put a hold on emigration. The huge jump in Iraqi immigration to the United States that began in 1992 reflects the large number of Iraqis admitted to the United States as refugees and regular immigrants as a result of the Gulf War and the paralyzing economic sanctions—which place strict limits on what can be sold to Iraq, and what Iraq can sell to other countries—that were still in place in Iraq at the end of 1999 (see pages 31-32).

## Syrians

Syrians are the fifth largest group of Arab immigrants to come to the United States since 1965. Between 1965 and 1992, 43,010 immigrants arrived from Syria. Syrian immigration over this period shows a relatively stable pattern, with a small rise in 1982 when the Israelis invaded neighboring Lebanon, and then regular annual increases beginning after 1988. As with immigrants from other Arab countries, this post-1988 increase may be due to the decline of lucrative jobs in the Arab Gulf countries. Post-1965 Syrian immigrants are a combination of relatives of earlier Arab immigrants, well-educated Syrians, such as doctors, pharmacists, and scientists seeking better job opportunities in the United States, and students who come to the United States for higher education and later decide to stay because of marriage or a job.

## Yemenis

Yemenis are the sixth largest group of Arab immigrants to come to the United States since 1965, with 10,097 immigrants from Yemen arriving between 1965 and 1992. Yemeni migration to the United States shows a rather stable pattern, with a rise in 1973, and again after 1990. While the 1973 rise does not appear to have an explanation, the reason for the rise after 1990 is clear. Like other Arabs, Yemenis suffered greatly from the Gulf War. In fact, more Yemenis lost their jobs permanently as a result of this war than any other group.

Yemenis are a unique group among modern Arab immigrants. Approximately 90 percent of Yemeni immigrants are unaccompanied men who come to the United States to work, save money, and support their families in Yemen. Few intend to stay permanently in the United States. Most Yemeni immigrants come as relatives of earlier immigrants and all of them are Muslims. Since the mid-1970s there has been a small migration of Yemeni families, but this has not grown into a large movement. Yemenis largely migrate to the same places they did during the years of the Great Migration and take on the same difficult jobs, although recently more Yemenis are going into business as shopkeepers.

# For More Information

Abraham, Sameer, and Nabeel Abraham, eds. *Arabs in the New World: Studies in Arab-American Communities.* Detroit: Wayne State University Press, 1983.

"The Arab Immigrants" *Aramco World Magazine,* September/October 1986.

Cainkar, Louise. *Gender, Culture and Politics Among Palestinian Immigrants in the United States.* Philadelphia: Temple University Press, in press. (Based on *Coping with Tradition, Change and Alienation: The Life Experiences of Palestinian Women in the United States.* Northwestern University: Unpublished Doctoral Dissertation, 1988.)

Cainkar, Louise. *Meeting Community Needs, Building on Community Strengths.* Chicago: Arab American Action Network, 1988.

Hooglund, Eric, ed. *Taking Root: Arab-American Community Studies.* Washington, D.C.: American-Arab Anti-Discrimination Committee,1985.

Naff, Alixa. *Becoming American: The Early Arab Immigrant Experience.* Carbondale: Southern Illinois University Press, 1985.

Naff, Alixa. "Arabs." In *Encyclopedia of American Ethnic Groups,* edited by Stephen Thernstrom. Cambridge, MA: Harvard University Press, 1980.

Orfalea, Gregory. *Before the Flames: A Quest for the History of Arab Americans.* Austin: University of Texas Press, 1988.

Swanson, Jon. "Sojourners and Settlers: Yemenis in America." *Middle East Report,* March/April 1986.

Younis, Adele. *The Coming of the Arabic-Speaking People to the United States.* New York: Center for Migration Studies, 1995.

*Louise Cainkar is a Research Assistant Professor with the University of Illinois. She received her Ph.D. from Northwestern University.*

# Community Profiles

There have been Arab communities in the United States since the late 1800s. The first group of Arabs to immigrate to the United States came from Greater Syria, particularly from the area that is present-day Lebanon. Most of these immigrants were Christians and were commonly referred to as Syrians. They came to the United States because of the economic opportunities available. The vast majority were men who only planned to stay for a few years, earn some money, then return to their home country. Most of these first Arab immigrants worked for many years as peddlers, traveling from house-to-house selling goods. As these Arab immigrants learned to speak English and adjusted to life in the United States, they assisted friends and relatives who wished to immigrate as well. After many years, some of the immigrants who initially planned to return to their home country decided instead to stay and began to bring their families over (see chapter 4).

As Arab immigrants settled, they established their own communities. At the turn of the twenty-first century, there are still Arab American communities that date back to the early period of immigration. Newer communities have been established by immigrants coming in the recent decades. This chapter examines some of the most important Arab American communities around the United States, how and when many immigrants settled, where they originally came from, and each community's special characteristics.

## Arab Americans and the U.S. census

When we study a community to find out how many people live there, where they come from, where they live and work, and how much education they have, we are doing demographic research. Demographic research also includes such basic information as how many people make up a certain community. As of 1999, there has been no accurate count of the Arab American population, not even by the federal government, so it is difficult to determine the size of the Arab American population. The U.S. Census Bureau is the federal government agency responsible for such a count because its primary function is to take a census (count) of the U.S. population every ten years. The last census was taken in 1990, and the next census will be taken in the year 2000. One goal of the census is to determine the populations of each of the various racial and ethnic groups around the country.

Two census forms are distributed by mail, a short form that 83 percent of U.S. households receive, and a long form that 17 percent of U.S. households receive. The manner of distributing the form to one of every six households (17 percent) is called random sampling. The purpose of the short form is to provide a count of the entire population and its racial composition or make up. Arabs are considered Caucasian, or white, and are thus included in that very large category, making it impossible to differentiate them from the rest of the group. The longer form contains many questions, including an open-ended question (fill in the blank) about a person's ancestry or ancestries.

This longer form is the only manner in which Arab Americans can claim their heritage and be counted. Although this system should provide a somewhat accurate count of the population, it does not. One of the reasons is because many people do not fill out this form, and therefore lose their only opportunity to actually be counted. This occurs among the

U.S. population in general, not just Arab Americans, as people are not aware of the importance of the census or find the many questions on the long form invasive (too personal). A 1999 study by Louise Cainkar and the Illinois Coalition for Immigrant and Refugee Rights shows that Arab Americans also have particular fears of the census, which may cause them not to respond. Persistent (continual) prejudice and discrimination against Arabs in the United States and stereotypical portrayals (distorted images) of Arabs in the American media (see chapter 13) cause many Arabs to fear any government efforts to track their home addresses, as is done in the census. Their stated fear is of a mass round-up or deportation (removal) of Arabs from the United States.

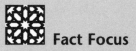 **Fact Focus**

- The United States is projected to have an Arab American population of five million people by the year 2000, making Arab Americans one of the fastest growing ethnic groups in the country.

- Arab Americans were involved in the Bread and Roses Strike of 1912, in which 20,000 textile workers went on strike (refused to work) until they received better working conditions and higher wages.

Another factor affecting an accurate count of ethnic groups is that third-generation Americans (people whose grandparents were immigrants to the Untied States) often identify themselves solely as Americans, not by their ethnic ancestry. In addition, many Arab American people have more than two ethnic heritages to claim. The form only allows for two, so people are forced to claim only part of their heritage. Since many Arab Americans are third-generation Americans, and some have more than one heritage, we can assume these circumstances affect the Arab count.

Because Arab Americans were undercounted in the 1990 census, we have to rely on other sources to determine or estimate the size of the population. Organizations such as Zogby International have estimated the population by speaking with Arab American religious leaders, schools, and social service agencies that can provide a more accurate count of the Arab American population. Zogby International has also studied the community by going to schools, churches, and mosques to count Arab Americans. This chapter relies heavily on the estimates provided by Zogby International, as well as those provided by the U.S. Census Bureau.

Arab Americans are among the fastest growing ethnic groups in the United States today. The 1990 census counted the Arab American community at 870,000, but Zogby International estimated in 1995 that the U.S. Arab American population was as high as three million. For a more accurate count in the year 2000 census, numerous organizations are working, through public education, to ensure that people of Arab heritage do identify themselves as Arab Americans. They want Arab Americans to be recognized as a large community so that they will have more influence politically and socially, and will be better able to promote the interests of Arab Americans as a group.

# Arab American community profiles

Arab immigrants have settled in many areas of the United States and have developed a number of communities. They tend to settle mainly in urban areas, or cities. (Ninety percent of Arab Americans live in urban areas as opposed to 74 percent of the rest of the U.S. population.) Of the entire Arab American population, 30 percent live in the Northeast, 27 percent in the Midwest, 22 percent in the South, and 21 percent in the West.

According to Zogby International, in 1995 the largest Arab American populations were found in (listed in descending order): California, New York, Michigan, Florida, Illinois, New Jersey, Massachusetts, Texas, Ohio, and Pennsylvania. Zogby International also noted that 40 percent of the Arab American population are first-generation immigrants who were born in the Arab world.

# Northeast United States

## Boston, Massachusetts

The first substantial wave of Arab immigrants to arrive in Boston came around 1880 and were mainly of Syrian descent. In 1910 more Syrians and Lebanese lived in Boston than in any other city in the country, except New York. The majority of early immigrants worked as peddlers while others worked in the textile or clothing industry as stitchers, cutters, and pressers. Those working in the textile industry became involved in unionizing (the organizing of workers into groups, called unions, to protect their rights). In fact, Arab Americans who were living in the town of Lawrence, just north of Boston, helped lead the famous Bread and Roses Strike of 1912. In this strike, 20,000 textile workers of thirty different nationalities refused to work for more than two months, until they received improved working conditions and higher wages. Some meetings for the strike took place in the basement of a Syrian church, and three of the leaders were Syrian American. The strikers were severely abused by the soldiers called in to end the strike. The soldiers killed a woman and a young Arab boy named John Ramey. The workers eventually won the strike due to their refusal to give in.

In the late 1990s roughly 80 percent of the Arab Americans in Massachusetts were born in the United States. There is also a significant population of recent immigrants, due in part to a heavy migration of Lebanese during the late 1970s and early 1980s. The proportion of the Arab American community in Massachusetts that is Lebanese is one of the highest in the nation. Additionally, there are growing communities from North Africa—mainly Egypt, Morocco, and Algeria. Other groups include Iraqis, Jordanians, Palestinians, and Saudi Arabians.

The size of the Arab American community in Boston is estimated to be between 100,000 and 150,000. There is no central community or neighborhood of Arab Americans, as there is in other cities. However, people generally congregate when there is a cultural event, such as concerts of Arabic music or other activities focusing on Arab culture.

Students from the Arab world attending universities in the Boston area number between 3,000 and 5,000 and are active in the community. After graduation, some choose to stay, while others return to their home country. There are Arab student organizations at Harvard University, the Massachusetts Institute of Technology, Northeastern University, Boston University, and Wesley College. Other active Arab organizations in the Boston area include the Arab Arts Network, the Arab American Cultural Group, the American-Arab Anti-Discrimination Committee, and the Algerian American Association of New England. Arabic media consists mainly of a weekly one-hour Arab television program and one Arabic music program.

Other cities in Massachusetts with significant Arab American populations include Lawrence, Fall River, Lowell, Lynn, Worcester, and Springfield.

## New York

The late 1800s marked the beginning of Arab immigration to New York. Most of the early arrivals were Syrians and Lebanese who worked as peddlers, and then eventually opened up stores. As people started to move away from New York City, they relied on the Arabic newspapers (the first of which was published in 1892) to inform them of events in the Middle East and news of Arab Americans in general. New York was also home to Kahlil Gibran (see chapters 12 and 18) and his literary circle. They and other educators and intellectuals helped to make New York City the center of Arab culture and business.

Between 1965 and the early 1990s, the Arab population in New York City almost doubled to an estimated 120,000, including both Christians and the recently arrived Muslims. In the late 1990s, 63 percent of the Arab American population in New York City was born in the United States. In addition to Syrian and Lebanese Americans, other groups present in New York City include Palestinian, Jordanian, Yemeni, Egyptian, Moroccan, and Sudanese Americans. Smaller communities include Iraqis, Algerians, Tunisians, Libyans, Saudis, and Kuwaitis. In addition to Christian and Muslim populations, New York City is home to between 30,000 and 60,000 Jews of Arab descent. About half of the Jewish population are descendants of Syrians who immigrated at the beginning of the twentieth century. Later, more Jewish immigrants from Syria arrived in New York City, along with Jews from Iraq, Yemen, and countries in North Africa. The Syrian Jews maintain many of their own institutions along Ocean Parkway and Kings Highway.

There are large Lebanese and Syrian communities in the Bay Ridge section of Brooklyn and in upstate New York cities. Newer Palestinian and Egyptian immigrants live in Brooklyn, Westchester County, and Syracuse. Moroccans, with an approximate population of 13,000, live around Atlantic Avenue in Brooklyn and in Astoria and Woodside in Queens. The Jordanian community in Yonkers, with an estimated population of 10,000, is the largest Jordanian community outside of Jordan, as well as the most politically powerful Jordanian community in the United States. Yemenis, with a population of 10,000, are most visible around Court Street and Atlantic Avenue in Brooklyn. The residences and businesses of Sudanese, who number around 8,000, are found on Coney Island Avenue, Cortelyou Road, and Avenue C, while others live in Upper Manhattan. Atlantic Avenue in Brooklyn has a concentration of Arab businesses.

There are numerous Arab American organizations, including student clubs at Columbia University, Hunter College, New York University, City College of New York, the College of Staten Island, and the Borough of Manhattan Community College. The radio station WNWK has weekly Arab programs discussing Arab and Islamic issues. Channel 67 in Brooklyn provides the community with 13 hours of Arabic programming a day. Other organizations include the Arab American Institute, the American-Arab Anti-Discrimination Committee, Algerian American National Association, Yemeni American Benevolent Association, Syrian Ladies Aid Society, Damascus Masonic Lodge, Syrian Young Men's Association, Sudanese American Organization, Sudanese Community in New York and New Jersey, and Friends of Lebanon.

## New Jersey

New Jersey has an estimated Arab American population of 80,000, 60 percent of whom are U.S. born. New Jersey has the highest percentage of Egyptians of any state, and they are located mainly in Jersey City. Palestinians are the largest nationality in Patterson, but are mainly concentrated in North Bergen along with Jordanians. A number of Syrians are located in Patterson, while Lebanese live mainly in Linden, and Sudanese are in Newark and Irvington. Syrian Americans comprise 28 percent of New Jersey's Arab American population, with the Lebanese close behind at 27 percent. Other Arab American groups in New Jersey include Iraqis, Assyrians, Jordanians, Moroccans, and Kuwaitis.

Historically, 80 percent of the Arab Americans in Patterson and West Hoboken were employed by the silk factories. Similar to the Syrian Americans working in the textile factories in Massachusetts, these Arab immigrants were conscious of the struggle for workers' rights and actively participated in labor disputes in their efforts to better their working conditions. Nowadays, the professions in which Arab Americans work are as diverse as the ethnic groups that comprise the Arab American community. Some of the fields in which people are working include medicine, technology, business, education, and entrepreneurship (being self-employed).

Christian churches can be found in various cities. There is a Melkite church in Patterson, as well as a Syrian Orthodox Church. A Coptic Church in Jersey City caters to the Egyptian population. The Muslim community is served by mosques located in Patterson, Jersey City, and Metropolitan New York. Other aspects of the Arab American community include Arabic newspapers and radio and television programs.

## Pennsylvania

Arab immigration to Pennsylvania began in Philadelphia in 1876, when the city invited exhibitors from other countries to come and participate in the Centennial Exhibition, celebrating one hundred years since the signing of the Declaration of Independence. Many people came from present-day Lebanon, and later headed west from Philadelphia, helping to begin the age of peddling. A few Arabs chose to remain in the Philadelphia area. Today, the greater Philadelphia area has an Arab American population of 20,000 to 25,000—approximately two-thirds of whom live in the city, while the other one-third lives in the suburbs. The three largest and most distinct communities are Lebanese Christians, who live mainly in southern Philadelphia, the largely Palestinian community of Germantown, and a primarily Palestinian community in the Feltonville area. The Arab American community is very visible, active both politically and socially.

The newest Arab American population of Philadelphia is comprised mainly of Iraqis, Algerians, and Moroccans. There has also been an increase in the number of Arab American professionals who attend college in Philadelphia and then decide to remain there. Because the cost of living is lower, a type of "secondary immigration" is taking place in

Philadelphia as people come from New York City and New Jersey to open stores and businesses.

Pennsylvania has an Arab American population of roughly 140,000 (of whom 83 percent are U.S. born). The majority of these are people of Lebanese and Syrian background. Western Pennsylvania, which includes the Pittsburgh metropolitan area, has a sizeable Arab American population. In the

**Workers in a Patterson, New Jersey, silk factory. Historically, 80 percent of the Arab Americans in Patterson were employed in silk factories.** *Reproduced by permission of Corbis Corporation (Bellevue).*

east, Allentown boasts of a substantial number of Syrians, and the towns of Wilkes-Barre and Scranton both have well-established Lebanese communities. Whereas the majority of Arab Americans throughout the state are second- and third-generation, in Allentown more than 65 percent of Arab Americans are first-generation.

There are numerous Arab American Christian and Muslim places of worship throughout the state. Eastern Orthodox and Maronite churches can be found in Pittsburgh, Philadelphia, Wilkes-Barre, Allentown, Eaton, and Newcastle. Mosques and Islamic organizations are found in Philadelphia, Pittsburgh, New Castle, and Eaton.

# Midwest

### Detroit and Dearborn, Michigan

Metropolitan Detroit is home to one of the largest Arab populations outside of the Arab world with an estimated population of 250,000 in the 1990s. Early immigrants to the Detroit area worked as peddlers, auto workers, and store owners. These first arrivals were predominately Christians, and most were from Lebanon and Syria.

In the early 1900s the Ford Model T automotive plant in Highland Park (a suburb of Detroit) drew many Arab immigrants to the area. They created the first Arab American community in Metro Detroit. Soon after, Arab Americans began moving to the south end of Dearborn (just west of Detroit) with the opening of the Ford Rouge automobile plant there. This plant, with its five-dollars-per-day wages, continued to draw new Arab immigrants to the city. Some workers decided to remain in the United States and started bringing their families, which resulted in another boom in the Arab population in the south end of Dearborn. During the late 1970s and 1980s, many new immigrants began to arrive as a result of the Lebanese civil war and the Israeli invasion and occupation of southern Lebanon. Many of these newer arrivals were also able to enter the auto industry, specifically because the children of the earlier immigrants who worked at the Ford Rouge automobile plant, having the benefit of education, were able to enter another sphere of work. This left many jobs

**Workers earning five-dollars-per-day on the Ford Motor Company's Highland Park plant assembly line in January 1914. This plant drew many Arab immigrants to the Metro Detroit area.**

open at the automobile plants, which were then assumed by newer immigrants.

Of the Arab American community in metropolitan Detroit, about 100,000 are of Lebanese and Syrian descent. At first, the Arab population was mainly Christian, but that has changed as more Muslims have immigrated, and the population in the late 1990s is approximately 50 percent Christian and 50 percent Muslim. The Syrian-Lebanese Christians generally live in the eastern communities of metropolitan Detroit, namely Eastpointe, the Grosse Pointes, St. Clair Shores, Harper Woods, Roseville, Mt. Clemens, and Sterling Heights. Lebanese Muslims are concentrated in the western area of metropolitan Detroit, especially Dearborn's south end, northeast Dearborn, and Dearborn Heights.

The second largest group in the Metro Detroit area are Chaldean Iraqis. The Chaldeans first came to the area around 1910, but the majority of the population did not arrive until the 1960s. They came mainly from a small town in Iraq named Telkeif and from the capital, Baghdad. Those coming from Baghdad had business experience that enabled them to open businesses in the metropolitan Detroit area. One can find numerous Chaldean supermarkets and shops throughout the area. Today, most Chaldeans live in the Seven Mile-John R area of Detroit and the suburban towns of Southfield, Oak Park, West Bloomfield, Troy, and Sterling Heights.

Palestinians are the third largest group at about 25,000 and live in the western suburbs of Farmington, Farmington Hills, Livonia, Westland, Garden City, West Bloomfield, Bloomfield Hills, and Dearborn. The Yemeni community with a population of 15,000 is located in southeast Dearborn and Hamtramck. The Yemeni arrived as early as 1910, but the majority did not come until the 1950s and 1960s. Egyptians are a more recent community and live in the northern suburbs. Most are Coptic Christians, although some are Sunni Muslims. Many Iraqis continue to migrate to the area, arriving mainly as refugees (people fleeing persecution who are given permission by the United States government to settle in the United States). Other substantial populations of Arab Americans are in Flint, Ann Arbor, and Lansing.

There are numerous active Arab American organizations in the Metro Detroit area. Some of the organizations include the Arab Community Center for Economic and Social Services (ACCESS), the American Federation of Ramallah, Palestine, the Yemen American Benevolent Association, the Arab American Institute, the American-Arab Anti-Discrimination Committee, the American Arab Chamber of Commerce, the American Lebanese University Graduates, the Arab American and Chaldean Council, the Bir Zeit Society, and the Warren Avenue Business Association. Media consists of Arabic radio and television shows and many newspapers, including *The Arab American News*. The main business district is in Dearborn along Warren Avenue, where there are many Arab American-owned businesses, restaurants, and shops that offer food and other items from Lebanon and provide services in Arabic. Another small Arab American business district is found in the neighborhood of the south end of Dearborn, on Dix and Vernor Avenues.

There are numerous mosques and religious organizations throughout the metropolitan area including the Islamic Center of America, the Islamic Institute of Knowledge, and the Islamic Mosque of America. Islamic media includes *The Muslim American,* a monthly newspaper. Christian churches include Catholic churches such as St. Sharbel Church in Warren and Orthodox churches such as St. George's Orthodox Church and St. Mark Coptic Orthodox Church. Chaldean Americans also have churches, including the Mother of God Church in Southfield and the Sacred Heart Chaldean Church in Detroit. Chaldean media includes television and radio shows and newspapers such as the *Chaldean Detroit Times.*

## Ohio

At the turn of the twenty-first century Ohio is home to 120,000 Arab Americans living mainly in Cleveland, Toledo, Columbus, Cincinnati, and Akron. More than three-fourths are Lebanese and Syrian. Of the state's Arab American population, 77 percent are U.S. born. A large number of newer Arab Americans have settled in Cleveland.

The most prominent Arab American labor activist was George Addes, who was a leader in the formation of the United Auto Workers in the 1930s. He became well known because of his participation in a strike in Toledo, Ohio.

Cleveland has an approximate Arab American population of 30,000. As with most other cities, the first Arab immigrants to the area were Lebanese and Syrian peddlers. In *Arab American Merchants and the Crisis of the Inner City, Cleveland: A Case Study,* it is noted that in the early part of the twentieth century, 80 percent of Arab American immigrants were self-employed. At the end of the century, newer immi-

**George Addes, a leader in the formation of the United Auto Workers (U.A.W.), became well known because of his participation in a strike in Toledo, Ohio.**
*Reproduced by permission of the Archives of Labor and Urban Affairs at Wayne State University.*

grants, many of whom are Palestinians and Muslims, continue to strive for self-employment. Arab Americans run more than 300 grocery stores, delicatessens, and restaurants in the city.

Organizations in Cleveland include the Cleveland Arab American Business Association, the Beit Hananina, El Bireh Society, the American Federation of Ramalleh, Palestine, Cleveland American Middle Eastern Association, Arab Community Center for Economic and Social Services (ACCESS), and the Council on American Islamic Relations. There are numerous Arab and Arab American student organizations at the various universities and colleges.

There are also large Arab American communities in Columbus, Cincinnati, Toledo, and Akron. Toledo is known among travelers for the Islamic Center of Greater Toledo, which is located close to the Ohio-Michigan border. Islamic centers are also present in each of the larger cities in Ohio. There are numerous Orthodox churches in Ohio, specifically in Cincinnati, Cleveland, Toledo, and Akron. Cleveland and Columbus are also home to a few Coptic churches.

## Chicago, Illinois

Illinois, which has the smallest percentages of Lebanese and Syrians, has a highly diversified Arab American population, including one of the largest Palestinian communities in the country. In the five-county area of metropolitan Chicago there are about 150,000 Arab Americans and 65,000 Assyrians (Aramaic-speaking Christians from present-day Turkey, Iran, and Iraq). The earliest Arab immigrants to Chicago were Syrian-Lebanese Christians, followed by Palestinian Muslims and a small number of Palestinian Christians. The Syrian-Lebanese immigrants assimilated (blended) more easily into American culture in Chicago than did other groups, partly due to their participation in the local Christian churches and their business successes.

Early Palestinian Muslims started out as peddlers and lived primarily on Chicago's south side. Later they moved to the southwest side and became the foundation of the Arab American community in that area in the 1990s. This Palestinian community on the southwest side of Chicago remains the most concentrated Arab population in the city today. After World War II (1939-45), Palestinian migration to the United States increased due in part to the Palestinian-Israeli conflict brought on by the United Nations' creation of an Israeli state out of Palestinian lands. Assyrians, Iraqis, and Jordanians also began their migration to Chicago, with the Assyrians and Iraqis settling mainly on the north side. By the late 1950s, Palestinian Muslims, along with Jordanians, began to open their own stores. It was estimated that by the early 1970s, Arabs owned 20 percent of all small grocery and liquor stores in Chicago.

Fifty-seven percent of the Chicago Arab American population is Palestinian and 20 percent is Jordanian. The rest of the population includes Egyptians, Iraqis, Syrians, Lebanese, Yemenis, and Assyrians. Due to the ongoing sanctions against Iraq brought about by Saddam Hussein's action in the 1990-91 Gulf War and the continuing Palestinian-Israeli conflict, it can be expected that the immigration of people from Palestine, Jordan, Lebanon, and Iraq will continue. The growing second wave of Arab Americans in Chicago also includes Assyrians and Egyptians.

There are numerous Arab American organizations in the Chicago area, including the Arab American Action Network, Arab American Medical Association, Arab American Lawyers Association, American-Arab Anti-Discrimination Committee, Ramallah Club, Association of Arab American University Graduates, and many local societies based on town or village ties. There is also an Arab Affairs Representative to the mayor. Numerous churches and mosques are found throughout the community. A number of Arabic supermarkets, restaurants, and cafes cater to the Arab American community. Arabic media consists of two Arabic newspapers and Arabic television and radio programs.

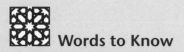

## Words to Know

- **Census:** the number of people in a given population.

- **Demographics:** the study of the characteristics of human populations and the classification of them into categories such as age, education, profession, or ethnicity.

- **Estimate:** a reliable judgment of size based on accurate information.

- **First-generation immigrants:** people who were born in one country and then immigrated to another.

- **Peddlers:** people who sold household goods door-to-door in areas not well-served by stores.

- **Refugees:** people who leave their home countries due to wars and other hardships and seek refuge elsewhere.

- **Second- and third-generation immigrants:** people who are born in one country but whose parents or grandparents were born in another country and immigrated to the country of the child's birth.

- **Unionize:** the process of workers forming groups, called unions, in order to protect their rights.

- **Urban:** pertaining to heavily populated areas, such as cities.

- **U.S. Census Bureau:** the federal office responsible for counting the number of people living in the United States.

# Southwest

## Houston, Texas

At the end of the 1990s, the Arab American population in Texas is 140,000, half of whom reside in Houston. The majority of the population is Lebanese, followed by Syrians, Palestinians, Jordanians, and Egyptians. The last decade of the twentieth century has seen a dramatic growth in the number of Arab Americans in Houston. Palestinians, Lebanese, Egyptians, Iraqis, Saudis, Moroccans, and Tunisians are the newest arrivals, along with Jordanians and many students from the Gulf region. They are joining the established immigrants who arrived mainly from Greater Syria (present-day Syria, Lebanon, Jordan, Palestine, and Israel) at the turn of the twentieth century. More than 60 percent of the current population was born in the United States, most of whom live in the southwest and northwest parts of Houston, although not in any specific neighborhoods.

Earlier arrivals to Houston were mainly Christian, although later immigrants represent both the Christian and Islamic faiths. The first wave of immigrants settled in Houston and Galveston because of work opportunities in the late 1890s and the early 1900s, while other groups started arriving after the 1948 Arab-Israeli War and the 1975-85 Lebanese Civil War. The first immigrants to Houston worked primarily as peddlers until they were able to earn enough money to open small businesses for themselves. It is these same immigrants who then used their earnings to send their children to college. These children have in turn become today's professionals in the Arab American community.

The major Arab American organizations in Houston include the Arab American Community and Cultural Center, the American-Arab Anti-Discrimination Committee, the Arab American Educational Fund, Arab American Medical Association, and the U.S. Arab Chamber of Commerce. Other community organizations include the Syrian Federation, the Egyptian American Society, the Lebanese Club, the Syrian Club, the Ramallah Club, the Palestinian Club, the Jordanian Club, and the Tunisian Club. The university students have formed numerous Arab American student organizations as well. There are also two Maronite churches, one Greek Orthodox church, and several mosques.

# West

## California

A large Arab American population can be found in the San Francisco Bay area, San Jose, Anaheim, and Los Angeles. Some estimates of the population in the 1990s are at 280,000, while other estimates are as high as 350,000, the majority being Egyptians, Assyrians, and Palestinians. The community is very diversified, and the population is equally split between foreign-born Arab Americans and U.S.-born Arab Americans. The first Arab settlers to come to California were Syrian-Lebanese, with newer immigrants arriving from Palestine and Yemen who have settled mainly in the San Francisco Bay area. Many Yemenis worked in the farms in California, alongside the mostly Latino farm workers. The fairly large Assyrian-Chaldean population is centered in Los Angeles, San Jose, Turlock, and San Diego.

## San Francisco

The San Fransisco Bay area—stretching from Berkeley to the west, San Francisco to the north, and San Jose to the south—has a population of about 200,000 Arab Americans. Mostly Palestinian, the population is largely concentrated in the immediate suburbs south of San Francisco. It was once estimated that Arabs owned 300 corner stores in San Francisco. There is a large Ramallah community that owns a church. There is also a large concentration of Arab Americans in San Jose. While most came from overseas, many also moved from San Francisco to the more suburban San Jose.

### Southern California

Southern California (Santa Barbara, Los Angeles, Anaheim, Orange County, and San Diego) has a large Arab American community estimated at several hundred thousand. The Arab American community as a whole is difficult to describe because it is very diverse and spread out. The most likely center for Arab activism may be found in Anaheim, a cohesive Arab American community. The city boasts several large Arabic supermarkets, numerous Arabic restaurants, cafes, several mosques and churches, and numerous Arab professional offices (doctors, pharmacies, etc.).

Southern California is home to more than eight Arab American publications, from weekly newspapers to monthly magazines. There are also four Arab American television programs, two of which are for entertainment and two that are religious (Muslim and Christian).

Organizations that are fairly prominent in California include the American-Arab Anti-Discrimination Committee (with chapters in San Francisco, Orange County and Los Angeles), the Arab American Institute, and the Council for American Islamic Relations. There are also numerous university student groups, including Arab clubs and Muslim student organizations.

Los Angeles and southern California are becoming major political and cultural centers as more immigrants come to the area.

# The future of Arab American communities

Arab American communities continue to prosper in many areas of the country, and are becoming more of a political and social influence in the nation as they become more economically prosperous and politically active and make their presence known. Many Arab American groups hope that the year 2000 census will produce a more accurate count of the community. To this end, they are educating Arab Americans on the importance of claiming their Arab heritage on the census forms.

# For More Information

Abraham, Nabeel. "Detroit's Yemeni Workers." *Middle East Report,* May 1977.

Abraham, Sameer, and Nabeel Abraham, eds. *Arabs in the New World: Studies on Arab American Communities.* Detroit: Wayne State University Press, 1983.

Ahmed, Ismael. "East Dearborn's Arabs: A Brief History." *Passport to the World,* May 1994.

Aswad, Barbara C., ed. *Arabic Speaking Communities in American Cities.* Staten Island, NY: Center for Migration Studies, 1974.

Aswad, Barbara C. *The Greater Detroit Arab and Chaldean Community.* The Arab World Festival Committee, 1986.

Bahhur, Riad, and George Shadroui. *Arab American Merchants and the Crisis of the Inner City, Cleveland: A Case Study.* Washington, D.C.: Arab American Institute, 1995.

Cainkar, Louise. *Meeting Community Needs, Building on Community Strengths.* Chicago: Arab American Action Network, 1998.

Cainkar, Louise, and the Illinois Coalition for Immigrant and Refugee Rights (ICIRR). *Don't Count Me Out: Immigrants and Census 2000.* Chicago: ICIRR, 1999.

David, Gary. "Behind the Counter: Iraqi-Chaldean Store Ownership in Metropolitan Detroit." In *Arab Detroit: From Margin to Mainstream,* edited by Nabeel Abraham and Andrew Shryock. Detroit: Wayne State University Press, in press.

El-Badry, Samia. "The Arab-American Market." *American Demographics,* January 1994.

Haiek, Joseph R. *Arab-American Almanac.* 4th ed. Glendale, CA: News Circle Publishing House, 1992.

Hajar, Paula. Various selections from *The Encyclopedia of New York City,* edited by Kenneth T. Jackson. New Haven, CT: Yale University Press, 1995.

Harik, Elsa Marston. *The Lebanese in America.* Minneapolis: Lerner Publication Company, 1987.

Hitti, Philip. *The Syrians in America.* New York: Geroge H. Doran, 1924.

Hooglund, Eric, ed. *Crossing the Waters: Arabic-Speaking Immigrants to the United States before 1940.* Washington, D.C.: Smithsonian Institution Press, 1987.

Kelley, Ron. "The Yemenis of the San Joaquin." *Middle East Report,* March/April 1986.

Naff, Alixa. *Becoming American: The Early Arab Immigrant Experience.* Carbondale: Southern Illinois University Press, 1985.

Sengstock, Mary C. *The Chaldean Americans: Changing Conception of Ethnic Identity.* New York: Center for Migration Studies, 1982.

Suleiman, Michael W. "The Arab American Left." In *The Immigrant Left in the United States,* edited by Paul Buhle and Dan Georgakas. Albany: State University of New York Press, 1996.

Suleiman, Michael W., ed. *Arabs in America: Building a New Future.* Philadelphia: Temple University Press, in press.

Younis, Adele. *The Coming of the Arabic-Speaking People to the United States.* New York: Center for Migration Studies, 1995.

Zogby, James, ed., and Pat Aufderheide and Anne S. Mooney, asst. eds. *Taking Root Bearing Fruit: The Arab American Experience.* Washington, D.C.: American-Arab Anti-Discriminatory Committee, 1984.

Zogby, John. *Arab America Today: A Demographic Profile of Arab Americans.* Washington, D.C.: Arab American Institute, 1990.

Zogby, John. *Arab American Demographics.* Zogby International, 1995.

*Jessica LaBumbard has a B.A. in Sociology and Spanish and is currently pursuing an M.A. in Intercultural and International Management.*

# Language

The native language of most Arab immigrants in the United States is Arabic, and many of their American-born children and grandchildren also speak Arabic as a second language. In addition to Arabic and English, some Arab Americans speak other languages native to the Arab world, including Berber and Chaldean.

## The origins and spread of the Arabic language

Arabic is the sixth most common first language in the world, and the thirteenth most spoken foreign language in the United States. It is the official language in the twenty-one countries that make up the Arab world (see chapter 1). Arabic is also used by Muslims worldwide for religious devotions, sermons, and prayer.

Arabic belongs to the Afro-Asiatic language family. A language family is a group of languages that are thought to have developed from a common parent language thousands

## Afro-Asiatic Language Tree

| Chadic | Semitic | Cushitic | Berber | Egyptian |
|--------|---------|----------|--------|----------|
| Hausa | Arabic | Somali | Tamazigh | Coptic |
| | Hebrew | Afar | Shilha | |
| | Ethiopic | | Riffian | |
| | Aramaic | | Kabyle | |
| |   -Chaldean | | Shawia | |
| |   -Assyrian | | Tuareg | |

of years ago. Language families are divided into subgroups and individual languages. For example, English belongs to the Germanic subgroup of the Indo-European language family. This subgroup also includes other Germanic languages, such as German and Dutch.

The Afro-Asiatic language family (also known as the Hamito-Semitic family) is divided into five subgroups of languages. These languages are spoken throughout the Middle East and North and Central Africa. The largest subgroup contains the Semitic languages, which include Arabic, Aramaic, and Hebrew (see language tree above). Arabic is thought to have developed in the Arabian Peninsula, and was spoken only there and in bordering areas to the north until the seventh century C.E. (common era, also called A.D.). At that time, the Arabic-speaking people, who had recently converted to Islam, began a period of expansion that carried the Arabic language throughout western Asia and North Africa, and even into Spain in southern Europe.

Arabic became the lingua franca (a language used to communicate between people who speak different languages) of the Muslim Empire. It was used for most government and commercial transactions, religious ceremonies, reading and reciting the *Qur'an* (also Koran; the Muslim holy book) and for scholarly, scientific, and literary writing. In the North African countries of Egypt, Libya, Tunisia, Algeria, and Morocco, Arabic slowly replaced the languages that were spoken there before the arrival of the Muslims. Some of these earlier native languages, such as Egyptian Coptic, have almost completely disappeared. Others, like the Berber languages of northwestern Africa, are still spoken today.

In western Asia—in what is today Syria, Iraq, Jordan, Palestine, and Lebanon—many of the people who became Muslims adopted Arabic, as did most Christians and Jews. A few Christian groups, however, including the Chaldeans and Assyrians, held onto their native languages. In Spain, Arabic was used by the Muslim rulers until 1492, when Queen Isabella and King Ferdinand succeeded in recapturing the south from them. In the next few decades, all Muslims were forced to convert to Christianity or leave Spain, and all use of the Arabic language was forbidden in that country.

In some areas, the population never adopted Arabic, even though they became Muslim. This is true of the Persian speakers of today's Iran; the Kurds found in modern Turkey, Iran, Iraq, and Syria; and the Turkish people of the Anatolian Peninsula (Turkey). Although Arabic never replaced their local languages, it did have a great influence on the vocabulary. Many technical, agricultural, and scientific terms in these peoples' languages have their origins in Arabic.

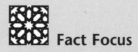

## Fact Focus

- Arabic is the official language of twenty-one countries in Asia and Africa.

- Arabic is written from right to left.

- The Arabic alphabet contains twenty-eight letters.

- Some English words from Arabic are almanac, calendar, magazine, sugar, and traffic.

- Arabic is spoken by over 400,000 people in the United States.

- Many Arab Americans are bilingual (speak two languages) in English and Arabic, and some even speak three languages.

## Written Arabic

The Arabic alphabet was adopted by many of the people ruled by Muslims, including those who never adopted the Arabic language. Even today, the Arabic script is used to write some of the Indo-European languages of western Asia, including Persian and Kurdish. Turkish was written with the Arabic alphabet until the 1920s, when they adopted the Latin alphabet.

Unlike English, Arabic is written from right to left. There are twenty-eight letters in the Arabic alphabet, and these letters have different forms, depending upon whether they come at the beginning, middle, or end of a word. The Arabic script is a source of pride for Arabs, and calligraphy—

# The Arabic Alphabet
# A Guide to Pronunciation

| | | |
|---|---|---|
| أ | alif | "a" as in *apple* |
| ب | ba | "b" as in *bat* |
| ت | ta | "t" as in *taffy* |
| ث | tha | "th" as in *thank* |
| ج | jiim | "j" as in *juggle* |
| ح | ha | "h" as in *hot* |
| خ | kha | "ch" as in *chutzpah* |
| د | dal | "d" as in *daffodil* |
| ذ | thal | "th" as in *that* |
| ر | ra | "r" as in *Iran* (roll the "r") |
| ز | zayn | "z" as in *zipper* |
| س | siin | "s" as in *summer* |
| ش | shiin | "sh" as in *shutter* |
| ص | sod | "s" as in *sorry* |
| ض | dod | "d" as in *dot* |
| ط | ta | "t" as in *taught* |
| ظ | za | "th" as in *other* |
| ع | ‹ayn | sound made in pronunciation of <u>aa</u>rgh (symbol ‹) |
| غ | ghayn | similar to "r" in *Paris* (French pronunciation) |
| ف | fa | "f" as in *favor* |
| ق | qaf | "c" as in *call* |
| ك | kaf | "k" as in *kettle* |
| ل | lam | "l" as in *lamb* |
| م | miim | "m" as in *manner* |
| ن | noon | "n" as in *nap* |
| ه | ha | "h" as in happy |
| و | waw | "w" as in *work*, or "oo" as in *moon* |
| ي | ya | "y" as in *yellow*, or "ee" as in *cheese* |

*Reprinted by permission from the supplement accompanying AMIDEAST's Arabic Alphabet Poster, available from AMIDEAST (1730 M Street, NW, Washington D.C. 20036).*

artistic handwriting—became a highly developed art in the Arab world during the golden years of the Muslim Empire.

## Change and variation in Arabic

Like all languages, Arabic has changed over time. The Arabic spoken at the time of the Prophet Muhammad (c. 570-632), before the Muslim expansion, is now referred to as Classical Arabic. This is the language of the Qur'an, and it is still used today for prayers and religious recitations. But the Arabic spoken by people in their everyday lives has changed greatly over the last fourteen centuries.

## Borrowing

Because the world is always changing, languages must continuously adapt by finding new ways to describe innovations and new ideas. One way that they do this is by borrowing words that already exist in other languages. During the time of Muslim expansion beginning in the seventh century, European languages borrowed many mathematical and scientific terms from Arabic, along with words referring to civil engineering and government administration. Arabic words that were adopted by the English language include: admiral, alchemy, alcohol, algebra, almanac, average, calendar, coffee, magazine, traffic, and zero.

Similarly, in recent years, technological innovations have created a need for new vocabulary to describe things such as television, computers, and pagers. The Arabic language sometimes borrows the English, French, or Spanish version of such words, which it modifies to fit Arabic pronunciation. For example, "television" is pronounced *te-le-fis-yon* in Arabic.

Because Arabic was spoken over such a large geographical area throughout history, it has had the opportunity to borrow from many different languages. These include local native languages spoken before the arrival of Arabic, as well as languages of the Europeans and Turks who colonized the Arab world in recent centuries. Moroccan Arabic, for example, borrowed words from the native Berber languages and from French and Spanish—the languages of the two European countries that colonized (governed) Morocco at the beginning of the twentieth century. Yemeni Arabic, on the other hand,

## English Words Adopted from Arabic Words

| | |
|---|---|
| Admiral | Cotton |
| Alchemy | Jasmine |
| Alcohol | Magazine |
| Algebra | Mattress |
| Almanac | Racquet |
| Atlas | Satin |
| Average | Sugar |
| Candy | Tambourine |
| Coffee | Traffic |
| Calendar | Zero |

has been influenced by the languages of the Turkish and British colonial governments.

## Spoken dialects and Modern Standard Arabic

The Arabic spoken in one country is not the same as the Arabic spoken in another. The different varieties of spoken Arabic are called dialects. Dialects of Arabic vary from country to country because each region of the Arab world was influenced by its own native (pre-Arabic) languages, as well as diverse colonial languages. Over time, these varying influences caused the spoken versions of Arabic to evolve differently from place to place.

The modern dialects of North Africa are quite different from those of the Middle East and the Arabian Peninsula. Sometimes it is even difficult for these Arabic speakers to understand one another because the words they use, and even their grammar, vary so much. For example, the phrase *How are you?* is pronounced *keefek?* in Lebanese, *izzayyak?* in Egyptian, *shlownak?* in Iraqi, and *la bas?* in Moroccan. This can make communication between different dialects rather complicated.

In spite of these differences, other factors have made it possible for Arabic speakers from such distant regions to communicate. First, mass media, such as television, radio, and movies, have allowed Arabic speakers from all over the world to see and hear each other. Because Egypt is considered the "Hollywood" of the Arab world, many Arabic speakers can understand the Egyptian dialect from watching movies and television programs. Second, modern means of transportation have allowed more people to travel, exposing them to other dialects.

Another factor that helps Arabic speakers communicate with one another is the existence of a common language known as Modern Standard Arabic. Just as Classical Arabic was the lingua franca during the time of Muslim expansion,

Modern Standard Arabic serves as the lingua franca of the Arab world today. Modern Standard Arabic is very similar to Classical Arabic, although the grammar (rules of language) has been simplified and new words have been added to reflect the needs of today's speakers. Almost all official documents, newspapers, books, and journals are written in Modern Standard Arabic. And people often use it in formal settings—such as newscasts, classrooms, and government administration—rather than speaking their local dialects.

Most people who are literate (can read and write) in Arabic can speak Modern Standard Arabic. While there are still illiterate people in the Arab world today (especially in mountainous and rural areas), the spread of public schooling and mass communications is rapidly exposing more and more people to both written and spoken Modern Standard Arabic. In fact, as more people learn this form of Arabic, some of the local dialects are sure to be lost just as they were during the first expansion of the Arabic language.

# Arabic and English among new immigrants

There are many varieties of Arabic spoken in the United States. Arab immigrants speak the dialects of their home countries, meaning that the most common dialects spoken in the United States are those of Lebanon, Syria, Palestine, Jordan, Yemen, and Iraq. While many Arab Americans can understand other dialects, it is sometimes difficult for them to communicate if the dialect spoken is very different from their own. But if they know Modern Standard Arabic, or are familiar with the Egyptian dialect from the movies and television, they can communicate with one another in Arabic. And eventually Arabic speakers from different countries who live in the same communities in the United States learn to understand each others' way of speaking.

## Learning English as a second language

Many Arab immigrants in the United States learn to speak English in addition to their native tongue. For some of them it is easy to learn a new language, but for others it can be

School-age children often learn English more quickly than their parents.
*Photograph by Diane Frank. Reproduced by permission of the Arab Community Center for Economic and Social Services (ACCESS).*

quite difficult. If Arabic speakers have studied English or learned another foreign language before coming to the United States, they may find it easier to pick up the new language. Because children in the Arab world often learn a second language at school from a young age, many Arab immigrants are bilingual (speak two languages fluently). People from Yemen, Egypt, and Palestine often know some English before arriving. And Lebanese people frequently speak French in addition to Arabic, since French is the second language of Lebanon. Knowing two languages—with their different alphabets, grammars, and vocabularies—makes learning a third language much easier.

Learning English is harder for those who never learned a second language prior to immigrating. It is also more difficult for those who did not learn to read and write fluently in their own language. This is the case for some older immigrants who come from small villages that did not have public schools until recently. Because they are not literate in

Arabic, learning English is much more of a chore, since they must not only learn a new grammar and vocabulary, but also the mechanics of reading and writing.

Another important factor in learning to speak a second language is the amount of exposure a person has to the language they are trying to learn. It is easier for new immigrants to learn English if they are forced to use the language on a daily basis at work or school in order to communicate with their coworkers and classmates. For this reason, school-age children often learn English more quickly than their parents do.

Learning English is especially hard for elderly people who do not work (such as those who, after retiring, come to join their adult children). But many Arab American organizations—including community centers, churches, and mosques—offer English language classes for these new immigrants. Even those who do not work or attend classes frequently pick up some English from interacting with neighbors and employees at stores and businesses. They also learn from their English-speaking children and grandchildren. And of course, the television offers people the opportunity to hear English, though not practice it, twenty-four hours a day.

## U.S.-born Arab Americans

Some Arab Americans born and raised in the United States speak Arabic at home with their families, while others speak English. In general, because they attend public school, they all become fluent in English no matter which language they speak with their parents. But the extent to which they are bilingual, and can speak, read, and write Arabic as well as they do English, depends upon the language spoken with families and close friends.

If Arab parents speak only English to their children, it is highly unlikely that the children will learn Arabic unless a grandparent or other relative lives with them and speaks Arabic to them on a daily basis. In some families, the parents speak Arabic to one another and to the children, but the children respond to them in English. These children feel more comfortable speaking English once they begin school and realize that English is the language of their peers (friends and classmates). In these cases, the children learn to understand Arabic well, but may never feel comfortable speaking it.

When parents and children do speak Arabic with one another, the children learn to speak the dialect of their parents, but may not learn how to read and write the language. Sometimes these children never become literate in Arabic, although they are fluent speakers. But in larger Arab American communities, parents have the option of sending their children to Arabic classes in a local church, mosque, or community center. Here the children learn to read and write Modern Standard Arabic or the Classical Arabic of the Qur'an.

It is common for Arab Americans who did not learn Arabic growing up to mourn the fact they have "lost" the language of their ancestors. First- and second-generation immigrant children often reject the language of their parents because it is not "cool" and makes them different from their peers, but as they grow older they often begin to learn about and appreciate the beauty of their parents' and grandparents' culture. Then they realize that by losing the Arabic language, they are losing an important part of their cultural heritage.

## Other languages spoken by immigrants from the Arab world

There are many native languages spoken in the Arab world besides Arabic, and some Arab Americans speak these other languages—often in addition to Arabic and English. Because language is one of the defining characteristics of Arab identity (see Chapter 1), some people in the Arab world whose native language is not Arabic may not consider themselves to be Arab. The ethnic minorities of the Arab world include Berbers, Chaldeans, Assyrians, and Kurds.

The Iraqi Chaldeans are considered ethnic minorities. Their native language, Chaldean, is an Afro-Asiatic language of the Aramaic subgroup. Unlike the majority of the Iraqi people, the Chaldeans are Christians who did not convert to Islam during the Muslim expansion in the seventh century. The Chaldeans originally come from an area in northern Iraq. They have retained their religion and their

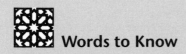

## Words to Know

- **Bilingual:** fluent in two languages.

- **Borrowing:** adapting a word from one language into another language. These borrowed words are sometimes referred to as loan words.

- **Classical Arabic:** the Arabic language which was spoken in the Arabian Peninsula at the time of the Prophet Muhammad and which was used to write the Muslim holy book, the Qur'an (Koran).

- **Dialect:** a particular local version of a language that can be understood by speakers of other forms of the same language.

- **Ethnic minority:** a group of people who identify themselves as being culturally different from the dominant group in the society.

- **First language:** the language a person learns at home or speaks most fluently. A second language is usually learned at school, or outside of the home.

- **Language family:** a group of languages thought to have derived from a common language thousands of years ago.

- **Lingua franca:** a language used to communicate between people who speak different languages.

- **Literate:** able to read and write.

- **Native language:** the language spoken by the original inhabitants of an area. (A person's native language is the language he or she learned first.)

- **Parent language:** a language from which two or more later languages evolved.

- **Second language acquisition:** learning to speak a second language.

native language in spite of the fact that they learn Arabic at school and use the Iraqi Arabic dialect to communicate with non-Chaldean Iraqis.

There are between 80,000 and 100,000 Chaldeans in the United States, and the largest community is in Detroit, Michigan. Many members of this community, especially the older generations, speak Chaldean in the home, and also speak, read, and write Arabic. The younger, U.S.-born Chaldean Americans are fluent in English, although they may understand, and even speak, Chaldean if they learn it at home. The Chaldean community tries to keep the language alive through classes offered in local churches. Like all immigrant communities, though, they know that with each passing generation fewer of their descendants will know how to speak the language that their ancestors held onto for so many centuries.

Another Aramaic language spoken in the United States is Assyrian, which is similar to Chaldean. Most Assyrian immigrants, who come from Northern Iraq and Syria, also speak Arabic as their second language. There is a large community of Assyrian speakers in Chicago and northern California.

Some Iraqi immigrants speak Kurdish as their native language. Kurdish, like English, is an Indo-European language. Many Kurdish immigrants also learn Arabic in Iraqi schools before coming to the United States.

Another group of native languages spoken in the Arab world are those of the Berber subgroup of the Afro-Asiatic family. These Berber languages (which are collectively called *Tamazight* by native speakers) were spoken by North Africans before the arrival of the Arabs in the seventh century. Although Arabic is now the official language, Berber languages are still widely spoken in today's Algeria and Morocco, and you can find Berber speakers in the United States among immigrants from these countries.

There are also ethnic minorities that migrated to the Arab world to seek refuge from wars, political turmoil, or the economic hardships of their homelands. These people often retained their native languages and cultural identity although they became citizens of Arab countries. This is the case with the Armenian people, who went to Lebanon, Syria, Egypt, Jordan, Iraq, and Palestine. Those who later immigrated to the United States, although they may not consider themselves Arab, do identify with Arab culture and speak the Arabic language.

# For More Information

Harik, Elsa Marston. *The Lebanese in America*. Minneapolis: Lerner Publication Company, 1987.

Sayegh, Lila. *First Arabic Handwriting Workbook and Tape*. Troy, MI: International Book Center, 1987.

Sayegh, Lila. *Learn Arabic through Words and Simple Phrases*. Troy, MI: International Book Center, 1987.

Shabbas, Audrey, and Ayad Al-Qazzaz, eds. *Arab World Notebook*. Berkeley, CA: Nadja (Women Concerned About the Middle East), 1989.

*Dawn Ramey is a Ph.D. candidate in Anthropology at Indiana University. She worked with the Arab Community Center for Economic and Social Services (ACCESS) from 1995 to 1999, and is currently conducting research on social justice issues for the Arab American community.*

# Religion

**7**

The two main religions practiced by Arab Americans are Christianity and Islam. Religion in the Arab American community is similar in many ways to religion in other American communities. Arab American Christians and Muslims share many of the same basic beliefs as Americans who are Catholic, Protestant, and Jewish. These include the belief in one supreme God who created the world.

Religion for Arab Americans does not only provide a system of beliefs about God and how people should live, it also brings together people from similar backgrounds. In churches and mosques, Arab Americans attend social, educational, and charitable events that allow them to meet and interact with other members of the congregation.

Before discussing the religions practiced by Arab Americans, it is helpful to understand the religious diversity of the Arab world. Arab Americans trace their ancestry back to the ancient, highly advanced civilizations that flourished around the Nile River in Egypt and the Fertile Crescent, an area that today includes the countries of Jordon, Lebanon, Syria, Iraq, Palestine, and Israel. These areas were the birthplace of three monotheistic religions: Judaism, Christianity, and Islam. Monotheism is the belief that there is only one God. Judaism was the first of the monotheistic religions to begin in the Middle East, followed by Christianity and, finally, Islam.

## Judaism and the beginning of monotheism

Judaism began almost 4,000 years ago in ancient Mesopotamia, in the area of the Tigris and Euphrates Rivers in present-day Iraq and Syria. In approximately 1800 B.C.E. (before common era, or "before Christ"), a man named Abraham, known as the founding father of Judaism and a prophet (a religious visionary and preacher), declared his belief in one Lord God. Abraham rejected the beliefs of his fellow citizens in the Greco-Roman Empire who were convinced that there were many gods. These people paid homage to the sun, moon, trees, and other objects in nature through prayer, offerings of grains, and animal sacrifices, hoping to be rewarded with health, good crops, and prosperity. At this time, it was common for people to make elaborate statues out of stone to represent the gods of their tribe or village. Therefore, Abraham's declaration that there was only one God was a new idea, one that strongly influenced the development of western (Christian European) civilization.

The followers of Judaism are known as Jews. They also believe in another important prophet, Moses. According to their tradition, the prophet Moses stood at Mt. Sinai, located in present-day Egypt, in the year 1250 B.C.E. and received from God the Ten Commandments and the Torah, or the Old Testament. Jews rely on their holy book, the Torah, for guidelines on how to treat other people and live a decent life.

Since the birth of Judaism, there have been Jewish communities throughout the Arab world. In the later half of the twentieth century, however, most Jews living in Arab countries—including Yemen, Iraq, Morocco, and Egypt—have immigrated to Israel or the United States for religious, cultural, or political reasons. When Jewish people immigrate to the United States from an Arab country, they often identify themselves as Jewish Americans rather than Arab Americans. Therefore, most Arab Americans are Christian or Muslim, not Jewish, even though in the Arab world people from all three religions can be found.

# Christianity

Christianity emerged 2,000 years ago when Jesus was born in Bethlehem, Palestine. Christians believe that there is only one God, and that Jesus Christ was God's son and the promised messiah, or savior. The teachings of Jesus, found in the Bible in the four gospels of Matthew, Mark, Luke, and John, include the virtues of good will, loving others as oneself, truth, honesty, and sincerity in thought and deed. The holy book for Christians is the Bible, which includes both the Old and New Testaments. Some Christians pray every day, but for many, the most important time for prayer is at the Sunday service in church, the place of Christian worship.

In the fifth century C.E. (common era, also called A.D.), the first major split in Christianity occurred. Today, several branches of Christianity exist, and Arab and Arab American Christians may belong to one of several churches. Despite small differences, most Arab American Christians share the same basic religious beliefs.

## Three Christian groups

There are three major Christian branches in the world, and within each of these groups smaller groups exist. The three branches are the Roman Catholic Church, the Protestant denominations, and the Eastern Orthodox churches.

The Roman Catholic branch of Christianity is the oldest, dating back to the fourth century. Roman Catholics consider the Pope in Rome to be their spiritual leader. It is believed

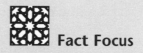 **Fact Focus**

- The Arab world is home to three well-known religions: Judaism, Christianity, and Islam.

- The first Arab American Mosque was built in 1923 in Highland Park, Michigan.

- Approximately 50 percent of Arab Americans are Christian and 50 percent are Muslim.

- Arab American Christians are more likely to be Catholic or Eastern Orthodox Christians than Protestants.

that God protects the Pope from making errors in terms of his spiritual teaching. This concept is called "papal infallibility."

The Protestant groups, which include the Presbyterians, Episcopalians, and Lutherans, emerged in the sixteenth century after the Protestant Reformation. The Protestant Reformation began in 1517 when Martin Luther, a Roman Catholic priest, criticized the church's sale of "indulgences"— certificates that were said to reduce the time a soul must stay in purgatory before reaching peace in heaven. Within a few years, there were millions of followers of the new Protestant faith. The focus in the Protestant denominations is the act of loving God and doing good deeds out of a sense of love rather than obligation.

Although there are Catholics and Protestant Christians in the Arab world and within the Arab American community, the majority belong to one of the Eastern Rite churches. In 1054 C.E., the Eastern Orthodox churches split from Roman Catholicism. This is known as "the Great Schism." One of the main reasons for this split was that the Eastern Orthodox churches did not consider the Pope to be the supreme authority on ethical (dealing with right and wrong) and spiritual (religious) matters. Instead, they decided that decisions affecting their faith should be made by consensus, or agreement, by the church members. Each of the Eastern Orthodox churches, including the Coptic Orthodox Church, the Greek Orthodox Church, and the Syrian Orthodox Church, have their own patriarchs, or leaders, that provide leadership and guidance to the community.

There are also Catholic churches in the Arab world. These Catholic churches, which include the Maronite and Melkite churches, accept the Pope in Rome to be their leader, but still have religious services in their native language of Arabic and continue their unique cultural rituals.

# Islam

Islam is the religion of the majority of Arabs and of approximately 50 percent of Arab Americans. It began with the birth of the prophet Muhammad (c. 570-632) in the town of Mecca, a famous trade center in present-day Saudi Arabia.

**An ancient handwritten copy of the Qur'an.**
*Reproduced by permission of Archive Photos, Inc.*

Muslims, followers of the faith of Islam, believe that in 610 Muhammad first heard the word of God through the angel Gabriel. His words were recorded in the *Qur'an* (also spelled Koran), the holy book for Muslims. Muhammad continued to receive revelations from God for the next twenty-two years. The word Qur'an means recitation, because its words were literally recited to Muhammad through the angel Gabriel.

Like Jews and Christians before them, Muslims believe in one Lord God. The word for God in Arabic is *Allah*. Islam means submission, and derives from a word meaning "peace." Muslims believe in submission to the will of God. In general, Muslims are more familiar with Judaism and Christianity than Jews and Christians are with Islam, because the religion of Islam recognizes all the prophets from Abraham through Jesus. These earlier prophets are mentioned in the Qur'an, and Jews and Christians are considered "people of the book." This means that Muslims respect the holy books of the Jews and Christians, and believe that the Jewish Torah and the Christian Bible contain divine truths. Because the Qur'an was revealed in Arabic, many Muslims all over the world learn to read Arabic in order to be able to read the Qur'an in its original language.

In the Qur'an Muslims find prayers, the history of the prophets, and guidance on ethical and spiritual matters. In addition, Muslims have two other important sources: the *Hadith,* sayings and acts of the prophet Muhammad, and the *Shari'a,* the code of Islamic law. Both of these derive from the Qur'an. The stories in the Hadith show how the prophet Muhammad handled various situations in daily life, and gives moral guidance to Muslims. In the Shari'a, Muslims find detailed explanations of legal matters, including laws on diet, marriage, divorce, and inheritance. For instance, Muslims should not drink liquor or eat pork, and they should eat only chicken or beef that is *halal,* meaning that it has been slaughtered according to Islamic law.

## The five pillars of Islam

In addition to the rules of the Shari'a, there are five commands—or pillars—that describe the important beliefs and obligations of Muslims. Muslims must follow these five pillars.

*Shahada:* This is the basic declaration of faith for Muslims, which says, "There is no god but God, and Muhammad is his messenger." This statement is central to Islam, and is recited by many Muslims daily because it affirms their belief in one God and in God's teachings, which were brought to humankind through the prophet Muhammad.

*Salat,* or prayer: Islam commands Muslims to recite prayers five times daily. These prayers are said at dawn, noon, mid-afternoon, sunset, and nightfall. A Muslim man or woman may pray anywhere, including a field, office, or university. Some Muslims prefer to pray with other Muslims in a mosque. A mosque is a place of worship for Muslims, as a church is for Christians and a synagogue for Jews. Just as Christians may gather together to pray at church on Sunday morning, congregational prayer in the Muslim community takes place at noon on Friday.

*Zakat,* or charity: This command reflects one of the most important principles in Islam—that all things belong to God, and human beings are trusted to share what they have with those who are less fortunate. Muslims must give 2.5 percent of their annual income to those in need.

*Soum,* or fasting: Every year in Ramadan, the ninth month of the lunar calendar, Muslims are expected to fast from sunrise until sundown, abstaining from food and drink. A Muslim is permitted to break the fast if they are sick, elderly, or on a journey. In addition, if a Muslim woman is pregnant or nursing, she can break the fast. In these circumstances, people must make up missed days at a later time in the year. If this is not possible, then they must feed a needy person for every day missed. During the month of Ramadan, many Muslims think about how they can be better people. Through the act of fasting, Muslims come to understand and sympathize with people who go hungry on a daily basis.

**Part of the five pillars of Islam is the pilgrimage to the sacred city of Mecca.**
*Reproduced by permission of the Library of Congress.*

*Hajj,* or pilgrimage: the annual pilgrimage to Mecca, the birthplace of the prophet Muhammad, is an obligation for people who are physically fit and financially capable of performing it. The Hajj takes place in the twelfth month of the lunar year, and about two million Muslim pilgrims arrive in Mecca each year, most wearing simple white garments that are meant to wipe away any distinctions of class or culture. In this way, it is believed that a Muslim from a wealthy family in Egypt or from a poor family in Detroit can stand equal before God. One of the special rituals of the Hajj is the circling of a site called the *Ka'ba* (Kaaba), which looks like an enormous black cube. Muslims believe that the Ka'ba is the place where the prophet Abraham and his son Ishmael were commanded by God to build a place of worship.

## Divisions within Islam

There are two main branches of Islam: *Sunni* and *Shi'a.* This division occurred shortly after the death of the prophet Muhammad in the seventh century C.E. With Muhammad gone, the Muslim community, called the *umma,* needed a new leader. The Sunnis believed that the new caliph, or successor, should be chosen through an election. They chose Abu Bakr, Muhammad's close friend, to be his successor. However, the Shi'a claimed that the line of succession should be through Muhammad's descendants. The Shi'a favored Muhammad's cousin and son-in-law, Ali, as his successor. In 680 C.E., one of Ali's sons, Hussein, led a rebellion against the ruling caliph, and the rebels were massacred. Hussein's martyrdom started the Shi'a movement that is known today. Currently, Sunni Muslims are the majority, making up about 85 percent of the world total, though there are large numbers of Shi'a Muslims in southern Iraq and Lebanon. Sunni and Shi'a Muslims both adhere to the five pillars of Islam, though they may have their own mosques and unique ceremonial rituals. There are many smaller divisions within Islam that may reflect the local culture and community.

One of the least understood branches of Islam is the *Druze.* The Druze trace their origins back to Cairo, Egypt, where they began as an Islamic reform movement in the eleventh century. While several individuals were important in establishing the religious principles of the Druze, Hakim is considered to be the founding father of Druzism. Two of the main reforms he introduced were the abolition of slavery and the separation of church and state. In spite of these reforms, the Druze still follow the five pillars of Islam. Along with the Qur'an, or Muslim holy book, the Druze have a collection of about thirty other manuscripts that outline specific Druze commandments and moral obligations. Today there are approximately one million members of the Druze faith worldwide. In the Arab world, the majority of the Druze community is found in Lebanon, Syria, Israel, and Jordan. In the nineteenth century, Druze immigrants began settling in other countries, including Central and South America, the Philippines, Europe, Canada, and the United States. Currently there are about twenty thousand Druze living in United States, with the largest American Druze community in southern California.

# Arab American Christians

Today, Arab American Christians make up about 50 percent of the Arab American community. Arab American Christians were the first Arab immigrants to settle in the United States, Canada, and South America. As early as the 1850s, Christians from Syria and Lebanon (then part of Greater Syria) were coming to America in search of economic prosperity and a better life. Greater Syria included the modern nations of Syria, Lebanon, Jordan, Palestine, and Israel. While there were some Muslims among this first wave of Arab immigrants, the majority belonged to one of three branches of Christianity: Maronite, Orthodox, and Melkite.

These branches of Christianity originated in the Arab world. The few Arabs who belonged to western Catholic or Protestant churches were converted by European missionaries in the nineteenth century. The missionaries, mainly from England and France, wanted Arab Christians to adopt forms of European Christianity.

Arab Christians, while sharing many of the same basic beliefs and values as European Christians, have their own patriarch (leader) and their own churches. Many celebrate the major Christian holidays according to the Eastern Orthodox calendar, rather than the Western calendar. This means that,

**Young Arab Americans at confirmation services at the Saint Nicholas Orthodox cathedral in Los Angeles, California.** *Reproduced by permission of Paul S. Conklin.*

for instance, while Christians in Italy or Ireland may celebrate Christmas on December 25, many Arab and Arab American Christians celebrate it on January 7.

# The Arab Christian churches in the United States

## Eastern Rite churches

Antiochan Orthodox: The first church was established in the 1890s in the city of New York. Most of the church's members come from Syria, Lebanon, and Palestine. Their patriarch is located in Damascus, Syria. The largest communities of Antiochan Orthodox are found in New York, Detroit, Los Angeles, and Massachusetts.

Assyrian Orthodox: The first congregation was founded in New York. The patriarch is located in Chicago. Today there are churches in Chicago, New York, and the San Francisco Bay area. Most members are of Iraqi, Syrian, or Iranian background.

Syrian Orthodox: The first church was established in West New York, New Jersey, in 1927 and in 1999 its patriarch is located in Hackensack, New Jersey. Today significant congregations are found in more than ten American and Canadian cities. Most of the several thousand members are of Syrian, Lebanese, or Iraqi origin.

## Catholic churches

Chaldean Catholic: The first congregation was established in 1947 in Hamilton, Michigan. Today churches are found in Chicago, Detroit, and California. Their patriarch is located in Baghdad, Iraq, and most members come from Iraq, although some come from Syria and Iran.

Coptic Orthodox: The first churches were found in the late 1960s in New Jersey and California. Large congregations are located in Los Angeles, Detroit, and New York. The patriarch is located in Alexandria, Egypt, and most members come from Egypt or Ethiopia.

Maronite: The first church was established in the 1890s in Boston, Massachusetts. Most church members are of

Lebanese origin. Today churches can be found in most large cities, including New York, Boston, St. Louis, Los Angeles, and Detroit.

Melkite: The first church was established in the early 1900s in Lawrence, Massachusetts. At the turn of the twenty-first century churches are found in Los Angeles, Detroit, and Boston. Members are mostly from Lebanon, Syria, Palestine, and Jordan, with fewer members from Egypt and Sudan. The patriarch is located in Damascus, Syria.

Syrian Catholic: One of the first churches was established in Jacksonville, Florida, in the 1950s. With members mostly of Syrian, Lebanese, and Iraqi origin, significant Syrian Catholic congregations are found today in Detroit and New York.

## Early Arab American churches

Among the pre-World War II (1939-45) immigrants from the Arab world, the majority were Christians, mainly from the area of Mount Lebanon. While some of these early immigrants were mobile peddlers and tradespeople, others settled in cities, towns, and rural areas in middle America. Like Polish, Irish, and Italian Americans, Arab American Christians established their own churches as a central part of their new communities. The first church established by Arab Americans was an Antiochan Orthodox church, founded by Father Raphael in New York City in the 1890s. Before World War II, Arab American Christians had established churches in the following denominations: Antiochan Orthodox, Melkite, Syrian Orthodox, Syrian Catholic (Jacobites), Maronite, and Assyrian Orthodox.

## Arab American Christian immigrants after World War II

After World War II, Arab immigrants to the United States began to come from many other regions and nations, including Palestine, Jordan, Iraq, Egypt, and Yemen. Once again, these new immigrants established their own churches, where they could continue to practice their religion the way they had in their homeland.

The Chaldean Catholics established their own church in America after World War II. Chaldean immigrants began emigrating from Iraq, Syria, and Iran at the turn of the twentieth century, though they did not have their own pastor (religious leader) or church until 1947. Until this time, they attended local Catholic churches in the communities in which they lived. In 1982, the Chaldean Catholics became even more independent when Pope John Paul II appointed Bishop Ibrahim Ibrahim to the Chaldean diocese (district) in California. Today, there are four Chaldean parishes in California, four in Detroit, Michigan, and two in Chicago, Illinois.

Another new religious community was the Egyptian Coptic Orthodox community. Coptic Christians began coming in significant numbers to America in the 1960s, and their first churches were founded between 1967 and 1969: one in New Jersey and one in California. In 1999 there were more than fifty-two Coptic churches in the United States. Currently, the largest Coptic Christian community is in California, but there are also active Coptic communities throughout the Midwest and East Coast, in places such as Michigan, New Jersey, and New York.

# Arab American Muslims

Among the first stream of immigrants from the Arab world to America, only 5 to 10 percent were Muslims. The few thousand Muslims, including Sunnis, Shi'a and Druze, who arrived in the years 1850 to 1924 were scattered throughout the United States. Like Arab Christian immigrants, they came to America seeking opportunities and a better life. However, it was more difficult for Arab American Muslims to practice their religion as they had in their homeland. Because Arab American Christians were more numerous, they were able to raise money to purchase land for their churches. Also, Arab American Christians who did not live in their own community often lived in cities or towns with Irish Americans, Polish Americans, or Italian Americans, where churches already existed that they could attend.

Many Arab American Muslims had to be adaptable in practicing their religion in America. There were no mosques (the Muslim house of worship) until 1923, when the first mosque was established in Highland Park, Michigan. The pace of life in America sometimes made it difficult for Muslims to follow the five pillars, or commands, of Islam. Muslim shop owners trying to build new businesses, or factory workers on a strict shift, had to struggle to find private space and time for the five daily prayers. Also, the Muslim day of rest is Friday, but in the United States Sunday is honored by the American government, employers, and schools as the day of rest. Many Muslims, therefore, found it difficult to attend the Friday mosque services for the noon-time prayer.

Arab American Muslims knew that the religion of Islam makes allowances for Muslims who are unable to fulfill all their obligations. At the turn of the twentieth century, some Arab American Muslims gathered in homes to pray and to celebrate religious festivals. While they may have wished for an *imam*—a Muslim religious leader—to lead them in prayer, Muslims do not require an imam to observe their religion. Some Arab American Muslims observe all aspects of their religion, while others choose to follow some commands, but not others. For instance, just as some Christians go to church on Sunday while others do not, some Muslims pray five times a day and fast during the month of Ramadan, while others do not.

## Early Arab American Muslim mosques

A few thousand Arab American Muslims arrived in the United States before 1924, when the Johnson-Reed Quota Act was passed by Congress. This act severely restricted immigration from southern and eastern Europe and from Asia, the continent where Greater Syria and other Arab provinces were located. Before 1924, Arab American Muslims were already living all over the United States, including Rhode Island, Minnesota, Massachusetts, North Dakota, and Iowa. One of the first sizable Arab American Muslim communities was located in Detroit, Michigan, and was founded at the beginning of the twentieth century. The largest Arab-Muslim community in the early 1900s, however, was located in Chicago, Illinois. Arab American Muslims soon found their way from the

**Muslims exit the Islamic Center in Washington, D.C.** *Reproduced by permission of Corbis Corporation (Bellevue).*

East Coast to the West Coast, and were spread out from Connecticut to Seattle, Washington.

The first mosque—established in Highland Park, Michigan, in 1923—survived only four years. In 1925, another mosque was founded in Michigan City, Indiana. The Arab-Muslim community of Michigan City purchased a cemetery and a building, which they divided into two—one for prayer and the other for Arabic language instruction and social events. This mosque is still in use seventy-five years later. Another important mosque and Islamic center was founded in Cedar Rapids, Iowa, in 1934. In 1971 the descendants of the original settlers of Cedar Rapids built a new one in its place.

## Arab American Muslims after World War II

After World War II, many more Muslims from the Arab world came to America. The increase in the number of new immigrants was due in part to the Hart-Cellar Reform Act passed in 1965, which lifted the former restrictions on immigration imposed by the Johnson-Reed Quota Act of 1924. The Hart-Cellar act allowed more Arabic-speaking immigrants to enter the country to obtain American citizenship. Since the 1960s, approximately 90 percent of the new immigrants coming from Arab countries, including Lebanon, Iraq, Yemen, and Palestine, are Muslim. Today, Arab American Muslims comprise about 50 percent of the Arab American community. Among the 6 to 7 million Muslims living in America, only about 1.5 million are Arab American. The rest are African American, or people from various other backgrounds, including Malaysians, Indians, Pakistanis, Iranians, and Africans. Arab Americans are only one part of the larger American Muslim community.

Today, the largest Arab American Muslim community is in Michigan's Detroit metropolitan area, but there are other thriving communities of Arab American Muslims in Illinois, Virginia, New York, Los Angeles, and Washington, D.C. In the last decade of the twentieth century, Americans have become more familiar with the religion of Islam, in part because of

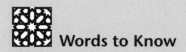

## Words to Know

- **Allah:** the name for God in the Arabic language.

- **Caliphs:** the religious and political leaders of the Muslim community after the death of Muhammad.

- **C.E. (common era):** another term for A.D., which means "after death" (referring to the death of the Christian figure Jesus Christ).

- **Druze:** a small branch of Islam developed in the eleventh century. The largest Druze community in the Arab world is in Lebanon.

- **Eastern Orthodox Christianity:** a branch of Christianity that split from Roman Catholicism in the eleventh century. It includes Antiochan, Coptic, Syrian, and Assyrian Orthodox churches. These are sometimes referred to as the Middle Eastern, or Arab, churches.

- **Hajj:** the Muslim pilgrimage to Mecca, the birthplace of the prophet Muhammad. All Muslims are obligated to do this once in his or her lifetime if they are financially and physically capable of doing so.

- **Hadith:** the sayings and acts of the prophet Muhammad.

- **Imam:** a Muslim religious leader. Imams lead the congregational prayers at noon on Fridays.

- **Monotheism:** the belief that there is only one God.

- **Qur'an:** also spelled Koran; the holy book for Muslims.

- **Ramadan:** the ninth lunar month during which Muslims fast from sunrise to sunset.

- **Salah:** the Arabic word for prayer.

- **Shahada:** the basic declaration of faith for Muslims that says, "There is no god but God, and Muhammad is his messenger." It is one of the five pillars of Islam.

- **Shari'a:** the code of Islamic law.

- **Shi'a:** a branch of Islam. The Shi'a have a significant following in Lebanon and southern Iraq. The majority of the people in the Middle Eastern (but non-Arab) country of Iran are Shi'a.

- **Sunni:** a branch of Islam. The majority of Muslims worldwide are Sunni Muslims.

the increase in the number of Arab Muslim immigrants. Some changes have been made that make life easier for Arab American Muslims and Muslims of every racial and ethnic background. For instance, in schools and universities that have many Muslim students, a special room may be set aside as a place where these students can go to pray, alone or together. Also, in schools and businesses where there are large numbers

**Muslim worshippers congregate on the sidewalk outside of the Al-Farooq mosque in Brooklyn, New York.** *Reproduced by permission of AP/Wide World Photos.*

of Muslims, the school district, school principal, or employer may excuse Muslims from class or work on Muslim holidays.

## Arab Americans in churches and mosques: learning, studying, celebrating

While Arab American Christians and Muslims may go to a church or mosque for religious worship, they have many other reasons to go. Just as other Americans may go to church hoping to make friends or to meet a potential spouse from their community, Arab American Christians often belong to churches where they are likely to meet others who come from a similar cultural background, sometimes from the same village or city. For instance, the St. Mary Orthodox Church in Livonia, Michigan, has many members from the Palestinian town of Ramallah. These families not share only a religion, but a history that includes being brought up in the Arab culture and migration from Ramallah, located in the Palestinian West Bank.

Another important service offered by Arab American churches and mosques is instruction in the Arabic language. Just as Jewish American children sometimes go to a synagogue to learn Hebrew, Arab American children may study Arabic in their local mosque or church. Arab American children born in the United States often learn to speak Arabic from their parents or extended family, but they do not have a chance to study Arabic grammar (rules of the language) and writing in their local public school. When a mosque or church offers Arabic language classes, these children have a chance to learn to read and write the Arabic language and to study grammar. This enables them to read letters from relatives living in the Arab world, and to read street signs and local newspapers if they visit an Arab country. Also, these children will be able to read the literature classics of the Arab world, just as they will read the classics of English language literature in American schools.

Arab American churches and mosques provide a place where various kinds of celebrations can take place, including weddings. In addition, Arab American Christians and Muslims may gather at their local church or mosque to package food for the needy around the holidays. Throughout the year, they may discuss matters such as cleaning up their neighborhood, local events, or world news. They may try to come to an agreement as to how they will respond collectively to new ethical questions (dealing with issues of right and wrong), or to a crisis in their community. New things happening in the neighborhood, city, or back in the Arab world are also discussed by members of the church or mosque. Arab American Christians and Muslims, like people in many other ethnic and religious communities, often see themselves as active members of both American society and the Arab societies from which they or their ancestors came.

# For More Information

Al-Faruqi, Ismai'l, and Lois Lamya. *The Cultural Atlas of Islam.* New York: Macmillan, 1986.

Al-Hussein, Hessein, and Ahmad Hussein Sakr. *Introducing Islam to Non-Muslims.* Lombar, IL: Foundation for Islamic Knowledge, 1990.

Boustani, Rafic, and Phillipe Fargues. *The Atlas of the Arab World: Geopolitics and Society.* New York: Facts On File, 1991.

"Christmas in Beruit." *Aramco World Magazine,* November/December 1971.

"Christians in the Arab East." *The Link,* November/December 1973.

Esposito, John L. *Islam: The Straight Path.* New York: Oxford University Press, 1998.

Hadda, Yvonne, and Adair T. Lummis. *Islamic Values in the United States.* New York: Oxford University Press, 1987.

Haddad, Yvonne. "A Century of Islam in America." *The Muslim World Today.* Occasional Paper No. 4. Washington D.C.: Islamic Affairs Programs, 1986.

Haneef, Suzanne. *What Everyone Should Know About Islam and Muslims.* Chicago: Kazi Publications, 1982.

Mostyn, Trevor, and Albert Hourani, eds. *The Cambridge Encyclopedia of The Middle East and North Africa.* New York: Cambridge University Press, 1988.

Shabbas, Audrey, and Ayad Al-Qazzaz. *Arab World Notebook.* Berkeley, CA: Najda (Women Concerned about the Middle East), 1989.

*Understanding Islam and the Muslims.* Washington, D.C.: The Embassy of Saudi Arabia, 1989.

Wormser, Richard. *American Islam: Growing up Muslim in America.* New York: Walker & Co., 1994.

## Web Sites

The History of the Druze in America. [Online] Available http://www.druze.com/history1.html (last accessed September 21, 1999).

*Alexandra Kalaydjian has an M.A. in Women's Studies with an emphasis on immigrant women from the Middle East. She is currently working on an M.A. in Social Work at the University of Michigan.*

# Work and Money

**8**

Immigrants to the United States have arrived from a number of countries, bringing with them different languages, cultures, and traditions. Despite these differences, they have one thing in common: the search for a better life. Immigrants hope to achieve a level of economic prosperity unknown in their own land. Because many are able to accomplish this, the United States has been called "the land of opportunity." Immigrants have achieved and continue to achieve prosperity through hard work and sacrifice. Immigrants also benefit from their own inventiveness by creating new niches—or positions—for themselves, doing jobs for which they are especially suited. In general, immigrants have succeeded because of their ability to combine the resources of their families and communities, allowing some immigrants to become more successful than people born in the United States.

Like other immigrants, people arriving from the Arab world want to find work in order to find prosperity. While the majority of the first waves of Arab immigrants were employed by others, many quickly began to invest in their own businesses and became known for their ability to operate them

**A Syrian man peddles food to two men on the streets of New York in the early 1900s.**
*Reproduced by permission of Corbis Corporation (Bellevue).*

successfully. These businesses primarily revolved around selling goods. Some sold household items door-to-door while others opened grocery and produce stores. Because of this, Arab Americans became known for their spirit of entrepreneurship, which means owning one's own business.

The history of Arab Americans at work spans from before the turn of the twentieth century. During this time, many changes have occurred in the Arab American community. As the community evolved, its work patterns changed as well. The children of earlier immigrants have been able to pursue careers different from their parents, thanks to higher education and the familiarity of American language and culture. But new arrivals continue to come from the Arab world and fill the vacancies left by older immigrants, keeping many of the entrepreneurial traditions alive. Although Arab American communities are more than a century old and much has changed, much has also stayed the same.

# Where do Arab Americans work?

People tend to rely on demographics—information on the size and distribution of human populations—to determine how many immigrants came from a specific country to the United States, when they came, where they settled, and how they made a living. One source of demographic information is the U.S. Census, which is compiled every ten years. The census provides information on data such as income, age, education level, ethnicity, and housing for the entire United States population (see chapter 5).

For a number of reasons, the census has not been as reliable for Arab Americans as it is for other ethnic groups, such as Asian Americans or African Americans. First, there has been no category on the census form where Arab Americans can designate their ethnicity. Second, Arab Americans whose families have been in the United States for many decades may not identify themselves on the census form as being Arab, but rather see themselves as being simply American. This is similar to how Americans of Italian, Polish, German, Irish, and other backgrounds view themselves. Third, recent Arab immigrants may be cautious about filling out such forms because of their experiences in their homeland, where some governments have used such information against them.

However limited the census numbers may be, it can be useful in providing a general understanding of Arab American employment patterns. In her 1994 article "The Arab American Market" in *American Demographics* Samia El-Badry used 1990 census data to describe where Arab Americans work. She found that Arab Americans tend to be better educated than the rest of the American population. Also, she found that Arab Americans are more likely to attend college, obtain graduate degrees, and have higher rates of employment.

## Fact Focus

- Early Arab immigrants often found work as peddlers: selling various household goods door-to-door or with a horse and buggy.

- Many Arab Americans value entrepreneurship (the desire to work for oneself, or owning one's own business).

- The Ford automobile plant in Detroit, Michigan, attracted many Arab Americans in the early 1900s because of its high wages: $5 per day.

- Well-known Arab Americans include the 1996 presidential candidate for the Green Party, Ralph Nader, New England Patriots quarterback Doug Flutie, and singer Paula Abdul.

According to El-Badry, 60 percent of Arab Americans work as executives, professionals, salespeople, administrative support personnel, and service personnel. This is compared to the rate of 66 percent for the American public at-large. The type of work done, however, varies from one city to another. For example, El-Badry found that Arab Americans living in Anaheim, California, and Cleveland, Ohio, tend to do sales work. In Bergen-Passaic, New Jersey, they lean toward administrative support jobs. Arabs in Boston can be found in education and health care jobs. In Detroit and Chicago, many are involved in manufacturing.

Another way of learning about Arab American employment is through anecdotal information. Anecdotal information is information gathered from reading, talking to people, and generally observing what is going on in a specific area. Anecdotal information tells us that there is a high rate of Arab Americans who operate their own businesses. These business include (but are not limited to) grocery and convenience stores, gas stations, restaurants, hotels, medical offices, law offices, engineering firms, and pharmacies.

Arab Americans are involved in every type of occupation imaginable. Arab American parents often encourage their children to enter into professional careers and become doctors, lawyers, engineers, and pharmacists. Others become teachers, professors, nurses, athletes, musicians, police officers, fire fighters, and politicians. In this way, Arab Americans are indistinguishable from other Americans in the type of work they do.

To get a better idea of the areas in which Arab Americans work, we can look to history as a guide. The history of Arab American work is one of change and adaptation. The only resources new immigrants have are personal motivation, the desire to succeed, and friends and family. Armed with these tools, Arab immigrants and their children have been able to prosper and become an integral part of the American economic system.

## Arab American work in history

Arab Americans came to the United States looking for economic opportunity for a number of reasons. Scholars usual-

Born in Kuwait, Munib Derhalli has lived most of his life in Portland, Oregon, where he attended Oregon Health Sciences University. The fields of medicine and dentistry have attracted many Arab Americans. *Reproduced by permission of Paul S. Conklin.*

ly classify these reasons into two categories: push factors and pull factors. Push factors include things that force people to leave their homeland, such as economic depressions, wars, famine, or natural catastrophes. Pull factors, on the other hand, include things that draw people from their homeland to another land, such as business opportunities, schooling, and the presence of family. Often, it is a variety of push and pull factors that contribute to the decision to come to the United States.

In the late nineteenth and early twentieth centuries, Arabs came to America out of both push and pull factors. One of the push factors was the declining silk trade: parts of Greater Syria (present-day Syria, Lebanon, Jordan, Palestine, and Israel) relied upon the sale of silk to others countries, and when this trade declined many people were affected economically. Another push factor was the increase in taxation and the recruitment of Arabs into the Ottoman army, due to the decline of the Ottoman Empire (see Chapter 2). These factors made many Arabs look to the West for a better life.

One of the major pull factors was that the United States was looking for labor for their factories, coal mines, and other industries. Some companies actively recruited Arab immigrants. Those not recruited would learn about opportunities and make their way to parts of the United States where they heard they could find jobs. This is the reason for large Arab communities in cities such as Detroit, Michigan; Toledo, Ohio; Wheeling, West Virginia; and locations throughout Pennsylvania.

Although immigrants may have been initially drawn by these jobs, not everyone remained in them. Many entered into business for themselves as soon as they were able. Since they often could not speak English and did not have a lot of money to buy a building or store front, they took to the road to sell goods from house-to-house and town-to-town. This practice was known as peddling. Peddlers would travel selling various goods and wares, mainly to housewives. Peddlers would often walk several miles every day, gradually saving enough money to invest in a horse and buggy. The peddler was such a part of the American landscape that playwrights Richard Rodgers and Oscar Hammerstein made a peddler a main character in their famous musical *Oklahoma!*

A whole industry arose out of peddling, in which Arab suppliers would station themselves in certain towns along the peddling routes that served as supply stations and resting points for tired peddlers. Some Arabs ran rest homes where peddlers could stay for a few days as they rested and bought additional items to sell. Gradually, as peddlers were able to save more money, some were able to give up the road and open grocery stores and produce stands. This was a major turning point in the development of Arab communities. Prior to this moment, Arab immigrants were primarily men who left their families in the "old country" and worked on their own. When they made money, they would send much of it back home. (Money sent back to one's homeland is known as remittances.) Once they settled down, they could send for their families and all could work together in the family store. Thus the store became the center of family life, with many families living above the store or in a back room.

Of course, not all Arab immigrants owned a business. Many more were employed helping to build the United States industrially. Arab immigrants were so connected to automotive manufacturing in the Detroit area that Arab communities sprang up right next to automotive plants. In one instance, the Arab community moved from Highland Park, Michigan, to Dearborn, Michigan, when the Ford automotive plant moved. These workers also assisted in the building of the nation's labor movement. For example, many who worked in Detroit's automotive factories also become active in the United Auto Workers labor union.

Wherever Arab immigrants found themselves, they were able to fit into the environment. Some immigrants that landed along the U.S.-Mexican border opened specialty stores catering to Mexicans and Mexican Americans. In the Southwest, Arab Americans sold Native American jewelry and crafts. In California, Yemeni Americans found work in the agricultural industry.

Hussein Fawaz stands near the employee entrance to Ford Motor Company's steel division in Dearborn, Michigan. Many Arab Americans have been involved in auto manufacturing in the Detroit area. *Reproduced by AP/Wide World Photos.*

## Current trends in Arab American work

A second major wave of Arab immigration began in the United States in the late 1960s and continues through the 1990s. Coming into an already established Arab community with more family networks, and sometimes more education and financial resources, these Arabs were able to establish themselves more quickly than earlier immigrants.

Even with these advantages, however, many newer immigrants face the same challenges as the earlier arrivals. Some have difficulties finding jobs in the same fields in which they were employed back in their own countries. For example, teachers, doctors, and lawyers often are unable to practice in the United States without first going back to school to get required certificates and degrees. Another barrier is that many

Joseph George, store owner, has shelves filled with a great assortment of goods from his native land of Lebanon. *Reproduced with permission of Paul S. Conklin.*

immigrants are coming from war-torn countries such as Lebanon, Palestine, Yemen, and Iraq—an experience that could make adjustment to their new life more difficult.

By embarking into entrepreneurial roles, a large number of newer immigrants follow in the footsteps of the earlier immigrants. Often newer immigrants are in a position to take the place of earlier immigrants who are moving out of store ownership and into other areas of employment. Others take manual labor, industrial, or agricultural jobs. For example, Yemeni migrant workers of California often travel in groups throughout the farming season, taking jobs harvesting a variety of fruits and vegetables. Even within this group, however, some workers are beginning to save their money in order to open up their own businesses.

While the recent immigrants are following the same general path as the earlier arrivals, they are doing so at a faster pace. For instance, new immigrants do not have to go through the process of building their financial reserves through peddling. Rather, by using family resources accumulated through years of living in the United States, some new immigrants are able to quickly establish themselves and get a business running in a relatively short time. Another reason for quicker success is that the earlier immigrants already paved the way for them to be successful.

Also, some immigrants are coming with more financial resources than those before them, enabling them to get ahead faster. Some recent immigrants come to the United States to earn college degrees, and once they graduate, they stay to enter into professional careers. Others come with professional degrees from their home countries. This movement has been called the brain drain, because some of the best and brightest people leave the Arab world to pursue opportunities in the United States.

The patterns of yesterday continue today, with second- and third-generation Arab Americans entering professional occupations while new immigrants fill their vacancies in manual labor production, store ownership, and agricultural work. As long as immigrants from the Arab world continue to arrive, this pattern will most likely continue.

## Roots of success and fruits of labor

The history of Arab American work has been long and varied. Despite the different trends and evolutionary steps, there are common themes that characterize how Arab Americans contributed to the American social and economic system. One is the spirit of entrepreneurship,

## A List of Famous Arab Americans and Their Jobs

| | |
|---|---|
| Paula Abdul | Singer/choreographer |
| Senator Spencer Abraham | Politician (Republican-MI) |
| Paul Anka | Singer/songwriter |
| Dr. Elias Corey | Nobel Laureate for chemistry |
| Dick Dale | Guitarist |
| Dr. Michael DeBakey | Surgeon/inventor of the heart pump |
| Jamie Farr | Actor |
| Doug Flutie | NFL quarterback |
| Jeff George | NFL quarterback |
| Khalil Gibran | Poet/artist/writer |
| J.M. Haggar | Founder of Haggar Slacks |
| Tony Ismai | Founder of the Alamo Flag Company (Dallas) |
| Col. James Jabara | U.S. Air Force jet ace |
| General George Joulwan | U.S. and NATO commander |
| Casey Kasem | Broadcaster |
| Candy Lightner | Founder of Mothers Against Drunk Driving (MADD) |
| Christa McAuliffe | Teacher/astronaut |
| Senator George Mitchell | Politician (Democrat-DE) |
| Ralph Nader | Consumer advocate, Green Party U.S. presidential candidate, 1996 |
| Kathy Najimy | Actor |
| Jacques Nasser | Ford Motor Company President and Chief Executive Officer |
| Paul Orfalea | Founder of Kinko's photocopying centers |
| Bobby Raha | Auto racer |
| Congressman Nick Rahall | Politician (Democrat-WV) |
| Edward Said | Professor/literary critic/social critic |
| Frank Saidy | Playwright |
| Jack Shaheen | Emeritus professor/author/film critic |
| Donna Shalala | Secretary of Health and Human Services |
| Tony Shalhoub | Actor |
| Vic Tayback | Actor |
| Danny Thomas | Actor/philanthropist |
| Helen Thomas | White House press correspondent |
| Stephen Yokich | Eighth President of the United Auto Workers (U.A.W.) |
| Frank Zappa | Singer/songwriter |

which has come to define the Arab experience and is still strong today. It lives on in the businesses that are operated by Arab Americans and in the stories of business ownership told by those whose parents and grandparents owned stores. Although today "mom and pop" stores are becoming less common, Arab Americans are establishing more professional businesses—law offices and computer sales and services for example.

Family is another factor. When asked about the secret behind Arab American success, the most common answer that people give is family support and the ability of families to work together. Even today, one can walk into an Arab-owned convenience or grocery store and see three generations working behind the counter. Family members also help one another find employment outside of family-owned businesses.

Arab American economic success is also due to the importance placed on education (see Chapter 9). Arab Americans have higher levels of high school and college education than the general U.S. population and many other ethnic groups. Close to 80 percent of Arab Americans have graduated from high school, and approximately 50 percent have a college degree.

Arab Americans derive great pride from their contributions to the United States. A list of some famous Arab Americans and their areas of work are given in on page 118.

The list on page 118 shows the great diversity of Arab American employment and the contributions made through their work. Despite the wide array of occupations, most Arab Americans cite family and community support as the main resource to help them reach their goals. Also, many talk about the pride they feel when reflecting on Arab contributions throughout history, such as the ancient civilizations of Sumer, Babylon, Assyria, and Phoenicia; the medical, technological, and scientific achievements of the Islamic Empire; and the contemporary contributions of Arabs and Arab Americans. Taken together, the history of Arab contributions to the world can be viewed in the context of Arabs working at their

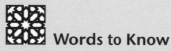

## Words to Know

- **Brain drain:** this occurs when many educated and highly skilled citizens of a country immigrate to another country in order to find work or better paying jobs, leaving their home country in need of educated and skilled workers.

- **Entrepreneurship:** self-employment; having your own business.

- **Peddlers:** people who sell household goods door-to-door in areas not well-served by stores.

- **Push factors:** things that force people to leave their homeland, such as economic depressions, wars, famine, or natural catastrophes.

- **Pull factors:** things that draw people from their homeland to another land, such as business opportunities, schooling, and the presence of family members who immigrated previously.

- **Remittances:** the money immigrants send to their home countries to support their families.

jobs and professions. Whether it is in the laboratory, grocery store, or assembly line, Arabs and Arab Americans continue to contribute and provide not only to their own families, but also to their communities, their societies, and the world.

# For More Information

Abraham, Nabeel. "Detroit's Yemeni Workers." *Middle East Report,* May 1977, pp. 3-9.

David, Gary. "Behind the Counter: Iraqi-Chaldean Store Ownership in Metropolitan Detroit." *Arab Detroit: From Margin to Mainstream,* edited by Nabeel Abraham and Andrew Shryock. Detroit: Wayne State University Press, in press.

El-Badry, Samia. "The Arab-American Market." *American Demographic,* January 1994, pp. 22-27, 30-31.

Kayal, P. M., and J. M. Kayal. *The Syrian-Lebanese in America: A Study in Religion and Assimilation.* Boston: Twayne Publishers,1975.

Kelley, Ron. "The Yemenis of the San Joaquin." *Middle East Report,* March/April 1986, pp. 22-36.

Naff, Alixa. *Becoming American: The Early Arab Immigrant Experience.* Carbondale: Southern Illinois University Press, 1985.

Saliba, N. E. "Emigration from Syria." *Arabs in the New World: Studies on Arab-American Communities,* edited by Sameer Abraham and Nabeel Abraham. Detroit: Wayne State University Press, 1983.

Sengstock, Mary C. *The Chaldean Americans: Changing Conceptions of Ethnic Identity.* Staten Island, NY: Center for Migration Studies, 1982.

Sengstock, Mary C. "Iraqi Christians in Detroit: An Analysis of an Ethnic Occupation." *Arabic Speaking Communities in American Cities.* Staten Island, NY: Center for Migration Studies, 1974.

Swanson, Jon. "Sojourners and Settlers: Yemenis in America." *Middle East Report,* March/April 1986, pp. 5-21.

Zenner, Walter P. "Arabic-Speaking Immigrants in North America as Middleman Minorities." *Ethnic and Racial Studies,* 1982, pp. 457-77.

*Gary David is an assistant professor of Sociology at Bentley College in Waltham, Massachusetts.*

# Education

9

## A brief history

Education and learning are highly valued by Arab Americans. This is due, in part, to a long history of scholarship in the Arab world, where the attainment of wisdom for a productive life was an important goal. For example, the earliest world writings and scripts were found in Mesopotamia (present-day Iraq) and Egypt. Beginning in the year 750 C.E. (common era, also called A.D.) and continuing through the fourteenth century, peoples of the Arab world—which spanned across North Africa, Mesopotamia, and the Near East—placed a very high value on learning and teaching. As a result, there was significant growth in the number of schools during that time. In the twentieth century, after independence from the European powers that governed them as colonies, Arab countries promoted mandatory primary (grade school) and secondary (high school) education for all children and free public universities.

Currently, in both public and private schools in the United States, Arab Americans are following in the same footsteps as their ancestors, taking education seriously and realizing the "American dream" of success.

## Statistics on Early Arab American Immigrants

Because Arab Americans were classified as "whites," they were not forced to attend segregated public schools as were African Americans, Asian Americans, Native Americans, and Latinos. For the same reason, there are no separate statistics available on the education of the early Arab American immigrants.

## The early immigrants

Arabs from the Middle East have immigrated to the United States since the turn of the twentieth century and in different stages (see chapter 4). For the most part, early immigrants adopted American culture and the English language easily, especially once they made the transition from being sojourners (people who were likely to return to their homeland after earning enough money) to settlers (people who intended to stay in the United States permanently).

The majority of the early Arab immigrants were Christians and they came mostly from rural areas in Syria and Lebanon. These immigrants had very little formal education and about half of them were illiterate (could not read or write) in both Arabic and English. They came with the intent of making new lives for themselves and a better future for their children. These immigrants worked hard and for long hours in grocery stores and as peddlers and factory workers, and they were determined to provide their children with a good education.

Most children of early Arab American immigrants attended public schools, while some, such as Arab Catholics, attended parochial (religious) schools. Meanwhile, they attempted to maintain their language and culture by teaching their children at home, in churches and mosques, and in community clubs.

## The second wave

Following World War II (1939-45), Arab immigrants were predominantly Muslim and came from Lebanon or Palestine (a smaller number came from Egypt, Syria, Iraq, Yemen, and North Africa). Many held professional degrees in medicine, law, and engineering, and came from an urban middle- and upper-middle-class background. These immigrants maintained strong ties to their national and Arab identities, but not necessarily to their religion. In other words, they were often secular (nonreligious) in their world views. Although most adapted to the American way of life, they continued to identify with the Arab world and to speak Arabic in the home.

Because of their educational and professional background, many of these Arab immigrants were able to live in more affluent suburban areas and to choose good school districts for their children. They were also able to help their children with the English language and school work. They attempted to teach their children Arabic at home and in churches, mosques, and community clubs. Some could also afford to send their children during the summers to their countries of origin to learn the Arabic language and culture. Sometimes the children would spend a year or two in their native country, living with relatives and attending school there.

## Recent immigrants

In 1965 the U.S. Congress passed a new immigration act that removed previous restrictions that favored immigrants from certain countries over others. Since then, larger numbers of Arab immigrants have been arriving in the United States. Some come to join family members who are already there, others come to improve their economic situation, and many come to escape wars and political unrest in their home countries. The majority come from six countries: Lebanon, Jordan/Palestine, Egypt, Iraq, Syria, and Yemen.

Recent immigrants are very diverse in terms of their level of education and professional background. A large proportion of the Egyptians and Syrians are professionals, such as doctors and lawyers. Lebanese and Palestinian immigrants have varying levels of education. Some are college-educated

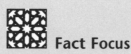 **Fact Focus**

- There are many Arab proverbs that reflect the importance of education, such as "Pursue knowledge all the way to China," "Childhood education is like etching on stone," and "Seek knowledge from the crib to the coffin."

- Al-Azhar University in Cairo was established in the year 975—two hundred years before Oxford University in England and one hundred years before the Sorbonne University in France.

- The Arabs invented the number zero, which made math and calculations much easier. The numeral system used in the West is of Arabic origin.

- Sixty-three percent of all Arab Americans aged twenty-five or over have been to college.

- Differences between Arab and U.S. cultures may cause conflict for Arab American students.

- Some Arab Americans attend school seven days a week.

professionals, while others work in jobs that do not require a college degree. Many Yemeni immigrants tend to have less formal education (no high school or no college) and work in blue-collar or manual labor jobs. Among Iraqi immigrants there are two extremes: highly educated professionals from urban areas, and people from rural areas with little or no schooling.

## Public education

Public schools across the United States are feeling the impact of international and national migration. This is reflected in the schools' student populations, which are becoming more ethnically, culturally, and religiously diverse. Public schools enroll students from different national origins, including Arab Americans who are at different stages of acculturation (adaption) to American culture. Some are newly arrived immigrants with limited knowledge of the English language and American culture, while others are American born and are both culturally adapted and fluent in the English language.

In the mid-1990s, minorities (Americans of non-European background or foreign-born Americans) made up 30 percent of public school students in the United States. These minorities include Latinos, African Americans, and Asian Americans. By the year 2020 it is expected that 40 percent of the public school population will be minorities.

In 1974, Congress passed the Equal Education Law, which makes education available to minorities and foreign-born students in their native language. Also, English as a Second Language instruction is also required in public schools across the United States, and many states have added laws to support bilingual (two language) and bicultural education. These programs provide training in the students' native languages along with English training, in order to help smooth the transition from one language to another. They also teach students about the history and culture of their native country along with American history and culture.

The change in the ethnic makeup of the school population is reflected in teacher education programs. Teachers are often required to take courses that focus on how to teach for diverse groups of students. This helps schools improve the teaching and learning that occurs in the classroom.

## Arab Americans and bilingual education

While the majority of Arab Americans (approximately 60 percent) are born in the United States and do not have any problems with the English language, 40 percent are foreign born. This means that some of the Arab American schoolchildren might have difficulties reading, writing, and understanding English in the classroom and while doing their homework.

Public schools in many cities—such as New York City, San Francisco, Chicago, Detroit, and Los Angeles—have seen a rise in the number of Arabic-speaking immigrants in the last two decades of the twentieth century. For example, in Dearborn, Michigan (a suburb of Detroit), approximately 50 percent of the school district population in the 1998–99 school year was of Arab background, and 38 percent of those students were enrolled in bilingual programs—meaning that these students were not completely fluent (having the language skills of a native speaker) in the English language.

Graduates at Fordson High School in Dearborn, Michigan, wear scarves under their mortar boards. *Reproduced by permission of Millard Berry.*

These differences pose certain challenges for teachers and students, both of whom are trying to overcome linguistic (language) barriers. Fortunately, there is a growing number of teachers of Arab background in the United States. These teachers often serve as mediators (go-betweens) between the school and the home, especially for newly arrived Arab immigrants. Parents feel more secure knowing that their children have teachers with whom they can communicate.

## Cultural diversity and public education

Sometimes cultural and religious differences affect how Arab Americans are treated in public schools. For example, some Muslim American Arabs wear traditional Islamic (religous) clothing. The girls will often wear the *hijab,* a head scarf that covers their hair and neck. This form of dress is distinct from typical student dress and may put-off other students. Although teachers often create classroom environments that are open to such differences, discomfort may still exist.

In schools where there are both Christian and Muslim students, there may be differences in how holidays are celebrated. Muslim Arab Americans will observe *Ramadan,* the Muslim holy month, while Christian Arab Americans will celebrate Christmas and Easter. School districts such as the one in Dearborn, Michigan, may accommodate religious practices by recognizing these holidays and allowing students to stay out of school on specific dates and/or to stay away from the cafeteria while fasting (going without food for a religious purpose, which is commonly done during Ramadan).

Because of religious and cultural reasons, some Arab American Muslim girls do not participate in after-school activities and sports, or in physical education and music classes. Schools strive to work with parents and community groups to find alternatives that respect the beliefs of the students. In schools with high populations of Arab American Muslims, separate physical education classes for girls may be offered.

Another challenge for some school districts is that Arab American girls may marry and have children while still in school. For example, among the Yemeni Americans, early

At the Al-Ghazaly School in Jersey City, New Jersey, the girls must begin wearing the hijab at the age of seven. *Reproduced by permission of AP/Wide World Photos.*

marriage is fairly common. Often Yemeni American girls continue to attend high school through pregnancy and soon after childbirth. Because of their large, supportive families, who help with childcare and other household responsibilities, the girls are able to finish school and raise their own children. The situation, however, can still be difficult for both schools and families, but because education is so highly valued, Yemeni American girls are likely to graduate with a high school diploma, even though they may not continue on to college.

Foreign-born Arab American students may also have difficulties adapting to the American public school system because they have been brought up in a society with different values. For example, school discipline, obedience, and respect for teachers are more emphasized in Arab countries. Some Arab American parents feel uncomfortable with the more relaxed discipline system in American public schools, and may even choose to send their children to private or religious schools.

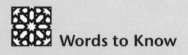

## Words to Know

- **Bicultural education**: programs that teach the history and culture of the students' country of origin alongside that of their new country.

- **Bilingual**: fluent in two languages.

- **Bilingual education**: programs that teach in the students' native languages along with the language of the country where they are living.

- **Curriculum**: the list of subjects schools choose to teach.

- **English as a Second Language**: English-language instruction for non-native speakers.

- **Fluent**: having the language skills of a native speaker.

- *Fousha*, **or Classical Arabic**: the language spoken at the time of the prophet Muhammad (seventh century), which is used in the Qur'an. Today it used for written communication (and therefore often called literary Arabic) but rarely spoken except in formal situations.

- **Linguistic**: pertaining to language.

- **Minorities**: groups within a society that are different from the majority of people, or that have less access to political and economic power. In the United States, these include citizens of non-European background and foreign-born Americans.

- **Parochial schools**: private schools run by a local parish or church.

# Private education: Islamic schools

Across the United States, private Islamic schools have been established to offer Muslim parents and students an alternative to the public school system. Islamic schools are not new—the first ones were established in Muslim countries more than 1,000 years ago.

As in the past, today's Islamic schools offer a standard curriculum (the same subjects that are taught in the public schools) along with religion and Arabic-language classes. These private schools provide the Arab American Muslim community and other Muslims with a sense of common political, cultural, and religious identity.

Because learning, prayer, and discipline are emphasized in Islamic schools, many parents are interested in sending their children to them. In 1999 in New York City alone, there are twenty-three Islamic schools. Islamic schools include diverse populations of students, including children of Egyptian, Yemeni, Pakistani, Indian, Iraqi, African American, and Bosnian background. As a consequence of their popularity, these private schools face the problem of overcrowding. To solve this problem in New York City, the Kuwaiti-financed Islamic Cultural Center of New York began to build a $10 million school for 1,000 students in Manhattan in the 1990s.

According to the Council of Islamic Schools in North America, there are at least two hundred Islamic schools nationwide. These schools

often obtain teaching materials from other countries. The most important text, which students learn by heart, is the *Qur'an*—the Muslim holy book.

While many Muslim Arab American students attend Islamic schools full time, others attend public school during the week days and Islamic schools on the weekends. Often these weekend schools are similar to the mosque schools of the past (see box on page 130). They focus on moral and religious education and the reading and writing of the literary— or classical—Arabic (*fousha*). Usually, boys and girls attend separate weekend schools or go to separate classrooms.

In general, Islamic schools in the United States are places in which the more established Muslim Arab American families can preserve cultural and religious roots and where newly arrived immigrants can find a community with which they can communicate as they adjust to American life.

**The American Muslim Society in Dearborn, Michigan, has a weekend school in the basement of a mosque. The school's 350 students study Arabic and the Qur'an.** *Reproduced by permission of Paul S. Conklin.*

# Islamic Schools of the Past

The golden age of Islam (750–1150 C.E.) was marked by the establishment and maintenance of a large network of educational institutions, including Islamic schools. Classical Islamic education was organized into six types of schools, all of which were primarily religious and most of which taught boys. Remnants of these schools are visible today, both in the Arab World and in the United States.

- The *maktab* or *kuttab* (writing school) focused on reading and writing. The instructor would teach children literacy skills. As the number of these schools grew, they became instrumental in spreading literacy among Muslims both in the East and West. Eventually, the maktab curriculum also included literature, grammar, proper etiquette and manners, calligraphy, swimming, and horsemanship.

- The *halgha* (circle school) focused on a particular teacher's teachings. The teacher usually sat on a cushion against a wall while students sat around him in a semicircle. The closer the student sat to the teacher, the higher the student's status in learning. Notebooks were usually checked by the teacher and discussions were characterized by passionate arguments and debate.

- The palace school, a school for royalty, had a similar curriculum to the maktab. In addition to a standard curriculum, however, the palace school focused on preparing its students for higher education, upper-class society, and employment in government and administration. Students were trained in the social sciences and taught how to be skillful public speakers.

- The *masjid* (mosque school) was the most common and longest lasting form of elementary education in Muslim societies. These schools were most effective in combining worship with learning. During the early period of Islam, there were 3,000 mosque schools in the city of Baghdad alone. These schools played a significant role in providing knowledge to Muslims. They continue to do so today.

- The *madrasah* (school of public instruction) provided a more advanced education than the other five types of schools. The madrasah schools believed strongly in teaching religious and political education, along with general education and specialized training. They often had the best professors and biggest libraries. Unlike the other schools, the madrasah was supported by funding from the state government.

- Bookshops were at first available only to the highly educated groups of people. With the expansion of bookshops across the Islamic world, however, book-dealers and copyists were important in making books available to the general public, students, and centers of learning. Libraries eventually formed, which students were free to use.

## Level of Education Attained by Arab Americans

| Level of Education | Percentage of Arab Americans |
| --- | --- |
| No High School | 17.6% |
| High School Diploma | 21.6% |
| Some College | 24.5% |
| Bachelor or Graduate degree | 36.3% |

*Zogby International, 1995*

# Educational attainment of Arab Americans

Overall, and according to U.S. Census statistics, Arab Americans have one of the highest educational achievement rates in the country: 63 percent of all Arab Americans aged twenty-five and over have been to college, compared to 45 percent of all non-Arab Americans.

The table above shows the level of education attained by Arab Americans.

Arab American achievement reflects the extent to which Arabs value education. There is a high level of educational diversity among Arab Americans, however, which means the level of education varies from one group to another.

# For More Information

Gibson, M. "Minorities and Schooling: Some Implications." In *Minority Status and Schooling: A Comparative Study of Immigrant and Involuntary Minorities,* edited by M. Gibson and J. Ogbu. New York: Garland Publishing, 1991.

Haddad, Y., and J. Smith. "Islamic Values Among American Muslims." In *Family and Gender Among American Muslims: Issues Facing Middle Eastern Immigrants and Their Descendants,* edited by Barbara Aswad and Barbara Bilgé. Philadelphia: Temple University Press, 1996.

McCarus, Ernest, ed. *The Development of Arab-American Identity.* Ann Arbor: University of Michigan Press, 1994.

Naff, Alixa. *Becoming American: The Early Arab Immigrant Experience.* Carbondale: Southern Illinois University Press, 1985.

Shamsavary, P., G. Nabi Saqeb, and M. Halstead. "Islam: State, Religion, and Education." In *World Religions and Educational Practice,* edited by Witold Tulasiewicz and Cho-Yee To. New York: Cassell, 1993.

Southeast Michigan Council of Governments (SEMCOG). *Patterns of Diversity and Change in Southeast Michigan.* Detroit: SEMCOG, 1994.

Suleiman, M. "Educating the Arab American Child: Implications for Teachers." Eric Document #392 864, 1996.

Suleiman, M. "Early Arab-Americans: The Search for Identity." In *Crossing the Waters: Arabic-Speaking Immigrants to the United States before 1940,* edited by Eric Hooglund. Washington, D.C.: Smithsonian Institute Press, 1987.

*Loukia K. Sarroub is a Ph.D. candidate in the College of Education at Michigan State University with concentrations in both education policy and social analysis and literacy education.*

# Family and Gender Roles

**10**

For immigrants and their descendants, it is often difficult to find a balance between adapting to a new culture while retaining the culture of their homeland. Culture includes many customs, such as language, dress, food, beliefs, traditions, and values (beliefs about what is right and wrong). Most immigrants retain some of the traditions of their home country, even after living in the United States for generations. This is true of the Arab American community as well.

There are many issues about adjusting to life in the United States that are controversial for Arab Americans, especially when the adjustments challenge values or beliefs that people hold dear. One issue important to many Arab Americans is the different roles of men and women and boys and girls in the family. When we speak of the different roles of males and females, we call these gender roles. This chapter discusses the history of the Arab American family and the diversity found among Arab American families across the United States.

Enjoying sweet tea, a waterpipe, and news of the day, an Arab American family unwinds in the late afternoon. In a ritual that almost resembles village life from ancient times, neighbors and relatives wave greetings and stop for a visit. *Reproduced by permission of Millard Berry.*

# The history of Arab American families

The history of Arab American families is closely tied to the history of Arab immigration (see chapter 4). When Arabs first started coming to the United States in the late 1800s, they were mostly men who came alone. Young men from Lebanon and Syria arrived in big cities and then spread out all over the country. They came to America to improve their families' economic situation. They often worked long hours to make enough money to open businesses in the United States and pay for their families to join them. These men were not only helping their immediate (nuclear) families— meaning wives and children—but also their extended families, which included parents, cousins, aunts, uncles, nieces, and even whole villages.

Although many of these first immigrants were unmarried men, others had wives and children who remained in the Arab world. Their wives would usually live with the extended family and continue to farm the family land and raise the children with the help of money received from their husbands in the United States.

In a few cases, women came with their husbands, or came alone, or with their children. Like the men, they often worked as peddlers, and some even found work in factories. One well-known case is Kahlil Gibran's mother, who came to the United States with her children and worked as a peddler (see chapter 12).

## Chain migration and the growth of Arab American communities

Over time, the pattern of men and women immigrating alone gave way to more families arriving together or coming shortly after the first member arrived. Often, one person from a village got established in an American city and then members of the family started to join the immigrant. Later more relatives and people from the same village would come. This pattern of migration is known as chain migration.

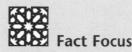

## Fact Focus

- Arab American families tend to have close relationships. They often live near one another, and spend a lot of time together. Sometimes family members are involved in each other's lives more than is common in most of the American population.

- Sometimes parents arrange their child's marriage to someone who they feel is responsible and will be able to provide a good home for their child and grandchildren.

- Arab American parents and teens may experience the "generation gap" when teens want to have the same freedom as their schoolmates and friends and parents want them to follow the traditional customs and values of their homeland in the Arab world. This causes debates over whether or not teens should be allowed to date, hang out after school with friends, have curfews, etc.

There were many reasons for this pattern of immigration. Families that were separated from each other wanted to be together. Also, new immigrants wanted the security of a community of people they already knew and whose customs they understood. The first immigrants would host the new arrivals in their homes, or find them housing in the same neighborhood. They would also help them learn English, find their way around the city, and, most importantly, help them find jobs.

In addition, the first immigrants created economic opportunities for the later ones. If they had started a business, they could hire family members and friends to work for them. In fact, many Arab American immigrants' first jobs were in a relative's or a friend's business. All of these factors have meant that life was often much easier for those immigrants who came after a relative or village member had already established themselves in the United States.

Because of the advantages of having families and friends live close to one another, we have seen the growth of Arab American communities (groups of people living near each other with common interests and ties). We find these communities in many cities where Arab Americans settled—New York, Detroit, Los Angeles, and Houston. In these communities new immigrants can find many of the comforts of home, including Arabic bakeries, grocery stores, restaurants, bookshops, and video stores. Arabic is spoken on the street, and Arabic newspapers or American newspapers published in Arabic are sold. There are also Arabic social clubs that hold public events, such as concerts and dinners.

## Assimilation and preservation of culture

Not all Arab immigrants have become part of an Arab American community within a large city. Historically, many of the immigrants assimilated (blended into) other communities where there were few, if any, Arabs present. These immigrants often found it harder to retain their culture and, especially, to pass it on to their children.

Some of the Arab immigrants who lived in the early communities pressured their families to assimilate. The United States was considered by many immigrants to be one of the best places on earth, and they felt very privileged to become a part of this society. They felt it was their duty to become "good Americans" and blend into mainstream society. Often, they did not teach their children Arabic, nor did they expect them to carry on Arab traditions.

But since 1965, when new U.S. immigration and political events in the Arab world caused many more immigrants to come to the United States, many changes have occurred in Arab American families. At the turn of the twenty-first century there is less pressure to assimilate or forget Arab culture. This is partially due to the fact that cultural diversity has become an accepted part of American society. Also, the large numbers of recent immigrants have increased the sense of connection with the Arab world among Arab Americans in general. Many Arab Americans are now more willing to display, rather than ignore, their Arab customs and values. In general children are not pressured to assimilate, but rather to preserve their Arab culture.

# Arab American families today

Most Arab Americans attach great importance to the family. They often explain that the family allows them to preserve many of the customs that they hold dear and to maintain their religion and language. Yet it is actually quite difficult to describe a typical, or average, Arab American family. This is due, in part, to the great diversity among Arab Americans in the United States. Where a family lives, when they first came to the United States, where they originally came from, what family members do for a living, how much money they make, and what kind of education they have all influence the family structure.

## Diversity in family and gender role patterns in the Arab world

It is also difficult to describe Arab American families because families in the Arab world vary greatly from country to country, and even from village to village (or neighborhood to neighborhood). Many people think that a traditional Arab family is one in which the mother stays at home and the father works. The story is much more complicated. In some situations, these roles are reversed. In rural areas in Egypt, for example, women work in the agricultural fields, take care of the family, and sell crops at the market, while men only do a few agricultural tasks and have a lot of leisure time. In other rural areas, women are not as active economically and stay home because it is considered more respectable for them to stay out of sight of men (except close relatives). In urban areas (cities) of the Arab world, many women work. Some are highly educated and have professional jobs. Others, with less formal education, may work as seamstresses in factories or as secretaries in offices.

## Words to Know

- **Assimilate:** when a person or a group drops their own culture (such as changing their name and style of dress) and adopts the majority culture, usually referred to as the dominant or mainstream culture.

- **Chain migration:** a continuous pattern of immigration in which once an immigrant has established himself in a new country he begins to bring other family members and friends.

- **Communities:** groups of people, often living near each other, with common interests and connections.

- **Culture:** the language, traditions, and values (beliefs about what is right and wrong) of a community or society.

- **Division of labor:** how work is divided between groups of people.

- **Extended family:** a whole group of relatives, including husbands, wives, children, parents, grandparents, cousins, aunts, uncles, nieces, and nephews.

- **Gender roles:** the different ways males and females are expected to behave in a society.

- **Hijab:** a head scarf worn by some Muslim women to cover their hair and necks.

- **Nuclear family:** a family consisting of husband, wife, and their children.

- **Values:** beliefs about what is right and wrong.

There are many other ways in which families and gender roles vary in the Arab world. In some countries people still have many children, while in others family planning and other factors have caused that number to drop. In some countries, girls are sent to high school and college if families can afford it, while in others girls are taken out of school at an early age and taught household chores.

All of this diversity affects the different patterns we see among Arab American families. Although the population is very diverse, some aspects of family structure are common to most immigrants from the Arab world and even many second- and third-generation Arab Americans. One of the most important of these is the value that Arab Americans place upon their extended family.

## The extended family

Some Arab Americans will share their home with members of their extended family—including grandparents, aunts, uncles, and cousins. They often tend to live close to extended relatives, so that their cousins and other distant relatives will be in the same neighborhood and will remain a large part of their social life.

There are many reasons why the extended family is so important for Arab Americans. One important aspect of the extended family is that it serves as a kind of social security. Family members look out for one another by giving economic assistance to rela-

An Arab American extended family crosses the street outside of the Yemen Cafe in New York. *Reproduced by permission of AP/Wide World Photos.*

tives in need. There is a strong respect for elders in the family, so that when parents grow old, they usually aren't sent to live in a nursing home but continue to live with their children, who take care of them.

Extended families also provide for other needs. Many Arab Americans socialize with their families. Families frequently spend evenings, weekends, and holidays together. Among younger people, siblings (brothers and sisters) and cousins often go out together to the movies or to restaurants. In general, Arab American families live close to one another and play a more important role in the social lives of their members than many other American families do.

Members of extended families provide other kinds of assistance to each other. They help with problems, give advice, and protect one another. While this is true in most families in the United States, among Arab Americans it is very common that family members serve the roles that school-

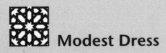

## Modest Dress

Many Arab Americans believe that to dress modestly is to show that one has strong morals and is trustworthy. Dressing modestly means dressing conservatively, or covering up, rather than showing off one's body. This is why some Arab American men tend not to wear shorts and sometimes wear a *taqiya,* a cap that covers the top of the head. Arab American women sometimes cover their heads with a head scarf called a hijab. The *hijab* is mainly worn by Muslim women, but there are many Christian women who also wear head scarves. Although some people feel that Arab women are not required by their religion or their culture to cover their heads, others say that it is mandatory for an upright Muslim woman to wear the hijab because there is reference to it in the *Qur'an* (Koran; holy book for Muslims).

The hijab means different things to different women. Many Arab American girls will start wearing the hijab when they are young. While girls sometimes feel pressure from family and friends to wear the hijab, Arab American women will often begin to wear it as a way of expressing pride in their heritage and respect for the value of modesty.

In general there is much diversity in the clothes Arab American women wear. While some choose to wear the hijab, others wear jeans, skirts, or dresses. There is no one style of dress for Arab or Arab American women.

mates, friends, and coworkers do for other Americans.

Of course, not all Arab Americans live close to their extended families. Like other people in the United States, Arab Americans sometimes move away from their relatives, making it difficult to see grandparents, aunts, uncles, and cousins who live in another city or state. In these cases they may only see their relatives on holidays and vacations, although family weddings and reunions sometimes provide them with extra opportunities to visit with extended family.

## Marriage

In the Arab world marriage practices vary enormously from country to country, and also depend on the economic and social situation of the family. This is also true for marriage practices among Arab Americans. In some cases, families arrange their children's marriage, either to someone from their home country or to another Arab American. In other cases, Arab Americans meet someone they like, but wait for their families' approval before getting engaged. And in other cases, Arab Americans choose their spouses and inform their families of their decision after it has been made. Each of these arrangements has its own advantages and disadvantages.

### Arranged marriages

In arranged marriages, the bride and groom might not know each other very well—or not at all—

before they become engaged. This is especially true when the family of an Arab American arranges a marriage to someone from the home country. In other cases, marriages are arranged to a distant cousin or family friend whom the bride- or groom-to-be has met and expressed an interest in. In either case, it is customary for the family to have the consent of the bride and groom before the marriage agreement is finalized.

Arranged marriages are common in some Yemeni and Lebanese American communities, but occur in any family in which the parents and children believe marriage is a decision that concerns the whole family. There are many reasons that families arrange the marriages of their children. First, because extended families are so close to one another, Arab Americans place great importance on knowing and liking a new addition to the family. And, it is not only the new son-in-law or daughter-in-law that matters—the parents of the newlyweds also feel it is important that they know and like the extended family of their child's spouse. They may check up on the other family's reputation to make sure they are responsible.

Another reason why arranged marriages are advantageous is that in some Arab American communities men and women tend not to date or socialize. This means that meeting a potential spouse may be difficult. So, as an alternative to staying single, some Arab Americans welcome the help of their parents in finding a spouse.

## Dating and meeting future spouses

As Arab Americans become more integrated into American culture, fewer marriages are arranged. Young Arab Americans start to socialize more with the opposite sex and become more accustomed to the idea that love is more important than the potential bride's or groom's family reputation. Sometimes, this can cause a conflict between parents and children: the parents would like to arrange the marriage in the traditional way and the children would like to choose a spouse on their own.

There are also conflicts over whether or not young men and women should be allowed to date. Many Arab American parents are resistant to the idea because they did

Hibat Abdelbaki receives gold jewelry from her fiance, Nader Oweis, at their engagement party at the Islamic Mosque of America in Detroit, Michigan. The bride-to-be felt slightly uncomfortable with the traditional ceremony that drew both families together. *Reproduced by permission of Millard Berry.*

not date and because it goes against the social norms they are used to. Young Arab Americans, however, have grown up in a culture that glamorizes dating and most want to be able to date just like their peers.

In families where dating is discouraged, there are still other ways of meeting potential spouses. Often, single men and women will get to know one another through work or school, at social gatherings such as weddings and conventions, or from living in the same neighborhood.

In some cases, the family will agree to dating once they have met the man or woman in question and see that they intend to marry their child. Sometimes this also involves meeting the family of the young man or woman. Once the two families have agreed that marriage is a possibility, then the man and woman can date to decide if they also agree to the match.

# Wedding ceremonies

Wedding ceremonies in Arab American communities are in many ways similar to those in the Arab world. They are large celebrations held in public halls or banquet facilities. In the past, wedding celebrations would last for up to a week, but this is very rare today because of the expense involved. Nowadays both Arab and Arab American wedding ceremonies are much shorter, usually lasting only one day.

Weddings are very festive occasions that offer families, friends, and community members an opportunity to come together and celebrate. Often family members from overseas will attend weddings if they are able to travel. Many people attend to honor the bride and groom with Arabic music, dancing, and food. Often, the bride and groom spend much of the evening seated on a platform, where they greet visitors and accept congratulations and gifts.

# Children

Arab American families tend to have fewer children than families in the Arab world, but many Arab Americans still prefer to have several children. One reason for having many children is that a large family provides a kind of safety net: people know that they have many family members they can rely on in times of need. Having many children also means that more people can economically contribute to the family. When children are old enough to work, they can help their parents in the family business, or get a job and give part of the money to their family.

Of course, Arab Americans are also quite fond of children, and the Arab culture places a high value on having many children. A big family creates an environment of emotional warmth that Arabs and Arab Americans value. However, it is difficult for many Arab Americans to continue the tradition of having large families in the United States because the cost of living is much higher and they simply do not have the incomes to support many children. As a result family size tends to decrease in Arab American communities over time.

## Raising children in the United States

Living in the United States sometimes challenges the values Arab immigrants bring from their homelands. This is often true of how people feel they should raise their children. Many of the values common to larger American society—such as teaching children individualism and independence—do not coincide with the values Arab immigrants bring with them to this country.

When parents raise their children, they want to instill in them values they believe are morally correct. For some Arab Americans, especially Muslims from rural areas, this may mean dressing modestly (not showing certain parts of the body), little socializing with children of the opposite sex, not dating, and showing respect for elders. Many parents are afraid that their children will pick up the negative things they see in American society—drug use, casual sex, violence, and individualism (putting one's own needs before those of the family and community). When parents worry that their children are picking up these traits, they usually make an extra effort to ensure their children learn the values that are a part of their ethnic heritage. But this can meet with resistance from young Arab Americans because they see their schoolmates live differently. This often causes conflicts between parents and children until a compromise is worked out.

There are numerous examples of how Arab American teens and their parents make compromises. For example, Selwa, a high school student, wanted to go out with a boy she liked. Her parents wanted her to be happy, but were worried about her being alone with a boy, so they sent her younger sister on the date with her as a chaperon. Although younger sisters can be annoying, Selwa was grateful to be able to go at all.

Even after high school, Arab American parents tend to retain control of their children until they are married. Both women and men are often expected to live with their parents until they are married. This sometimes causes clashes. In one case, Nadia, a college student, wanted to move into an apartment during her senior year in college. Her father said no. She was frustrated, but instead of moving out she decided that her father's happiness was more important to her than having her own apartment. She stayed at home, but her parents let her come and go whenever she wanted. They found a compromise that suited everyone.

Not all Arab American youth are resistant to their parents' attempts to have them follow Arab customs. Many young Arab Americans are also proud of their heritage and like to show respect for their culture. Living according to the standards their parents set is a part of this respect. Young Arab Americans who live in communities with large numbers of people with Arab backgrounds often socialize together. This is because other Arab American youth understand what their parents expect of them and how they are supposed to dress and act. Having friends who understand is important for anybody; for Arab American children it is often difficult to explain their parents' strictness or values to non-Arabs.

## Gender differences among Arab Americans

As with marriage, family, and child rearing patterns, there is an immense diversity in the way that gender roles—

the different ways males and females are expected to behave—affect the lives of Arab Americans. In some ways, differences between men and women, or boys and girls, are very similar to those found in mainstream American society. For example, in both American society and Arab societies women have historically held the primary responsibility for child rearing and housework, while men were responsible for earning the family's income.

In both the Arab world and in the United States, recent years have brought changes in this traditional division of labor. Now it is more common for men to share in the responsibility of raising the children and women to be more active in earning money for the family. But there is also an incredible diversity, both in the United States and among Arab Americans, in the division of labor between men and women. Some families still have a stay-at-home mother who cares for the house and the children, while the father earns the family's income. In other households, women earn part, and sometimes all, of the family's income, and men may take a more active role in housework and childcare.

Among Arab Americans many factors contribute to different patterns in the division of labor. Families that came from small villages in rural areas, or from working class (non-professional) backgrounds, may have a more pronounced (extreme) division of labor between men and women. Women have primary responsibility for childcare and maintaining the home, while men are the primary wage earners. Women do all of the cooking, serve the food, and clean up after dinner. Girls are expected to learn household chores at an early age and help their mothers in the kitchen. Boys are taught auto mechanics and household chores, and may be expected to get a job or work in a family business to contribute to the family income.

Arab Americans from urban areas, from highly educated or professional families, or who were born and raised in the United States are less likely to have such a defined division of labor between men and women. Girls are expected to get an education just as their brothers (although they often still learn to cook and help with the household chores more than boys). Both women and men work outside of the home, and men may help with childcare and housework (although these tasks

tend to fall more to women, while men do more household repairs and auto care, as is true in many American families).

Observant Muslim women honor the Qur'anic injunction to be modest and conceal their "adornments" from men who are not close relatives. Only the hands and face are exposed in public. *Reproduced by permission of AP/Wide World Photos.*

## Attitudes towards women's roles

During the 1960s and 1970s American society underwent many changes in the attitudes towards women's roles. One movement that promoted these changes was the women's liberation movement, which is known as feminism. This movement called for an end to the rigid differences in gender roles between men and women. Women wanted to be able to work and earn equal pay as men. They wanted the freedom to decide whether they would be housewives and mothers, professionals, or both. Similar movements have occurred around the world in almost all societies, to varying degrees.

In the Arab world, feminist movements began a century ago. In Egypt during the early 1900s, women demonstrated in the streets for legal and social equality, including equal access to jobs and education and the right to appear in public unveiled. Since then, many women all over the Arab world have fought for the right to an education, paid jobs, and freedom to choose their dress and lifestyle. One of the first Arab American women's rights proponents (someone who promotes an idea) was Afifa Karem. This dynamic journalist wrote for many Arab American newspapers in the late 1800s and early 1900s, insisting that women be accepted as equal participants in society and respected in all of their roles—whether workers, mothers, or wives.

Attitudes about gender roles among Arab Americans have been affected by women's movements, but also by other struggles for equality in the United States. Arab American women have been working to reform attitudes about Arab women—those held by Arabs and others. Like other American women, they have fought for equal pay, equal opportunities, respect, and freedom from sexual harassment. Furthermore, Arab American women have needs similar to those of all other American women: health care for themselves and their families, access to affordable childcare, and the ability to educate their children so that they can succeed.

## For More Information

Aswad, Barbara, and Barbara Bilgé, eds. *Family and Gender Among American Muslims*. Philadelphia: Temple University Press, 1996.

*Benatt Chicago (Daughters of Chicago): Growing up Arab and Female in Chicago* (video). Produced and directed by Jennifer Bing-Canar and Mary Zerkel. Chicago: American Friends Service Committee, 1996.

Eisenlohr, Charlene Joyce. "Adolescent Arab Girls in American High School." In *Family and Gender Among American Muslims,* edited by Barbara Aswad and Barbara Bilgé. Philadelphia: Temple University Press, 1996.

Fernea, Elizabeth. *Women and the Family in the Middle East: New Voices of Change.* Austin: University of Texas Press, 1985.

Kadi, Joanna, ed. *Food for Our Grandmothers: Writings by Arab-American and Arab-Canadian Feminists.* Boston: South End Press, 1998.

Najor, Deborah. "Selma's Weddings." *Michigan Quarterly Review,* Fall 1992.

Rodseth, Lars, Sally Howell and Andrew Shryock. *Arab World Mosaic: A Curriculum Supplement for Elementary Teachers.* Dearborn, MI: The

Arab Community Center for Economic and Social Services (AC-CESS), 1994.

Shabbas, Audrey, and Ayad Al-Qazzaz, eds. *Arab World Notebook*. Berkeley, CA: Najda (Women Concerned About the Middle East), 1989.

Shakir, Evelyn. *Bint Arab: Arab and Arab-American Women in the United States*. Westport, CT: Praeger, 1997.

*Tales from Arab Detroit* (video). Directed by Joan Mandell, produced by The Arab Community Center for Economic and Social Services (AC-CESS) and Sally Howell, Ho-ho-Kus, NJ: New Day Films, 1995.

Tucker, Judith. "Arab Family in History: 'Otherness' and the Study of the Family." In *Arab Women: Old Boundaries, New Frontiers*. Bloomington: Indiana University Press, 1993.

*Karen Rignall, an anthropologist, did her graduate work at the University of Michigan at Ann Arbor and has conducted research in Egypt and Morocco.*

# Holidays and Celebrations

## 11

Throughout the year Arab Americans celebrate many religious and cultural holidays. Some of the religious holidays, such as Christmas, are celebrated by most other Americans. Others, such as Eid al-Fitr and Eid al-Adha, are celebrated only by Muslims. American holidays, such as Thanksgiving, the Fourth of July, and Labor Day, are observed, too. Arab Americans celebrate events that are important in a person's life as well, including birthdays, graduations, and marriages. Village and town reunions, ethnic festivals, conferences, and banquets are also held. Whatever the occasion, holidays and celebrations play an important role in preserving culture and reinforcing important values. Family and friends get together to enjoy home-cooked Arabic food, music, dance, storytelling, and traditional games such as backgammon.

## Adjusting to the new world

When Arab Americans first arrive in the United States they tend to celebrate holidays just as they were celebrated in their home countries. For example, they celebrate Mother's

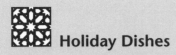

## Holiday Dishes

Some of the favorite food dishes prepared for holidays are:

- Tabbouleh: a salad of chopped parsley and tomato mixed with cracked wheat.

- Shish kabob: lamb or beef barbecued on skewers.

- Hummous: a dip made from garbanzo beans.

- Kibbeh: a meatball made from ground lamb and cracked wheat.

- Stuffed grape leaves: grape leaves stuffed with either rice and ground lamb or rice and chopped vegetables.

Day on the first day of spring, March 21, rather than the first Sunday in May. With time, some of the Arabic traditions are replaced by popular American traditions, especially among Arab Americans who are born in the United States. Bridal showers, for example, replace the Arabic tradition of bringing gifts to the home of the newly-wed couple. In many celebrations, American foods are eaten alongside Arabic foods.

## Religious holidays and celebrations

Arab Americans have been coming to the United States since the late 1800s. The majority of the early immigrants were Christians. They came first from Syria and Lebanon (at that time Lebanon was part of Syria), and later from Iraq, Palestine, and Yemen. Since the 1970s the majority of Arab American immigrants to the United States are Muslims from a variety of Arab countries, including Lebanon, Palestine, Iraq, Egypt, and Yemen (see chapter 4). It is currently estimated that 50 percent of Arab Americans are Muslim and 50 percent are Christian. For this reason, some Arab Americans observe Muslim holidays and some observe Christian holidays.

## Muslim holidays

Muslim holidays occur according to the lunar calendar, which has 354 days—eleven days less than the Gregorian calendar used in most of the world. The Gregorian year has twelve months, and is based on the 365-day rotation of the earth around the sun. The lunar calendar also has twelve months, each starting with the new moon and having twenty-nine or thirty days. Muslim holidays always fall on the same date on the lunar calendar, but fall eleven days earlier than the previous year on the Gregorian calendar. For example, the Muslim holiday Eid al-Fitr fell on February 11 in 1997, on January 30 in 1998, and on January 19 in 1999. The same rule applies to all Muslim holidays (see table on page 154).

Some Muslim holidays, such as Eid al-Fitr and Eid al-Adha, are festive occasions. Others mark important historical milestones, including the birth of the Prophet Muhammad. Some holidays are sad occasions, such as Ashura, which honors the death of the Prophet Muhammad's grandson Hussein. All of these dates are important not only to Arab American Muslims, but also to Muslims worldwide.

Because of the small number of American Muslims, estimated at six million, their holidays are rarely mentioned by the media or noticed by the general public. But Eid al-Fitr and Eid al-Adha are as important to Muslims as Christmas and Easter are to Christians. Often, American Muslims have to go to school and work on these holidays. Some people take personal vacation time during these holidays so that they are able to celebrate them with their families and communities.

# Ramadan

*Ramadan* is the month in which Muslims believe that the prophet Muhammad received his first revelation from God in the form of the *Qur'an* (also spelled Koran) the holy book for Muslims (as is the Bible for Christians). Ramadan is considered the holiest month for all Muslims. During Ramadan Muslims are supposed to fast from sunrise to sunset, abstaining from eating, drinking, and smoking during that time. (Children, pregnant and nursing women, and sick people are not required to fast.) In this month, devout Muslims

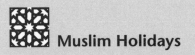

## Muslim Holidays

| Muslim Holiday | Date on Lunar Calendar | | Date on Gregorian calendar | | |
|---|---|---|---|---|---|
| | *Month* | *Day* | *1997* | *1998* | *1999* |
| Eid al-Fitr | Shawal | 1 | Feb. 11 | Jan. 30 | Jan. 19 |
| Eid al-Adha | Dul Hijja | 10 | April 18 | April 7 | March 26 |
| Ashura | Muharam | 10 | May 18 | May 7 | April 26 |

spend more time on spiritual activities, such as going to the mosque, praying, and reciting the Qur'an. Ramadan is also a month of peace, forgiveness, and giving. In some cities of the Arab world, wealthy individuals set up large tents and serve free food after sunset throughout the month.

While fasting is important to Muslims, so is the ritual of breaking the fast, which varies from one community to another. Lebanese and Palestinian Americans, for example, break their fast by drinking water or apricot juice and by eating two or three dates. Arab Americans from North Africa break their fast with soup. Some people's main meal is a feast that includes soup, salad, vegetable stew, and rice and chicken or lamb. Among Yemeni Americans, however, a favorite Ramadan dish is *Asida* (chicken or lamb broth cooked with flour). Traditional Ramadan desserts include *katayef* (a folded pancake filled with nuts or cheese), *kinafa* (a cheese pastry), *baklava* (thin sheets of pastry layered with nuts and butter), and milk pudding.

Although Ramadan is a holy month, it is also a festive one. For some children, the rules of discipline are bent a little—they can stay up longer, visit their friends, and go shopping. Ramadan is also a month in which the extended family, neighbors, and friends get together to break the fast. Families rarely break the fast alone. After breaking the fast, people go shopping or visit each other. Desserts, coffee, and tea are served to guests all night long.

The last day of Ramadan is called the *Waqfa*. During the Waqfa people prepare for the upcoming Eid al-Fitr by

cooking, cleaning, and doing last-minute shopping for clothes and food.

# Eid al-Fitr

Eid *al-Fitr* is also known as *Eid al-Sagheer* (the small holiday). The word *fitr* in Arabic means "breakfast" and it is called Eid al-Fitr (the holiday of breaking the fast) because it comes at the end of Ramadan, the month of fasting. Eid al-Fitr lasts for three days and is a happy occasion, especially for children. On the first day of the Eid, children wear new clothes bought especially for the occasion and receive gifts and money from relatives and friends.

Adults also dress up during this holiday. They begin the first day of the Eid very early by visiting their elder relatives and then attend the Eid prayer at the mosque. The rest of the three days are filled with visits to family and friends,

Katayef, a popular sweet during the month of Ramadan, being prepared on the first day of the month. Pious Muslims refrain from drinking, eating, and smoking during the month, which ends with a three-day feast. *Reproduced by permission of Corbis Corporation (Bellevue).*

Muslims bend in prayer marking Eid al-Adha, observing the day that the prophet Abraham attempted to sacrifice his son to God. *Reproduced by permission of AP/Wide World Photos.*

lots of food, and homemade *ka'ak* and *ma'moul* (date and nut cookies) made especially for this occasion. No alcohol is served, since Muslims are not supposed to drink alcoholic beverages.

In some Arab countries, such as Yemen, children start the Eid by going around the neighborhood collecting candy, money, and gifts—similar to what Americans do on Halloween. In the United States, however, it is difficult for Yemeni American children to do this unless they live in a neighborhood that has other Yemeni Americans familiar with this custom.

## Eid al-Adha

*Eid al-Adha* is also called *Eid al-Kabeer* (the big holiday) because it is celebrated for four days. The word *adha* in Arabic means "sacrifice." This holiday comes on the tenth day of the lunar month Dul-Hijja. It observes the prophet Abraham's attempt to sacrifice his son Ishmael to God, and the miraculous appearance of a lamb to be sacrificed in the son's place. Arab American Muslim families celebrate this holiday by purchasing a lamb. They give part of it away to the needy, and cook the rest for their holiday dinner with family and friends.

As with Eid al-Fitr, the day before Eid al-Adha is called Waqfa and is also dedicated to the tasks of cleaning, shopping, and cooking. This Eid is as festive as Eid al-Fitr, and other than the tradition eating lamb, the two holidays are celebrated in the same way. Eid al-Adha comes at the end of the Hajj, or pilgrimage.

## The Twelve Months of the Lunar Year

Each month starts with the new moon.

- Muharram
- Safar
- Rabi' Awal
- Rabi' Thani
- Jamad Awal
- Jamad Thani
- Rajab
- Sha'ban
- Ramadan
- Shawwal
- Dul-Qi'da
- Dul Hijja

# The Hajj

All financially and physically able Muslims are required to make a pilgrimage, or *Hajj,* to the city of Mecca, Saudi Arabia, at least once in their lifetime. Muslims from around the world come to Mecca in the first week of the lunar month Dul Hijja to perform a series of rituals and prayers. On the tenth day of Dul Hijja, they end the Hajj on Mount Arafat, where it is believed that the prophet Abraham attempted to sacrifice his son.

In the old days, before modern transportation, the Hajj was a difficult and dangerous journey, so a person's safe return from the Hajj was celebrated by the whole community. Although going on the Hajj is much safer now, people continue to celebrate this occasion as a significant religious accomplishment.

Arab Americans celebrate the return of their relatives from the Hajj by decorating their homes with lights and tree branches. Sometimes a banner that says "Hajj Mabrook" or "Hajj Mabroor," "Congratulations" or "Blessed Pilgrimage" is placed across the front porch. For a few days friends and relatives come

**Arabs on a pilgrimage to Mecca. All financially and physically able Muslims are required to make a pilgrimage, or Hajj, to the city of Mecca at least once in their lifetime.** *Reproduced by permission of Corbis Corporaton (Bellevue).*

to the home of the person who has just returned from the Hajj and who is now called "Hajji" (male) or "Hajja" (female). In addition to sweets, coffee, and tea, guests are served dates and holy water brought back from Mecca.

## Ashura

*Ashura* comes on the tenth day of the lunar month Muharram. (The word Ashura is derived from the Arabic word *ashra,* which means "ten.") On this day the prophet Muhammad's grandson Hussein and his family were killed. The first ten days of the month of Muharram are a mourning period, especially for the *Shi'a* (See-ah)—a group of Muslims who believe that Hussein was the rightful leader of the Muslim people (see Chapter 7). During these ten days all signs of joy are shunned, including music, dance, television, picnics, and weddings, and women cannot wear makeup. For ten consecutive nights, devout Shi'a go to the mosques, read verses from the Qu'ran, chant religious songs, and recite the story of *Karbala,* the battle in which Hussein was killed.

## Christian holidays

It is estimated that 50 percent of Arab Americans are Christians. Most Arab Christians are the descendants of the very first Christians in the Arab world, and their churches are among the oldest in the world. Most Arab American Christians come from Lebanon, Syria, Jordan, Egypt, Iraq, and Palestine.

In addition to the more commonly celebrated Christian holidays of Easter and Christmas, Arab American Christians observe Lent (a period of fasting before Easter), Palm Sunday, Saint Barbara's Holiday, and the Rogation of Nineve (observed mostly by Chaldeans and Assyrians).

# Christmas

Christmas is a special time for the extended family to get together, have elaborate meals, observe religious services at midnight, and exchange gifts. Although many Christians in the Arab world celebrate Christmas on January 7, in the United States the majority of Arab Americans celebrate Christmas on December 25. The Egyptian Coptic Church, however, continues to celebrate Christmas on January 7.

A few days before Christmas, special ka'ak and ma'moul (date and nut cookies) are made. Children usually help by decorating the cookies, which are served during Christmas to family and guests. They are also given as gifts to the elderly who cannot make their own.

On Christmas day the family comes together for dinner. In addition to turkey, the dinner includes lamb, rice, *kibbeh* (meatballs), and grape leaves. In Arab countries, children get new clothes for Christmas and receive money from adult relatives and gifts from their parents. The tradition of gift-giving is mostly limited to children, though adults may give their elderly parents simple gifts. In the United States, exchanging numerous and expensive gifts has become a very important component of Christmas for Arab American Christians, and even for some Muslims.

# Rogations of Nineve

Three weeks before Lent (the period of fasting prior to Easter; see below), Chaldean and Assyrian Americans (who are Catholics from Iraq and Syria) fast for three days from midnight to midday, abstaining from meat and dairy products. These three days are called the Rogations of Nineve. They commemorate the time when it is believed that the prophet Jonas was sent by God to the people of Ninevah to warn them to repent in order to avoid the destruction of their city.

# Lent

Arab Americans observe Lent for forty (or sometimes fifty) days before Easter by abstaining from meat, eggs, and

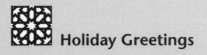

## Holiday Greetings

During the holidays, Arab Americans greet each other by saying "Eid mabrook" ("Blessed Holiday") or "Kul sana wa inta salem" ("May you be safe this year and every year"). These are the Arabic greetings for all holidays, including Christmas, Mother's Day, and birthdays.

dairy products. Elaborate vegetarian meals, referred to as *Siami,* are cooked during this period. Rules of fasting have been eased in modern times. Now many Arab Americans, especially the young, observe Lent by giving up only one food item that they really like, such as chocolate or french fries. During Lent, Arab American churches hold a special mass every Wednesday evening. In these masses people recite chants called *taraneem* in Arabic.

# Palm Sunday

Palm Sunday occurs the Sunday before Easter. It commemorates the entrance of Jesus Christ to Jerusalem before his death. (In Jerusalem, Palestinian Christians observe this day by reenacting the entry of Jesus Christ to their city.) Arab American Christians celebrate this holiday by attending special church services. Children wear new clothes bought especially for the occasion and enter the church carrying palm branches decorated with flowers (similar to the palms people waved before Jesus as he entered the city) and colorful ribbons with candles of all shapes and sizes.

# Easter

Among Arab Christians, Easter, which honors the day it is believed that Jesus Christ rose from the dead after being crucified an a cross, is the most important Christian holiday. The two days before Easter are called *Al-Juma' Al-Hazena* (Sad Friday—the Friday Jesus was crucified) and *Sabt Al-Noor* (Bright Saturday). Easter day is called *Ahad Al-Suroor* (Happy Sunday).

As with Christmas, Arab Americans celebrate this holiday by baking special date and nut cookies and by coloring eggs (which symbolize new life). On Easter day people wear new clothes and visit their relatives (especially the elderly), and the traditional "good morning" greeting is replaced by "Christ has risen." Families get together for a very elaborate meal that marks the end of the long fasting period of Lent. A

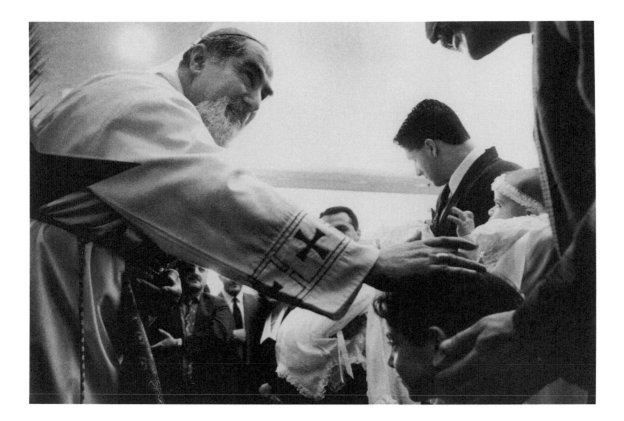

typical Easter dinner includes baked ham, baked turkey, lamb, rice, hummous (garbanzo bean spread) and tabbouleh (parsley, tomato, and cracked wheat salad).

**A priest at the Mother of God Church in Southfield, Michigan, which serves the Chaldean Community, praises a young boy who came to be baptized.**
*Reproduced by permission of Millard Berry.*

## Saint Barbara's holiday

Many Arab Americans observe December 4, the day that marks the death of a Christian saint named Barbara who was executed by her father after she refused to deny her belief in Jesus Christ. The day is observed simply by cooking a special dish called *Burr-ba-ra*. It is made of wheat grain, sugar, cinnamon, and a variety of nuts and raisins.

## Celebrating important life events and accomplishments

Most societies celebrate events that mark important accomplishments and changes in individuals' lives. These in-

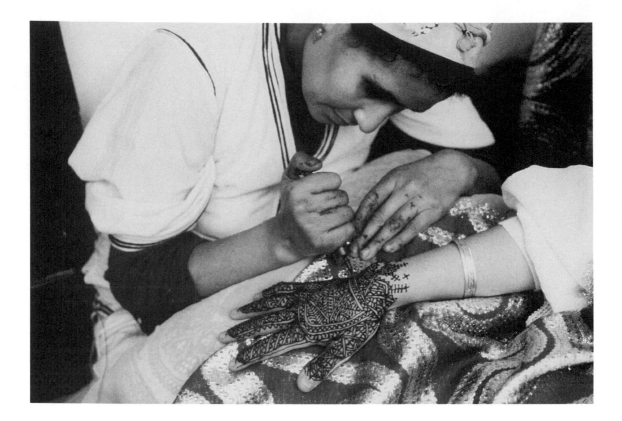

A bride-to-be has an intricate henna pattern painted on her hand. Henna designs are a traditional mark of beauty for a wedding day. *Reproduced by permission of Corbis Corporation (Bellevue).*

clude weddings, births, christenings (services marking a child's entrance into the church), graduations, first jobs, and first homes. For Arab Americans the most important of these are weddings and births, although they celebrate other occasions in the same way that other Americans do.

## Weddings

For Arab Americans, marriages are very festive occasions. Marriages are important because they not only bring together the bride and the groom, but also unite their two extended families (see Chapter 10). In many towns and villages in the Arab world, celebrating a wedding involves the whole village, and the celebration may last for up to seven days. This elaborate celebration is modified in the United States, where weddings only go on for one or two nights. Nonetheless, a few days before the wedding, relatives, including second and third cousins, start arriving from various cities to join the festivities. Every night a dinner is held at a different family household to welcome the incoming guests. People enjoy good food, catch up on family news, and give advice to the bride and groom about the secrets of a good marriage.

Weddings are usually held at a community center or a banquet hall. It is almost impossible for an Arab American couple to have a small wedding. Close and distant relatives, friends, and neighbors must be invited. The best food and desserts are served, along with the traditional wedding cake. An Arabic band usually plays, and people dance and sing until late at night. It is a common custom to throw dollar bills on the bride and the groom while they are dancing.

Since weddings can be very costly, the parents of the bride and the groom help pay for it, and often give money and gifts to the new couple to help them start their new life together. After the honeymoon, relatives and friends invite the newlyweds for family dinners. They also visit the couple at their home, bringing them gifts.

# The henna night

Henna night takes place on the night before the wedding, when the female relatives of the bride come to her home to decorate her body—especially her hands and feet—with henna (a natural dye made from the leaves of the henna tree). While the bride gets the most elegant and detailed designs, other female relatives also get their hands and feet decorated. It is said that if young unmarried women are decorated with the bride's henna they will have good luck and find a suitable husband. During the henna night, women dance and sing special songs. Food, sweets, and non-alcoholic drinks are served.

In the United States, the henna night tradition is practiced by only a few Arab American communities, including Yemenis, North Africans, and Palestinians. To reduce the pressure on the busy bride and her family, sometimes the henna night is held one week, rather than one night, before the wedding.

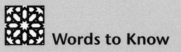
## Words to Know

- **Ashura:** observed during the first ten days of the Muslim month of Muharram, it commemorates the assassination of prophet Muhammad's grandson Hussein.

- **Baklava:** a dessert made of thin sheets of pastry layered with nuts, honey, and butter.

- **Country of origin:** the country in which a person is born.

- **Debkeh:** a special group dance performed in many Arab countries.

- **Eid:** the Arabic word for holiday.

- **Eid al-Adha:** a Muslim holiday that marks the end of the pilgrimage, it commemorates events in the lives of the prophet Abraham and his family.

- **Eid al-Fitr:** a Muslim holiday that marks the end of Ramadan, the month of fasting.

- **Extended family:** a family that includes grandparents, uncles, aunts, and cousins.

- **Hafla (plural haflat):** a get-together that is a cross between a concert and a party.

- **Hajj:** the Muslim pilgrimage to Mecca, the birthplace of the prophet Muhammad. All Muslims are obligated to do this once in his or her lifetime if they are financially and physically capable of doing so.

- **Henna:** a dye made from henna tree leaves that is used to color hair and to decorate hands and feet.

## Births

Many Arab Americans consider children to be blessings from God, and like to have large families. Traditionally the birth of a boy is more celebrated than that of a girl (although this is changing) because boys carry on the family name and are expected to take care of the parents when they get old.

When a child is born, the grandmother stays with the family of the newborn for a few weeks (usually forty days) to help with the baby and the household chores. After a birth, relatives and friends come to congratulate the parents and bring gifts. A traditional gift for the newborn is a golden cross or a verse of the Qur'an, and a blue bead to protect the child from

- **Hummous:** a dip made from garbanzo beans, tahini (sesame seed butter) and garlic.

- **Karbala:** a city in southern Iraq, where Muhammad's grandson Hussein was killed.

- **Kibbeh:** a meatball made from ground lamb and cracked wheat.

- **Lunar calendar:** a calendar that divides the year into twelve months, each starting with the new moon. The lunar calendar has 354 days, eleven days shorter than the Gregorian calendar used in the West.

- **Mecca:** located in modern Saudi Arabia, it is the most important holy city to Muslims worldwide.

- **Muhammad:** the prophet believed by Muslims to be the most recent and final messenger of God.

- **Qur'an:** also spelled Koran; the holy book for Muslims.

- **Ramadan:** the ninth month of the Islamic lunar calendar, during which Muslims fast from sunrise to sunset.

- **Shi'a:** a branch of Islam. The Shi'a have a significant following in Lebanon and southern Iraq. The majority of the people in the Middle Eastern (but non-Arab) country of Iran are Shi'a.

- **Tabbouleh:** a salad of chopped parsley and tomato mixed with cracked wheat.

evil. A special pudding, called *karawyah* or *moughli,* made with spices and nuts, is usually served to the guests. Some Arab Americans will celebrate the fortieth day after a child's birth by having a family dinner and by decorating the hands and the feet of the mother with henna. It is believed that it takes a woman forty days to totally recover from giving birth.

# Celebrating Arab American identity and culture

Like other ethnic minorities in the United States, Arab Americans try to preserve their culture and pass it on from one generation to another. Arab Americans also try to main-

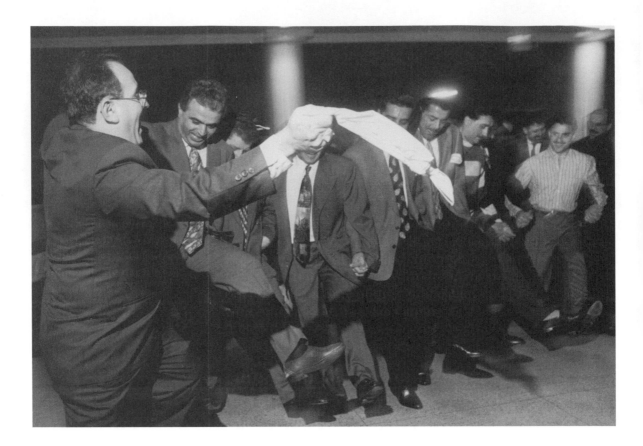

The head of an energetic debkeh line leads a crowd of revelers at an ACCESS (Arab Community Center for Economic and Social Services) annual dinner. *Reproduced by permission of Millard Berry.*

tain contact with their extended family and members of their town of origin, who may be dispersed throughout the world. Family and town reunions, community banquets, conventions, and festivals all allow Arab Americans to preserve and celebrate the culture of their homelands and to maintain ties with other people from back home.

## Family and town reunions

Many Arab Americans dedicate one long weekend—such as the Fourth of July or Labor Day weekend—to a family or a town reunion. These reunions may be small, including only the children and grandchildren of one or two grandparents or great-grandparents. Or they may include hundreds, or even thousands, of members of a large extended family.

One reason why Arab American family reunions can be so large is that some Arab Americans come from a village where most, if not all, of the people trace their background to a common ancestor. If many members of that village immigrated to the United States (as is often the case), then a family reunion could include people as loosely related as tenth cousins.

For example, Lebanese Americans who trace their origin to the Lebanese village of Karoun get together every Labor Day weekend. More than four hundred people travel from different cities in the United States, Canada, and even South America for this reunion. They stay in one hotel and hold a Saturday banquet and a Sunday picnic.

 **Ramallah**

Some Arab Americans who come from small villages can trace their ancestors to one couple, or to two or more brothers. For example, there are more than 75,000 Palestinian Americans who came originally from the town of Ramallah and who trace their ancestry back to seven brothers, meaning that they are all related to one other.

The largest Arab American reunion is the four-day convention of the American Federation of Ramallah, Palestine, which has been taking place since 1959. The size of attendance ranges from three thousand to five thousand people depending on the hosting city. Detroit and San Francisco are the most popular places because they have the largest number of people from Ramallah. These reunions are festive occasions with lots of food, music, dancing, and games.

## Banquets and conventions

Arab Americans belong to a variety of political, social, and professional associations that hold banquets, conventions, and other cultural events. Some of the most well-known of these associations are the Arab American University Graduates (AAUG), the Arab American Medical Association, and the American-Arab Anti-Discrimination Committee (ADC), (see chapter 13).

The conventions and banquets of these associations serve a variety of purposes. In addition to maintaining contact among their members, keeping them informed about the group's activities and strengthening the organization, conventions and banquets celebrate Arab culture and offer their members the opportunity to socialize. Many Arab Americans refer to the banquet as a hafla, or party. No matter what the occasion might be, the evening program usually includes a dinner, speeches or lectures, then live music and debkeh—a group line dance.

## Festivals

Arab Americans usually take part in local festivals that celebrate ethnic diversity. Sometimes Arab Americans organize their own festivals. These festivals often feature traditional Arabic food, clothing, art, films, music, and dance. Among the largest Arab American festivals in the United States are the Mahrajan Al-Fann (Festival of the Arts) in New York City, the Ana Al-Arabi (I Am the Arab) Festival in Washington, D.C., the Arabic Festival in San Francisco, and the East Dearborn Arab International Festival in Dearborn, Michigan.

## For More Information

Ghazi, Suhaib Hamid. *Ramadan.* New York: Holiday House, 1996.

Najor, Julia. *Babylonian Cuisine: Chaldean Cookbook from the Middle East.* New York: Vantage Press, 1991.

Rodseth, Lars, Sally Howell, and Andrew Shryock. *Arab World Mosaic: A Curriculum Supplement for Elementary Teachers.* Dearborn, MI: The Arab Community Center for Economic and Social Services (ACCESS), 1994.

Shabbas, Audrey, and Ayad Al-Qazzaz, eds. *Arab World Notebook.* Berkeley, CA: Najda (Women Concerned About the Middle East), 1989.

*Teaching about Islam & Muslims in the Public School Classroom.* 3rd ed. CA: The Council on Islamic Education, 1995.

Winchester, Faith. *Muslim Holidays.* Manakto, MN: Bridgestone Books, 1996.

*Anan Ameri is the Cultural Arts Director of the Arab Community Center for Economic and Social Services (ACCESS). She received her B.A. from the Jordanian University in Amman, Jordan, her M.A. from Cairo University in Egypt, and her Ph.D. in Sociology from Wayne State University in Detroit, Michigan.*

# Health and Environmental Issues

**12**

Research on Arab American health is still in the early stages at the end of the twentieth century even though Arabs have immigrated to the United States since the end of the nineteenth century. The first articles and studies on health issues concerning Arab Americans didn't appear until the 1980s. While there are large-scale health studies on other ethnic groups, little has been done on Arab Americans and data on Arab American health patterns remains sketchy.

## Arab American diversity and health

Because of their diversity, Arab Americans present health researchers with some rather unique challenges. Arab Americans come from twenty-one different countries, and health, climate, and environmental conditions vary greatly among these countries. The amount of biological and environmental differences (diversity) among Arab populations has not yet been determined. Therefore, when researchers lump together Arab Americans who come from different countries and regions of origin, the data results may be confusing or misleading.

Arab Americans also come from multiple religious backgrounds, the largest groups being Muslims and Christians. Religion may influence what people wear, what they eat, and how they behave. Yet the impact of religious differences on health has not been adequately studied.

Another important factor affecting Arab Americans' health is the adjustment to the American lifestyle—including diet and exercise—for new immigrants. This is an important scientific question for all immigrant groups, and because Arab Americans are a relatively new group to the United States, they are in a unique position to provide some of the answers.

## Arab American health patterns

When Arab Americans began immigrating in significant numbers during the 1880s, there were no researchers gathering data on their health before or after they arrived in the United States. The information now available on the health of the first wave of Arab American immigrants comes only from anecdotal (stories of individual cases) information. In order to find out about the health of these immigrants, it is necessary to look into the few written accounts of the time.

Most of the early wave of Arabs that immigrated to the United States between 1880 and 1924 were from Lebanon, which was part of Greater Syria (present-day Syria, Lebanon, Jordan, Palestine, and Israel) at that time and under Ottoman Turkish rule (see chapter 2). Lebanon suffered a series of crushing environmental, economic, and political blows during this period. These included the blockade of the country by Allied forces during World War I (1914-18), the destruction of the silk industry—upon which Lebanon's economy depended—and the famine (starvation) brought on by locusts and unusually dry weather. Public health and sanitation (waste removal) in the Arab world during the early 1900s was not as advanced as in the United States, either.

The early wave of Lebanese immigrants came to the United States seeking a better life for their families. American Christian missionaries living in the Lebanese mountains spread many stories of how wonderful life in the United States would be for them. Many Lebanese immigrants believed that they could easily strike it rich in the United States, and that their troubles would be over when they reached America. They also expected to be healthier and have better food and housing. But what they found after they immigrated to the United States was different from what they expected.

## Life in the immigrant quarter

At the end of the nineteenth century, the large cities of the East coast, such as New York and Boston, became center points for immigrants looking for a new life. In each of these cities, there were large immigrant quarters or neighborhoods. Sometimes people of the same ethnic background found comfort living in isolated neighborhoods, such as "Little Italy" in New York. In other cases, the immigrants lived in multicultural neighborhoods. Often the immigrants came to the country with little money and only the few possessions they could carry. The ethnic quarters provided low-rent housing and a place to start their new lives.

### Fact Focus

- Early Arab immigrants' health was affected by their lifestyles—including living in crowded cities and working as factory workers and peddlers.

- In spite of the healthy Arab diet, Arab Americans may be overweight and suffer from high cholesterol due to the large amount of fat, sugar, and meat in the American diet.

- For Arab Americans it is sometimes harder to get enough exercise in the United States due to dependence on cars for transportation. In the Arab world, people walk much more.

- A high percentage—between 35 percent and 45 percent—of Arab Americans smoke, putting them at high risk for lung cancer and other smoking-related diseases.

Life in the ethnic quarters came at a price. The housing in these areas was often poorly constructed and lacked acceptable heating, hot water, adequate sanitation, and proper ventilation. The small apartments that lacked heat or hot water were called "cold water flats." For many newcomers to the United States, this was all that could be afforded. As a result, these apartments—also known as tenement houses—were often over-crowded. Epidemics of diseases such as the flu, tuberculosis, small pox, and measles easily swept through these neighborhoods and killed thousands of people.

### Boston's south end in the 1920s

Arab immigrants were among those who settled in the cities on the eastern coast in the late 1800s and early

Many immigrants came to the United States with little money. Ethnic quarters, or neighborhoods, provided low-rent housing that was often poorly constructed and lacked acceptable heating, hot water, sanitation, and ventilation. *Reproduced by permission of the Library of Congress.*

1900s. A famous Arab American who settled in the ethnic quarters in the South End of Boston was the poet and artist Kahlil Gibran. During the 1920s, he immigrated from Lebanon with his mother, Kamila, two sisters, Marianna and Sultana, and half-brother, Peter. At first Kahlil's mother supported the family by carrying a fifty-pound pack of household goods, embroidery, and items from the Arab world to sell in the suburbs of Boston. She walked many miles every day to sell her wares. Although it was rare for women to do this type of work, she needed to support her children. The family soon had enough money to open a small shop. Kahlil went to the community public school and his artwork and poems were quickly recognized by his teachers. He was destined to become one of the world's beloved poets.

The story of Kahlil Gibran's family, however, is not a happy one. Within eight years of coming to the United States, Kahlil's mother died of cancer and his half-brother and one of his sisters died of tuberculosis. The Associated Charities, a group devoted to helping immigrants in Boston's South End, reported 42 percent of the families in the area came to their association for help because of illness, and one-third of those people had tuberculosis. Tuberculosis is very contagious (easily passed from person to person) and it often sweeps through communities, causing epidemics. Tuberculosis was a huge problem for all immigrants in Boston during the late 1800s and early 1900s.

In Kahlil Gibran's day, the poverty and bad conditions that immigrants lived in often led them to be unfairly stereotyped as being "disease ridden" and as having "criminal tendencies." People in those days confused environmental conditions in which one lived with biology (a person's physical make up). Today we recognize that people in Boston's South End were working very hard, but living under very bad conditions. In a letter to a cousin living in Lebanon and wanting to immigrate to Boston, Kahlil Gibran warned of his area's high unemployment rate and poor health conditions. Kahlil Gibran also suffered health problems—tuberculosis and a diseased liver— and died at the age of forty-seven.

So while many of the early Arab immigrants were making and saving money, they also faced serious health concerns. Kahil Gibran's is one of the few existing stories telling about the problems early Arab immigrants faced. Many of the Arab immigrants from that generation only wanted to talk about their successes. Great-grandparents and grandparents simply say that they came to the United States, found a job, and made a life for themselves. What they do not talk about is how hard it was for them. This is why the picture of their lives is often incomplete.

Kahlil Gibran as a teenager in Boston. Gibran moved from Lebanon to Boston's South End when he was twelve years old. *Reproduced by permission of the Library of Congress.*

## Health in the second wave of Arab immigrants

Conditions in the immigrant quarters in America's big cities improved over time. During the second wave of Arab immigration, from 1924 to 1952, Americans became aware of the poor conditions in the ethnic quarters and slums of the United States. Social work and charities expanded and began to change the way people in the United States viewed poverty, disease, housing, and work conditions. Housing laws began requiring proper lighting, heating, ventilation, and sanitation in buildings. These changes had an effect on people's health. Severe disease epidemics decreased due to improvements.

Before conditions improved, child labor was also a big problem in America's factories. It remains uncertain if Arab American children worked long hours in unsafe factory conditions—but many immigrant children did. Between 1924 and 1952, child labor laws were passed to protect children from long hours and unsafe working conditions. These laws also resulted in an improvement in immigrants' health and safety.

Just as Arab immigrants were beginning to benefit from better conditions, they were hit with a new problem. In 1924, the United States entered a period of fearing foreigners. Laws were passed that sharply reduced the number of new immigrants—especially those from Far and Middle Eastern countries, which included Arab nations. The Oriental Exclusion Act of 1924 and the Johnson-Reed Quota Act of 1924 almost completely stopped the flow of immigrants from Arab countries. These laws created many hardships for Arab families, including separating loved ones. If someone had immigrated to the United States before these laws were passed, the rest of their family could not come to join them (see chapter 4).

During this period, the world went through some very difficult times—particularly World War I and World War II (1939-45). Several thousand Arab Americans served in both wars for the United States. There are no accurate counts of how many Arab Americans gave their lives for their new country or how many came back wounded. Diseases, such as the flu epidemic that struck soldiers and the American population after World War I, took many lives. Although some diseases were declining, new diseases and the wars continued to take lives.

It is also not very clear what life was like for many Arab Americans during the second wave of immigration to the United States. People were busy working and not writing about their lives. It was not until the 1970s that studies began on Arab American culture and life.

# Health in the third wave

Although Philip Hitti wrote one of the first books about Arab Americans in the 1900s, it was not until the 1970s that other researchers began studying Arab Americans. Anthropologists and social scientists such as Barbara Aswad and Mary Sengstock researched the Arabs and Chaldeans living in metropolitan Detroit. They were interested in describing their culture and communities. They discovered that most of the Arabs and Chaldeans in Detroit originally came from agricultural villages in the Arab world. Arabs are not usually thought of as farmers, but throughout the history of the Arab world, large numbers of Arabs have been farmers. Moving from small farming villages to large cities is a major change in lifestyle.

## Health and the move from rural to urban life

After the 1950s life in the United States changed radically. Better housing laws, improved work conditions, and better sanitation made life safer and healthier for everyone in America—especially immigrants. Mass vaccinations for polio and small pox made these contagious diseases nearly extinct. But these improvements were accompanied by other changes, which sometimes proved harmful to people's health. One such change was the worldwide movement of people from rural, or farming, areas into heavily populated urban areas. In the industrial age after World War I, more jobs became available in big cities. Cities grew in size all over the world as millions of people made the shift from rural villages and small towns to big cities.

Although cities had seen an improvement in public health thanks to improved living conditions and the elimination of contagious diseases, the shift from farming to urban life brought a different set of problems. Today, people are plagued with long work hours and many stresses. Heart disease, diabetes (high amounts of sugar in the blood), high blood pressure, obesity (being overweight), and high cholesterol (which slows the flow of blood to the heart) are the new health epidemics of our age. These diseases are not contagious, however, in that a person cannot catch heart disease from another person. They are caused by poor lifestyle choices, including stress, lack of exercise, and poor diets full of junk food.

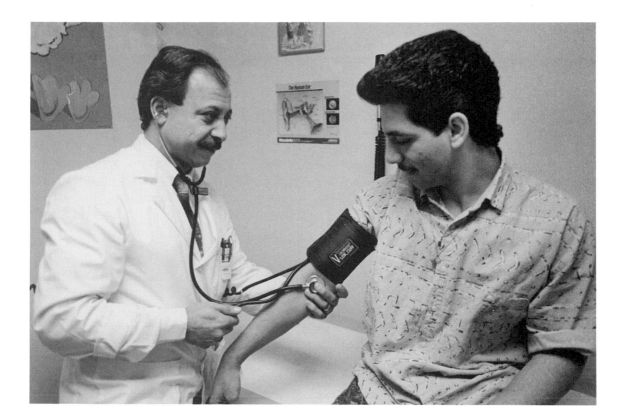

# Arab American health today

Researchers have began to look at immigrants and minorities (members of less-affluent ethnic groups) to see if everyone in the United States suffers equally from these diseases. What researchers are finding is that many minority and ethnic groups have higher rates of many diseases than the majority, or dominant, population.

In the 1990s research began on patterns of disease in Arab Americans. The Arab Community Center for Economic and Social Services (ACCESS) in Dearborn, Michigan, started some of this research by surveying people (asking questions) about heart disease and other illnesses. They found that Arab Americans are at a higher risk for heart disease than the majority population.

Interested in how people adapt to life in the United States and how new and different patterns of work, eating, and exercise effect health, Dr. Rosina Hassoun did a study on

Although cities have seen an improvement in public health thanks to improved living conditions and the elimination of many contagious diseases, people today are plagued by a different set of problems—including heart disease, high blood pressure, and high cholesterol. *Reproduced by permission of the Arab Community Center for Economic and Social Services (ACCESS).*

diet, health, and high blood pressure among Arab Americans. Her research found that Arab Americans may suffer higher than normal rates of high blood pressure, diabetes, and high cholesterol. The most important factor causing an increase in these diseases appeared to be changes in the diets of Arabs immigrants once they come to the United States. Her survey showed that Arab immigrants ate more red meat, sweets, and fats than they did previous to immigrating. Her study also suggested that diabetes rates could be two to three times higher in Arab Americans than in the general population in Michigan. The same problems could be seen in other ethnic groups, including Hispanics, African Americans, and Native Americans.

A high rate of smoking among Arab Americans is another serious health risk factor. Between 35 percent and 45 percent of Arab Americans smoke. Smoking has been linked to cancer and researchers are afraid that many Arab Americans are at a high risk of getting cancer. Not enough research has been done, however, to determine cancer rates among Arab Americans.

## Environmental issues and Arab Americans

Today's Arab Americans do not suffer from the same work- and lifestyle-related illnesses that may have plagued early immigrants, including bad backs (peddlers carried heavy packs) and contagious diseases (such as the flu and tuberculosis), but work environments still play an influential role in the health of Arab Americans. In Detroit, Arabs Americans settled in the south end of Dearborn, a suburb located near the automobile factories. Like many other immigrants, they were attracted to the good pay provided by the car manufacturing plants. Over time, the south end of Dearborn became home to a large number of Yemeni Arabs, whose community lies in the heart of an industrial area. Unfortunately, the industries in that area have historically produced large amounts of toxic air pollution. Better air pollution laws have reduced the amount of toxic pollution; however, pollution levels remain a concern. In the meantime, the Arab community in Dearborn is learning about environmental health issues and

Arab American students play soccer in the shadow of the massive Ford Motor Company Rouge Plant. The south end of Dearborn, Michigan, is surrounded by heavy industry. *Reproduced by permission of Millard Berry.*

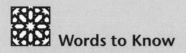

## Words to Know

- **Majority:** the social or ethnic group that is most numerous and powerful within a society.

- **Minority:** a group, especially an ethnic group, that is less numerous and has less resources than the majority, or dominant ethnic group.

- **Public health:** the overall health of a city's or country's inhabitants, which is promoted through public education, vaccination programs, school lunches, sanitation, and other government programs designed to benefit large numbers of people.

- **Rural:** pertaining to sparsely populated areas, such as farms and villages.

- **Sanitation:** sewage disposal, waste removal, and other measures taken to promote better health for the public.

- **Urban:** pertaining to heavily populated areas, such as cities.

how to protect their right to a clean environment.

Another work-related environmental threat to the health of Arab Americans is the use of pesticides on farms where they work. Yemeni workers in northern California, in conjunction with the United Farm Workers, organized to protest the use of dangerous pesticides. In a 1973 incident, a Yemeni farm worker was killed by local authorities during a protest strike.

## Arab Americans and health care

Another concern of Arab Americans is how well the American health care system cares for Arab and Muslim patients. The Arab Community Center for Economic and Social Services (ACCESS) and many other researchers are trying to educate doctors and nurses in the United States about Arabic culture and the needs of Arab and Muslim patients. They argue that healthcare givers should work to provide more humane care, and to respect the privacy and special dietary needs of all patients.

## New directions in Arab American health

Arab American health patterns and problems appear to have changed over time. The early Arab immigrants were more concerned with contagious diseases than are Arab Americans today. Chronic diseases such as high blood pressure, heart disease, and diabetes, however, are the health problems of Arab Americans at the end of the twentieth century.

The good news is that improvements in diet, exercise, and education may help prevent these illnesses. Researchers and health workers in Arab American communities are helping to raise awareness and to provide Arabic-language health information and culturally sensitive health care. Environmental researchers are educating Arab Americans about the dangers of pollution, and new research is being conducted to further the knowledge and ability to improve the health of Arab Americans.

An important step in this direction was the First National Conference organized by ACCESS on Health Issues in the Arab American Community, held in Detroit from April 30–May 1, 1999. This conference brought together researchers, educators, healthcare providers, community service organizations, and public policy makers from around the country. The hope is that this conference will be followed by others like it, resulting in improved research on Arab American health and, ultimately, a healthier Arab American population.

## For More Information

Affaf, M., and J. G. Lipson. "Assessing Arab-American Health Care Needs: Research Note." *Social Science and Medicine,* 1989.

Cabadas, Joseph. "Rouge Paint Facility Critics Raising Concerns." *U.S. AutoScene,* 1997.

Gibran, Jean, and Kahlil Gibran. *Kahlil Gibran: His Life and World.* New York: Avenel Books, 1981.

Naff, Alixia. *The Arab Americans.* New York: Chelsea House Publications, 1988.

*Rosina Hassoun holds a Ph.D. in Biology/Medical Anthropology from the University of Florida at Gainsville. Hassoun is currently an adjunct assistant professor in the Department of Anthropology and the Bailey Scholars Program at Michigan State Univeristy.*

# Civil Rights and Social Justice

13

Arab Americans have become a vital part of American society. Both as individuals and as a community, they have made important contributions to American life. Yet all too often they face discriminatory treatment—unfair treatment on the basis of their group identity. Arab Americans have organized to oppose discrimination and to educate the public about Arab Americans and the Arab cultural heritage. They have yet to fully convey to their fellow Americans, however, the true picture of their historical, social, and cultural identity.

In the United States, all citizens are granted certain civil rights by laws and documents such as the Constitution and the Bill of Rights. These include the rights to freedom of speech and religion, the right to vote, and the right to equality before the law. Sometimes, however, the rights of certain groups are ignored or violated. One of the most obvious examples of this in U.S. history has been the treatment of African Americans, who only recently received legal equality and still suffer from economic and racial discrimination.

Arab Americans have also suffered violations of their civil rights. For this reason organizations such as the Ameri-

**Rudolph Valentino holds Agnes Ayres in a still from the 1921 movie _The Sheik_.** *Reproduced with permission of Corbis Corporation (Bellevue).*

can-Arab Anti-Discrimination Committee (ADC) were founded to protect the rights of Arab Americans. In addition to combating laws that treat Arab Americans unfairly, the ADC and other similar groups also work to ensure that Arab Americans do not suffer from other forms of social injustice, such as: discrimination in the workplace and at school, violence resulting from prejudice against Arabs, and the promotion of negative stereotypes of Arabs in films and the media.

This chapter discusses some of the major issues of civil rights and social justice that concern Arab Americans. The issues of social justice—equal treatment of all groups in a society by others—include stereotyping, discrimination, and violence against Arabs. The civil rights section deals with institutional and legal discrimination, including airport profiling, the 1996 Antiterrorism and Effective Death Penalty Act, and the use of "secret evidence" in cases against Arab Americans.

## Representations of Arab Americans in the media

One issue of concern to Arab Americans is the way in which they are portrayed in the media. Films, television, and the news media often present stereotypes—or distorted images—of the Arab world that do not represent reality.

Such negative media images often justify discrimination. These stereotypes can be found in a variety of media, including textbooks and novels, news programs and newspapers, movies, and television shows. Below are discussed two of the most common sources of stereotypes of Arab Americans: Hollywood movies and the news.

## Arabs in the eye of Hollywood

Throughout the history of cinema, all ethnic groups have been a subject of stereotyping at one time or another. African Americans were commonly represented as happy-go-lucky buffoons in early cinema, and Asian men were often portrayed as treacherous and conniving. Today, while filmmakers and movie-goers are more sensitive to stereotypes of these ethnic groups, stereotypes of Arabs and Arab Americans are just as prevalent as they were in the early days of the film industry. Over and over, the rich and complex civilization of the Arab world is reduced to a few distorted images.

Beginning with Rudolph Valentino's role in the 1921 movie *The Sheik,* many films have relied on the image of the Arab sheik—the leader of a bedouin tribe of desert nomads. He is seen in a desert oasis with camels, tribesmen, and a

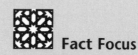 **Fact Focus**

- The first major Hollywood portrayal of an Arab character was Rudolph Valentino's role in the 1921 movie *The Sheik.*

- Bedouins comprise only about 2 percent of the population of the Arab world. Most Arabs live in cities.

- Disney altered the lyrics to a song in the cartoon movie *Aladdin* after protests from Arab Americans.

- In 1998 the soap opera *Days of Our Lives* portrayed an Arab harem, complete with belly dancers and a bloodthirsty sultan, until protests caused the producers to change the locale to the Caribbean.

- Arab Americans are disproportionately (more than people of other groups) singled out for embarrassing searches and questioning at airports.

- U.S. President George Bush continually referred to the Iraqi president Saddam Hussein as *Sadam,* badly mispronouncing his first name as a deliberate insult rather than using his last name as is the custom with world leaders.

harem (a large number of women often shown in belly dancing costumes). This image does not represent the great majority of Arabs. Historically, the Arab world has been centered in urban society, not the desert. Bedouins (pronounced BED-O-wins) today comprise only about 2 percent of the population of the Arab world. Likewise, the image of the Arab woman belly dancer is more myth than reality. Most Arab women's lives are in many ways similar to those of American women—they raise families, go to school, work, manage homes, and socialize. Yet these images of rich bedouin sheiks, desert nomads, and belly dancers persist in the mind of many people who are unfamiliar with the reality of Arab society.

Another common stereotype is that of the Arabs as terrorists, people who kill civilians for political purposes. Films like *True Lies, Executive Decision,* and *The Siege* portray Arabs hijacking airplanes and threatening the United States with bombs.

Arabs have also been portrayed in Hollywood as barbaric or bloodthirsty. In Disney's cartoon film *Aladdin* the theater version contained a song that referred to the Arab world as a place "where they cut off your ear if they don't like your face." After protests by the American-Arab Anti-Discrimination Committee (ADC), Disney executives agreed to change the lyrics to something less offensive in the video version.

Desert sheiks, belly dancers, and terrorists are no more representative of Arab society than cowboys, bank robbers, and supermodels are of the United States. But while Americans know that images of cowboys don't realistically represent life in the United States, they are less likely to understand that rich sheiks and belly dancers don't represent Arabs. This is because most people in the United States are not familiar with everyday life in the Arab world.

What is missing amid the Hollywood stereotypes are images of Arabs as normal people. In films and other forms of popular culture, it is difficult to find portrayals of Arabs in the reality of their everyday lives. As media analyst Jack Shaheen has commented, "Rarely do we see ordinary Arabs, practicing law, driving taxis, singing lullabies or healing the sick." Also missing are images of Arab Americans, who continue to be an almost invisible ethnic group in the United States. In short, the mainstream Hollywood film industry has yet to produce a film that adequately portrays Arab civilization, Arab efforts

to develop their own countries, or Arab American participation in American civic, cultural, or artistic life.

## Political bias in the news

Just as Hollywood has promoted stereotypes of Arabs through films, the news media has promoted inaccurate images of Arabs through its use of language and its biased coverage. One problem is that the media tends to use the word "terrorist" more often in reference to acts of violence committed by Arabs and Muslims than to those committed by other groups. This leads the public to associate violence with Arabs or Muslims in general. There are many forms of political violence in which innocent civilians are threatened or killed, but when Arabs and Muslims are not involved, the news media is less likely to call this violence an act of terrorism. For example, when Christian groups bomb abortion clinics, it is rarely referred to as "Christian terrorism."

**Disney agreed to change offensive lyrics in the video version of the cartoon film *Aladdin* after protests from the American-Arab Anti-Discrimination Committee (ADC).** *Reproduced by permission of the Walt Disney Company. All Rights Reserved.*

A related problem is that when bombings and other acts of violence are carried out in the United States, the media often jumps to the conclusion that Muslim or Arab groups were involved. In 1995, when the Oklahoma City Federal Building was bombed and 168 people died, the news media immediately reported the assumption that Arabs or Muslims were to blame.

Arab Americans are also concerned with the fact that the media does not give them sufficient opportunity to voice their opinion on issues that concern them. Instead, the media often interviews non-Arab American officials or politically biased analysts. For example, when the media discusses the impact of the 1991 Gulf War on Iraqi people, we rarely hear from Iraqi Americans who may have relatives in Iraq or from Iraqi immigrants who came to the United States after enduring as much as nine years of hardship caused by the war.

According to the estimates of the United Nations International Children's Emergency Fund (UNICEF) and other United Nations (UN) agencies, UN/U.S. economic sanctions banning the export of goods—including food and medicine—to Iraq with the hope of removing Saddam Hussein from power may have killed over a million innocent Iraqi civilians. The media has never presented this tragic, human suffering to the American people in an effective manner. Often, when Arabs are perpetrators of violence, the headlines are dramatic and vivid; when Arabs are the victims of violence, the news is buried and almost invisible.

One reason for the lack of Arab sources in the media is that there are very few Arab Americans working as mainstream news reporters, editors, and producers. To remedy this situation Arab Americans need to enter these professions in increasing numbers and the mainstream media must hire Arab Americans who have links to their community and understand the culture and the concerns of Arab Americans for visible news positions.

## Discrimination at work

Negative stereotypes often affect Arab Americans on the job, especially when stereotypes are held by their supervisors and coworkers. These stereotypes are reflected in different kinds of discrimination and harassment.

## The American-Arab Anti-Discrimination Committee (ADC)

The largest Arab American organization devoted to fighting discrimination of all types is the American-Arab Anti-Discrimination Committee (ADC). Founded in 1980 by former senator James Abourezk, this organization in the late 1990s has a national membership of 10,000 and is involved in a variety of activities aimed at promoting equality for Arab Americans on all levels.

In important cases that affect the whole Arab American community, ADC files legal suits against the government and against companies and organizations that discriminate against employees and clients. In addition, ADC works diligently to educate the public about discrimination against Arabs and Arab Americans and to counteract negative stereotypes by promoting more realistic and positive images of Arab Americans. Other organizations that work towards the same goals are the Arab American University Graduates (AAUG) and the Arab American Institute (AAI).

**James Abourezk, founder of the American-Arab Anti-Discrimination Committee.** *Reproduced by permission of the Corbis Corporation (Bellevue).*

Some forms of discrimination are more psychologically harmful than physically or financially damaging, such as when coworkers make inappropriate jokes about Arabs that are based on ethnic prejudices. In 1996 an Arab American living in Boston, for example, filed complaints about being called offensive names by his coworkers. The man's supervisors allegedly joined in with the name-calling and did not discipline the other workers. Many Arab American children tell similar stories about being harassed by classmates at school.

In other cases, Arab Americans are denied jobs and promotions due to more severe levels of discrimination. For instance, in South Carolina in 1997 an Arab American man

Attorney, civil rights activist, and former president of the American-Arab Anti-Discrimination Committee (ADC) Abdeen Jabara has used his legal skills to defend the rights of Arab Americans. *Reproduced by permission of Abdeen Jabara.*

with two master's degrees—and an accent—called for information about an engineering job. He was told that the job had been filled. Something aroused his suspicion, so his wife also called to ask about the position. She had no accent. The company told her that the job was still open.

Another issue in the Arab American struggle for equal treatment in the workplace is the freedom to practice their religion. This can be especially challenging for Arab Muslim women. In 1996, for example, a department store in Virginia fired a Muslim woman because she insisted on wearing the *hijab,* or head scarf, as she believed was required by her religious tradition. Similar problems have been reported by Muslim women across the country. Arab American and Muslim organizations protest these actions because they violate the constitutional rights to freedom of religion guaranteed to all Americans. Because of these protests, some companies have recognized the rights of their employees to retain their religious dress.

Arab Americans have fought and won numerous other cases of discrimination. In 1994 an Arab American who had endured repeated ethnic slurs by his coworkers won $100,000 in a lawsuit. The New York City Commission on Human Rights awarded three Egyptian Americans $10,000 in 1991 after years of religious and ethnic harassment by their employer. In 1998, after complaints that city agencies discriminated against Arab American businesses in awarding contracts, the city of San Francisco officially recognized Arab Americans as a minority group with the same privileges as other groups. These victories have come as a result of the efforts of Arab Americans and non-Arab American individuals and organizations working together to address widespread discriminatory practices.

## Anti-Arab discrimination and U.S. foreign policy

In the late twentieth century anti-Arab discrimination has been closely related to U.S. foreign policy in the Arab world. Whenever the media reports that there is a national crisis related to the Arab world, Arab Americans become targets of harassment and violence stemming from ethnic prejudice. This is because the language used by the news—as well as photographs, drawings (including cartoons), and film footage—often centers solely on the negative aspects of the people being blamed for the crisis. This promotes anti-Arab attitudes and bigotry against the Arab-American community, fostering a climate of hostility that encourages violent acts.

Since the late 1970s there has been an increase in hate crimes—personal attacks based on ethnic prejudice—against Arab Americans. There were significant numbers of hate crimes reported against Arab Americans following the U.S. bombing of Libya in the 1980s, during the 1991 Gulf War against Iraq, and during the first few days after the 1995 Oklahoma City bombing (when Arabs and Muslims were immediately, but falsely, accused).

During the Gulf War against Iraq, Arab Americans were the targets of widespread hostility, harassment, and physical attacks. Bombs were planted and shots fired at Arab

American stores, Arab American-owned businesses, and mosques. People were beaten and their property vandalized. Many people received death threats.

The rise in anti-Arab discrimination and violence affected young people as well. In Dearborn, Michigan, there was a bomb threat at Fordson High School, where 50 percent of the students are Arab American. The Fordson basketball team reported anti-Arab insults at games, and some other high school teams refused to play the Fordson team. In Brooklyn, New York, six girls attacked a sixteen-year-old Arab American girl walking home from school. They beat her, tore off her scarf, and called her names.

## Threats to civil rights by official agencies

One of the issues that most concerns Arab American civil rights groups is that they are sometimes discriminated against by law enforcement agencies that are working to combat terrorism. Arab Americans suffer disproportionately from airport security policies and immigration proceedings. Law-abiding citizens are unfairly singled out, harassed, and even deported because they are suspected of being terrorists or associating with terrorist organizations. Such actions violate basic first amendment rights to freedom of speech, association, and political activity.

In the 1980s the Justice Department formulated a contingency plan for the mass arrest of Middle Eastern residents of the United States in the event of an unspecified national emergency. They were to be held in prison camps in Louisiana and Florida prior to deportation. During World War II (1939-45), a similar policy caused hundreds of thousands of Japanese Americans to be put into concentration camps, often losing their homes and jobs.

In 1996 Congress passed the Antiterrorism and Effective Death Penalty Act that gave the Federal Bureau of Investigation (FBI; a federal law enforcement agency) expanded surveillance powers (permission to spy) over the legal and peaceful activities of immigrant communities and organizations. It allows for the deportation of non-citizens on grounds of suspected links to organizations abroad that the U.S. government has designated as terrorist. The Antiterrorism and Effective Death Penalty Act also states that U.S. citizens can be given a ten-year prison sentence for donating funds to humanitarian programs—such as medical clinics, orphanages, or schools—that are affiliated with terrorist organizations.

Arab American spokespeople have pointed out that these policies violate the civil rights of individuals who have committed no crime or act of violence, but only have engaged in peaceful, legal, constitutionally protected political activities. The result has been that Arab Americans now think twice before engaging in political activities such as sending a letter to an editor of a newspaper or magazine regarding the U.S. policy towards Israel or calling the White House to request an end to the sanctions against Iraq.

 **Some Examples of Hate Crimes Against Arab and Muslim Americans During the Gulf War**

- In Los Angeles, an Arab American Catholic bishop was attacked near his home and left injured and unconscious.

- In Mississippi, barbershops refused service to Arabs.

- In San Diego, a bomb was discovered in the rest room of a mosque during Friday prayers.

- In Tulsa, Oklahoma, evening prayers were interrupted by rocks thrown through windows and a nearby Muslim school was vandalized.

## Secret evidence

Arab Americans are also concerned about laws that permit the use of "secret evidence" in legal proceedings. Secret evidence refers to evidence that is kept secret from defendants—those accused of wrongdoing—and their lawyers. Both the 1996 Antiterrorism and Effective Death Penalty Act and the 1996 Immigration Bill allow for the use of secret evidence against immigrants and foreign visitors in order to deport them. The problem with secret evidence is that the defendants are unable to defend themselves against accusations since they do not know what they are being accused of. This makes it impossible to prove their innocence.

For example, in 1997 a thirty-one-year-old Lebanese citizen was deported. He had lived in the United States for ten years and was married to a U.S. citizen. He was deported be-

**Words to Know**

- **Civil rights:** the rights of individuals as guaranteed by laws, the Constitution, and the Bill of Rights. Such rights include the right to freedom of speech, freedom of religion, the right to vote, the right to equality before the law, and the right to engage in political activity.

- **Discrimination:** the unfair treatment of individuals or groups on the basis of their group identity, rather than on the basis of their personal merits. Some discrimination is the act of prejudiced individuals; some discrimination is institutionalized in laws, regulations, or policies of government agencies, corporations, or other agencies.

- **Hate crime:** a criminal offense committed against a person or property that is motivated by the offender's bias against a race, religion, or ethnic group. Such crimes include physical assault, vandalism or destruction of property, and even intimidation through threatening words or conduct that causes others to have a reasonable fear of bodily harm.

- **Prejudice:** unjustified prejudgments about others on the basis of their group identity. This usually refers to unreasonable negative opinions and feelings about other groups.

- **Profiling:** a system used by airports to help employees choose which passengers to single out for questioning and searches. It involves looking for certain characteristics that are thought to be more likely to identify a potentially problematic passenger. People of Arab descent have frequently been singled out as potential terrorists.

- **Sheik:** the leader of a family, village, or tribe.

- **Social justice:** fair and equal treatment of all groups in a society by others, and equal access to a reasonable standard of living and lifestyle.

- **Stereotype:** an oversimplified and misleading image or idea about a group of people—including racial, ethnic, cultural, and religious groups. Stereotypes usually portray people in a negative and distorted way.

cause he donated a small amount of money for the care of a young relative in an orphanage in Lebanon, which was run by an organization on the State Department's "terrorist list."

Out of the twenty-four cases in which secret evidence was used, thirteen involved Arabs; the other eleven cases were Irish. The Irish cases were suspended when a peace agreement was made with the Irish Republican Army. As of 1999, only Arabs continue to be the targets of this deportation policy.

## Airport profiling

In 1996 TWA Flight 800 mysteriously crashed in the Atlantic Ocean, killing 230 people. The cause of the accident was never determined, but airport and flight security became the focus of public attention. Some of the policies put into effect by the Federal Aviation Administration have fostered anti-Arab discrimination at airports. First, a profiling system was designed to specify the characteristics of persons most likely to commit an act of terrorism. Several airline manuals list ethnic factors in their profiling: Arab names, birth in an Arab country, and travel to or from an Arab country.

The effect of this profiling system has been that Arab Americans are commonly singled out for scrutiny—or inspection—in airport check-in lines. This involves a humiliating process of questioning, interrogation, and intrusive searches. Most often, it means that all items of personal belonging will be seen and handled in public view.

In one documented case in 1997, a Syrian mother and her five-year-old daughter were traveling from Buffalo, New York, to Detroit, Michigan. A hand-search of their bags was carried out while other passengers watched. An airline employee accidentally damaged one of the woman's sweaters, and after the woman asked for formal documentation of the damage the employee responded by shouting at the woman, calling security, and threatening her with arrest.

## Arab American gains in civil rights and social justice

In spite of individual, institutional, and legal discrimination, Arab Americans have been successful in combating discrimination in recent years. For example, in 1987 Arab Americans won acknowledgment from the Supreme Court that they were protected under existing U.S. civil rights legislation from discrimination based on ethnicity.

Some deportations based on secret evidence have also been prevented. In one case in 1999, a judge ruled that the government's evidence against an Arab American failed to establish any connection with a terrorist organization and that the accused man was an upstanding, responsible citizen.

Arab American leaders now regularly meet with presidents, congressional leaders, secretaries of state, and the FBI in order to ensure that the concerns of their community are being heard. In 1999, there are six Arab Americans in the House of Representatives and one in the Senate, and Arab American educator Donna Shalala is Secretary of Health and Human Services.

Because of the committed involvement of thousands of Arab Americans, the Arab American community is increasingly becoming a recognized and respected part of America's multicultural landscape. It is no longer so easy for public or private agencies to disregard the rights of Arab Americans or denigrate (belittle) their culture and heritage.

# For More Information

Abraham, Nabeel. "Anti-Arab Racism and Violence in the United States." In *The Development of Arab-American Identity,* edited by Ernest McCarus. Ann Arbor: University of Michigan Press, 1994.

Conklin, Nancy Faires, and Nora Faires. "Colored and Catholic: The Lebanese in Birmingham, Alabama." In *Crossing the Waters: Arabic-Speaking Immigrants to the United States before 1940,* edited by Eric Hooglund. Washington, D.C.: Smithsonian Institution Press, 1987.

Michelak, Lawrence. "Cruel and Unusual: Negative Images of Arabs in American Popular Culture." Washington, D.C.: American-Arab Anti-Discrimination Committee, 1988.

"1991 Report on Anti-Arab Hate Crimes." Washington, D.C.: American-Arab Anti-Discrimination Committee, 1991.

"1996–1997 Report on Hate Crimes and Discrimination Against Arab Americans." Washington, D.C.: American-Arab Anti-Discrimination Committee, 1997.

Shaheen, Jack. *Arab and Muslim Stereotyping in American Popular Culture.* Washington, D.C.: Center for Muslim-Christian Understanding, 1997.

Shaheen, Jack. "The Comic Book Arab." *The Link,* November/December 1991.

Shaheen, Jack. *The TV Arab.* Bowling Green, OH: Bowling Green State University Popular Press, 1984.

Stockton, Ron. "Ethnic Archetypes and the Arab Image." In *The Development of Arab-American Identity,* edited by Ernest McCarus. Ann Arbor: University of Michigan Press, 1994.

Suleiman, Michael. *The Arabs in the Mind of America.* Brattleboro, VT: Amana Books, 1988.

*Marvin Wingfield is the Director of Education and Outreach for the American-Arab Anti-Discrimination Committee, an Arab-American civil rights organization.*

# Organizations and Political Activism

**14**

## How and why Arab Americans organize

Arab Americans, like all ethnic, racial, and religious groups in the United States, organize themselves for a number of reasons, many related to how they have been treated by other Americans. Since the late 1800s Arab Americans have created institutions to meet their needs as immigrants, as American citizens, as professionals, as activists, and as a people proud of their cultural heritage.

## The first Arab immigrants

When the first immigrants came to America from the Arab world, the majority of Americans were descendants of European settlers and immigrants or slaves. Part of a large wave of "new" immigrants from 1880 to 1920, the Syrians were considered strange and different from previous immigrants. Syrian (called after the area of Greater Syria—now Lebanon, Syria, Jordan, Palestine, and Israel—where most of them originated) names, appearance, language, religious customs, clothes, and food were unique (see chapter 4).

In those days, many native-born Americans were worried that these new arrivals, with such foreign habits, could not become "American." The immigrants were encouraged—in school and at work—to replace their homeland traditions and loyalties with American ones, a process called "Americanization."

Integrating into American culture strongly influenced how and why early immigrants organized. The first institutions were religious, since most Arab immigrants, although Christian, belonged to Eastern churches—Orthodox, Maronite, and Melchite—not Protestant or Catholic churches like most Western Europeans. Many fewer Muslims came at that time, but mosques (places of worship for Muslims) began to appear in the 1920s and 1930s (see chapter 7).

These early Arab Americans also formed clubs with people from their hometown to socialize, help newcomers adjust, and keep in touch with their families and friends back home. Both the churches and clubs of this early period were places where Arab immigrants could keep and celebrate their native culture. Newspapers printed in their native Arabic language also helped the immigrants keep up with news from the home country (see Chapter 19).

The early Syrians did not organize around politics for several reasons. They came from areas that were occupied by the Ottoman rulers of Turkey (see chapter 2), and so they had no tradition of modern democracy (electing their leaders). Citizenship and voting were a new experience to the Syrians, as was loyalty to a nation state. So in the political arena, the early Arab immigrants kept a low profile and did not form, like other European immigrants, organized ethnic voting blocs that would draw attention to themselves.

## Race and citizenship

Shortly before World War I (1914-18), the courts began to question whether Syrian immigrants should be excluded from U.S. citizenship. Their country of origin was in western Asia and other Asians had been barred from citizenship since the 1880s (especially through the Chinese Exclusion Act of 1882). Syrian leaders appealed these court challenges with proof that Syrians are Caucasian (white) by racial origin, even if their skin and hair color were darker than most Europeans. What became known as the "Yellow Race Crisis" was the first political issue that faced the Syrian immigrants, and it remained an issue until the end of the war. Added to the question of racial identity was the wartime atmosphere that questioned the loyalty of immigrants from countries (such as Ottoman Turkey) at war with the United States and its allies (see chapter 3).

## Assimilation and acceptance

By the mid-1920s, the anti-immigrant feelings in the country had grown, and quotas—or fixed limits—were placed on the number of new immigrants from outside northern Europe. The Johnson-Reed Quota Act of 1924 limited the number of immigrants coming to the United States to no more than 2 percent of that group's foreign-born population in the 1890 census. Very few Arabic-speaking immigrants were admitted into the United States for a period of three to four decades. During this period, the American-born children of Arab immigrants began influencing the way in which the Arab American community organized itself.

## The era of federations

Beginning in the 1930s, social clubs and churches that served the immigrants in a local community recognized the benefit of coming together to share cultural expression. The form this took was a large summer picnic (called a *mahrajan*) that began in Bridgeport,

### Fact Focus

- Arab Americans have been forming their own institutions since the late 1880s and 1890s; political organizations, however, emerged mainly after the Arab-Israeli war of 1967.

- Hundreds of Arab Americans hold public office as members of congress, cabinet secretaries, governors, state legislators, judges, mayors, and local officials. Seven Arab Americans served in the U.S. Congress in 1999.

- Eighty-two percent of Arabs living in the United States are U.S. citizens. Their voter participation is close to that of the national average, and their political affiliations are divided between Republican, Democratic, and independent parties.

- Arab Americans are active in issues that are international (Middle East peace, human rights, democracy), national (civil rights, immigration, religious tolerance), and local (education, community relations, cultural exchange).

- Today there are hundreds of Arab American organizations that represent this ethnic community in politics, civic life, public service, legal and human services, and religious and cultural expression, in addition to social, fraternal, and professional associations.

Connecticut, and attracted thousands of members of smaller clubs in surrounding states. The mahrajat soon gave birth to a formal federation, or union, of the smaller clubs—the Federation of Syrian and Lebanese American Clubs. This federation was organized by regions of the United States (eastern, midwestern and southern). In 1950 the National Association of Syrian and Lebanese American Clubs was formed.

The link of these federations to the Eastern Rite churches that served most of the Arab immigrants and their families encouraged the much smaller Muslim community to organize as well. In 1952, the first Federation of Islamic Associations was founded and called on Muslim communities in the United States and Canada to organize themselves into local associations to administer to the religious needs of their members.

# The turbulent 1960s and 1970s

By the 1960s, Arab American organizations entered a dramatic new era. The civil rights movement challenged the conscience of the country to uphold the rights of African Americans. It also empowered other racial and ethnic minorities to express more publicly and proudly their unique heritages, needs, and concerns.

Advances in civil rights protections laid the foundation for changing social attitudes about diversity and American identity. At the same time, new immigration laws passed in the 1960s allowed immigrants from all regions of the world, including the newly independent nation states of the Arab world, to come to America without quotas. A wave of newcomers from many Arab countries—students, professionals, workers, and refugees fleeing wars—came to America and revitalized the Arab American community that was mostly American born and assimilated (integrated into mainstream American culture) and had less direct ties to the "old country."

## The Arab-Israeli conflict and Arab American activism

As America was becoming more tolerant and welcoming of non-white or non-European cultures and communities,

Mary Lahaj, a delegate from South Weymouth, Massachusetts, at the 1988 National Democratic Convention. *Reproduced by permission of Paul S. Conklin.*

a crisis was created by the Arab-Israeli conflict. The conflict began when the international body the United Nations decided to create the state of Israel out of Palestinian lands in 1948 to establish a safe homeland for Jews. (Nearly six million Jews were systematically slaughtered during World War II on the orders of German leader Adolf Hitler.) Eight hundred thousand Palestinians lost their homes and had to leave the country. Tensions exploded during the war in June 1967, in which Israel occupied Jordanian, Egyptian, and Syrian territory. The crushing defeat of Arab countries in that war, and pro-Israel/anti-Arab attitudes in the United States, created a new type of political organization.

The 1967 war convinced many Arab immigrants, students, and American activists of Arab heritage that Americans needed to hear both sides of the Arab-Israeli conflict if they were to hold fair and objective opinions. A group of Arab Americans in education and other professions formed the Association of Arab-American University Graduates (AAUG) in 1967 to provide that voice. Many leaders of AAUG had been active as students in the Arab student organizations that formed in the 1960s on many U.S. campuses. Arab Americans also organized charitable groups to help Palestinian refugees who lost their homes in 1948 and 1967.

By 1973 the National Association of Arab Americans (NAAA) had been founded as another national organization to monitor America's Middle East policy and provide information to the U.S. government to help improve U.S.-Arab relations. The NAAA leadership added new elements: American businessmen and professionals of Arab background leading a program that tried to counter the strong influence the supporters of Israel had in the U.S. government.

## An Arab American human service organization

Throughout the 1970s, a new Arab American identity emerged that went beyond politics. In 1972 the Arab Community Center for Economic and Social Services (ACCESS) was founded in Dearborn, Michigan. Its mission was to offer Arab immigrants services to help them adjust to their new life, including legal services, job placement, family counseling, language training, youth clinics, and cultural programs. ACCESS became the pioneer and model for activists in other Arab American communities to focus on service-related programs.

## Stereotypes and backlash

The 1970s was a period that convinced many Arab Americans that the more controversial Middle East politics became, and the greater the misunderstandings about Arab causes, the more important it was to be active in public affairs.

The political activism of the 1970s brought negative attention to Arab American groups. Supporters of Israel were well organized, influential, and able to discredit the people and organizations that supported Palestinian rights and other Arab issues. As the conflict continued and Palestinian resistance to Israeli policies increased, Arab Americans and their allies were often viewed suspiciously, or as "anti-American," by U.S. government agencies. Portraying Arab issues as anti-American became worse during the late 1970s. Higher oil prices that caused gasoline shortages in the United States created a climate in which Arabs were seen as "enemies" to the country, and negative stereotypes became commonplace.

Arab stereotypes, now both with political and economic roots, seeped into American popular culture. Television programs, movies, and novels portrayed Arab characters as villains, and as a result the American public began to think of Arabs as enemies (see chapter 13).

This negative public image was especially hard to accept for the several million Americans of Arab heritage. Like so many other minority groups, Arab Americans needed to work hard to correct these images and protect themselves from public backlash. Backlashes against Arab Americans sometimes occur after a conflict between an Arab country or group and the American government or its citizens. Some people take their anger and frustration out on Arab Americans. Even when problems happen in non-Arab countries (such as when U.S. citizens were taken hostage in Iran in 1978), the backlash results in negative feelings about Middle Eastern people as a whole.

## Advocacy, coalition building, and recognition

Anti-Arab feelings pushed Arab Americans to organize further to protect their rights. In 1980, the American-Arab Anti-Discrimination Committee (ADC) was founded as an advocacy organization. Advocacy organizations promote the interests of a particular group of people—building public support for them and defending their rights. ADC defends Arab Americans who are victims of discrimination and challenges the media and schools when they promote biased information about Arabs.

## Selected Arab American Figures in Politics and Public Affairs

James Abourezk: U.S. Senator from South Dakota (1978-84); cofounder of the American-Arab Anti-Discrimination Committee (ADC; 1980).

Spencer Abraham: U.S. Senator from Michigan beginning in 1994; former co-chair of the National Republican Congressional Campaign Committee and Deputy Chief of Staff for Vice President Dan Quayle.

Ismael Ahmed: Community activist and Director of the Arab Community Center for Economic and Social Services (AC-CESS) in Dearborn, Michigan, the largest community center in the United States serving the needs of Americans of Arab descent.

Philip Habib: U.S. Diplomat; Undersecretary of State for Political Affairs, Reagan Administration; Middle East Peace negotiator.

Ray LaHood: U.S. Representative from Illinois beginning in 1994; Chief of Staff for House Minority Leader Robert Michel; former state legislator.

Candy Lightner: Founder of Mothers Against Drunk Driving (MADD), a national grassroots advocacy and public interest organization; served a term as president of the American-Arab Anti-Discrimination Committee (ADC).

M.T. Mehdi: Founder of Action Committee on American-Arab Relations (1964); early advocate for Palestinian rights and outspoken critic of U.S Middle East policy.

The 1960s and 1970s were also a period when more immigrants and refugees were coming to America from Arab countries, and community organizations were called on to attend to their needs on the local level. Like in the early 1900s, these immigrants and refugees needed help in understanding their rights.

But unlike the early 1900s, American society in the 1980s and 1990s was more tolerant and respectful of the culture and traditions brought by immigrants. If the early immigrants focused mostly on being accepted in a country dominated by a western, European-based culture, the later Arab Americans spent as much time and energy forming institutions to keep alive their culture, language, and religious beliefs. Hundreds of American communities have mosques and

George Mitchell: U.S. Senator from Maine (1980-95); special advisor to President Bill Clinton and chairman of peace negotiations in Northern Ireland.

Ralph Nader: Champion of consumer protection and founder of numerous advocacy groups, including Public Citizen; independent U.S. presidential candidate in 1996.

Nick Joe Rahall II: U.S. Representative from West Virginia beginning in 1977; Dean of the Arab American Congressional Delegation.

Richard Shadyac: Executive Director of the American Lebanese Syrian Associated Charities (ALSAC)-St. Jude Children's Research Hospital; cofounder of the National Association of Arab Americans and the American-Arab Association (AMARA).

Donna E. Shalala: U.S. Secretary of Health and Human Services beginning in 1993; former Chancellor of the University of Wisconsin.

John H. Sununu: White House Chief of Staff (1989-90); governor of New Hampshire (1982-88); host of CNN's *Crossfire* and frequent political commentator.

Helen Thomas: Chief White House correspondent for United Press International and dean of the White House press corps.

James J. Zogby: Founder of the Arab American Institute (1985) and several other Arab American organizations; media commentator on Arab American issues and U.S.-Arab relations; co-chairman of the National Democratic Ethnic Coordinating Council.

Islamic centers where Arab Muslim families worship and teach their children Arabic and the Muslim holy book, the *Qur'an* (also spelled Koran). Arabic-language newspapers, magazines, and television and radio programs are available in most major cities. Community centers now exist in several urban centers as a place for social events (weddings, youth activities) and a resource for services immigrants need (legal advice, job training, counseling, etc.).

## Arab Americans and political involvement

Arab Americans have also organized around their rights as citizens and responsible voters. In 1985 the Arab American Institute (AAI) was founded to train Arab Americans in electoral politics—the activities of political parties, campaigns, and elections. One of AAI's goals is to organize Arab Americans into groups of voters—or constituencies—and volunteers who could be mobilized around elections to respond to matters of local, national, and international policy. AAI helps local communities register new voters, educate voters on important issues, and reminds them to vote on election day. It also serves as a bridge between Arab American constituents and government officials.

## Public service

Arab Americans have served in all levels of public (government) office. While most elected officials have been the American-born children or grandchildren of immigrants, some are naturalized citizens—people who became citizens after immigrating to the United States. Since the early 1960s, there have been members of Congress who are of Arab descent; in the late 1980s, the majority leader of the U.S. Senate, George Mitchell, was an Arab American. In the 106th Congress (1999/2000), six U.S. representatives and one U.S. senator traced their roots to the Arab world.

Outside Congress, Arab Americans have served as cabinet secretaries, governors, White House chiefs of staff, ambassadors, attorneys general, and state legislators. There are several Arab American mayors and many more judges and members of city councils and school boards. They serve on government advisory boards and commissions—from the U.S. Commission on Civil Rights to state and local bodies. By the late 1990s, about fifty Arab Americans were running in an election campaign every year. Some are elected in places where many Arab Americans live (such as Dearborn, Michigan), while others come from areas with small populations of Arab Americans (New Hampshire). Ralph Nader, an Arab American, even ran for president in the 1996 elections.

## Campaigns and elections

In the 1980s, Arab Americans began to organize into clubs and caucuses (meeting groups that determine policy) of the local and state Democratic and Republican parties. Since

the 1988 presidential campaigns, Arab Americans have held a large cultural event at the national nominating conventions of both major parties. Arab Americans also run as delegates, or representatives, at national conventions; in 1996 more than eighty Arab Americans participated in the process of nominating the presidential candidates.

Arab Americans also bring issues to the attention of the political parties and candidates. In 1988, AAI organized an effort to have the presidential campaigns endorse (support) statehood for the Palestinian people. Although it was a very controversial (highly debated) foreign policy issue, hundreds of Democratic delegates signed petitions to support it as a consideration for their party's platform (set of policies). Although it did not win enough support to become formally adopted as a party position, for the first time an Arab American issue was debated on the convention floor.

**Arab American congress members from the 106th Congress (1999-2000).**
*Reproduced by permission of the Arab American Institute Foundation.*

To bring the concerns of Arab American voters to the Democratic and Republican parties, national Arab American advisory councils were formed in the early 1990s. By the 1996 national conventions, the parties noticed the work of Arab American activists and recognized their role in helping them to reach their constituencies (voters). By 1996, the Democratic Advisory Council was so involved in mobilizing ethnic voters for President Bill Clinton's re-election campaign that it helped form a new body in the national party: the National Democratic Ethnic Coordinating Council. Democrats of Arab descent are now joined by those of Irish, Italian, Greek, Polish, and other backgrounds to have a voice in party decisions. Similar efforts are underway in the Republican Party, especially through the New Majority Council that reaches out to immigrant and minority voters.

# Voting

Voting is the most basic way citizens participate in politics, and mobilizing Arab American voters has been a priority in recent years. The process has four major concerns: voter registration, voter education, candidate support, and voter turnout on Election Day.

## Voter registration

Arab Americans began organizing voter registration drives in the 1980s, especially in highly concentrated communities such as Dearborn, Michigan. When the Arab Voter Registration and Education Committee (AVREC) formed in that city shortly after the mayoral elections of 1986, approximately 20 percent of the city's Arab population was registered to vote. AVREC organized drives to deputize, or appoint, Arabic-speaking registrars to register voters, to take forms door-to-door in Arab neighborhoods, and to have registration tables at social, cultural, and religious events. There are now thousands of registered voters in that Arab American community, which makes them a voting bloc—a significant group of voters—in all local elections. AAI has helped communities in several states to increase voter registration. A national database of Arab American voters and volunteers

from more than thirty states is maintained in AAI's office in Washington, D.C.

## Voter education

Once citizens are registered to vote, they need to know who and what they are voting for. Local and national groups provide Arab Americans with this information through voter guides that summarize the positions of candidates on important issues, town meetings, and candidate forums. At these public events, elected officials and candidates are invited to meet their Arab American constituents, speak about their campaigns, and answer questions from the voters.

**Arab Americans participating in the 1992 Democratic Convention.** *Reproduced by permission of the Arab American Institute Foundation.*

There are now thousands of registered voters in the Arab American community of Dearborn, Michigan, thanks to voter registration drives. *Reproduced by permission of the Arab American Institute Foundation.*

Some community groups make public endorsements supporting a particular candidate to encourage the support of other Arab American voters.

## Candidate support

Arab American voter groups have shown support for specific candidates by volunteering in their campaigns and raising donations. In the early 1980s some Arab American fund-raising efforts were rejected by certain candidates because the candidates were afraid that an Arab American endorsement, or statement of support, would anger their Jewish voters and donors. Nonetheless, Arab Americans continued to work hard with party leaders to protect the rights of voters in their community to give public support to candidates of their choices. Today, most candidates welcome Arab American support. Arab Americans are just starting to form political action committees (PACs) to coordinate candidate support. In 1998 the Washington-based Arab American Leadership PAC donated funds to support the campaigns of more than fifty members of Congress.

### Get-out-the-vote

The final step in voter participation—once people are registered and informed—is to actually vote on Election Day. Arab American "get-out-the-vote" activities can be nonpartisan (unconnected to a party or candidate) or partisan (done in cooperation with a particular party or campaign). In 1998 a nonpartisan effort to increase the Arab American vote focused on three main communication tools: fliers and posters (in Arabic and English); public announcements (at mosques and churches and on Arabic radio and television programs); and phone banks, where volunteers call lists of Arab American voters at home to remind them to vote. Voters whose English is weak can ask for help reading the ballot from bilingual volunteers. In some neighborhoods, these resources significantly increased the Arab American voter turnout.

# Shaping the policy debate

The third arena for Arab American political involvement is expressing opinions on matters of policy. Policy refers to a plan or set of principles that guide the decisions and actions of public officials. Arab Americans have been organized around policy issues for many decades, especially since the 1967 Arab-Israeli war. They have worked both to promote their viewpoint and to defend their rights when they are threatened.

Many Americans of Arab descent closely follow what the U.S. government says and does about matters in the Middle East. In times of conflict, they worry about the safety and welfare of their relatives and friends in Arab countries. When Congress or the U.S. State Department consider matters that may be harmful to American interests in the Middle East, Arab American groups organize to tell the government their viewpoint and request certain actions.

Some organizations limit their work to a particular country (for example the American Task Force for Lebanon, the Center for Policy Analysis on Palestine, and the Iraq Founda-

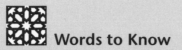

## Words to Know

- **Advocacy organization:** an organization that tries to build public support for an idea, plan, or group.

- **Americanization:** learning the customs, language, and rules of American society and letting go of native customs and traditions.

- **Arab-Israeli conflict:** the political struggle that began with the creation of the state of Israel in 1948 on Palestinian land.

- **Assimilate:** when a person or a group drops their own culture (such as changing their name and style of dress) and adopts the majority culture, usually referred to as the dominant or mainstream culture.

- **Backlash:** a reaction against a group of people due to a particular event or conflict with another group that may result in discrimination or violence.

- **Cabinet secretary:** the appointed public official who serves as the head of a government department that advises the president.

- **Caucus:** a subgroup in a committee or political party.

- **Civil rights:** the rights of an individual to equal treatment and equal access to the benefits of society, including housing, free speech, employment, and education.

- **Civil rights movement:** a movement, which was especially strong in the 1960s, that advocated civil rights for minorities in the United States.

- **Coalition:** two or more groups working together towards a common goal.

- **Constituency:** a group of voters represented by an elected official.

- **Controversial:** a subject that causes disagreement or debate.

- **Delegate:** a person elected to represent a candidate or district at a convention.

- **Deputize:** to authorize someone to perform certain duties.

tion), while others, such as the National Association of Arab Americans (NAAA) and the Association of Arab-American University Graduates (AAUG), focus on U.S. relations with the broader Arab world. Still other organizations, including the Arab American Institute (AAI) and the American-Arab Anti-Discrimination Committee (ADC), balance their attention between U.S.-Arab relations and the needs of Arab Americans as immigrants, citizens, workers, and members of the American family.

- **Electoral politics:** activity related to electing candidates to public office.

- **Endorsement:** a statement of public support or approval for a candidate.

- **Federation:** a union of groups joined by an agreement or common purpose.

- **Greater Syria:** a part of the Arab world under the Ottoman Empire (the sixteenth century through the nineteenth century) that included present-day Syria, Lebanon, Jordan, Palestine, and Israel.

- **Loyalty:** firm support or faith in one's country, family, friends, or beliefs.

- **Mosque:** the Muslim place of worship, similar to a church for Christians.

- **Naturalization:** the process by which immigrants become U.S. citizens.

- **Platform:** a statement of beliefs of a group.

- **Policy:** a general plan or principle that governments, politicians, and organizations use to help them make decisions or take action.

- **Political Action Committee (PAC):** a group set up to raise and spend money on candidates for public office.

- **Quotas:** pertaining to immigration, limits that are placed on the number of immigrants from a particular country who come to live in another country.

- **Refugees:** people who leave their home countries due to wars and other hardships and seek refuge elsewhere.

- **Stereotype:** an oversimplified and misleading image or idea about a group of people—including racial, ethnic, cultural, and religious groups. Stereotypes usually portray people in a negative and distorted way.

- **Voter registration:** signing up to be able to vote in elections.

- **Voting bloc:** a group of voters organized to the support of a candidate or elected official.

Sometimes decisions made by a government official or agency can have a direct impact on the lives of Arab Americans. Arab American organizations become advocates to protect the rights of the ethnic community. Advocacy work can address both individual problems and ones that affect a large group of people. For example, in the mid-1980s the ADC brought a lawsuit to the Supreme Court on behalf of a professor who was discriminated against because of his national origin. That case changed the way people can sue for damages when they face ethnic discrimination. As another example, several Arab American organizations challenged certain parts of the 1996 Antiterrorism and Effective Death Penalty Act that they believed were unconstitutional. Similarly, during the Gulf War, Arab American advocates worked with local and national governments to speak publicly against the anti-Arab backlash of 1990 and 1991, and when changes in immigration laws targeted people from Middle Eastern countries more than others, Arab American advocates spoke out.

In addition to reacting to crises and problems, Arab American advocacy has also been proactive, meaning that it works to strengthen existing policies that are favorable to the community, draw public attention to important issues, or prevent harmful actions from taking place. Examples of proactive advocacy include a group asking a city council to proclaim "Arab American Day" so that the community can recognize the ethnic contributions of their Arab American neighbors. Another example is a resolution introduced in Congress in 1998 to honor the contributions of Muslims in America, a step taken to draw positive attention to a group that has suffered from negative stereotypes.

## For More Information

Abu-Laban, Baha, and Michael Suleiman, eds. *Arab-Americans: Continuity and Change*. Belmont, MA: Association of Arab-American University Graduates, 1989.

Kasem, Casey. *Arab Americans Making a Difference* (brochure). Washington, D.C.: Arab American Institute Foundation, 1997.

McCarus, Ernest. *The Development of Arab-American Identity*. Ann Arbor: University of Michigan Press, 1994.

Naff, Alixa. *The Arab Americans*. New York: Chelsea House, 1988.

Naff, Alixa. *Becoming American: The Early Arab Immigrant Experience*. Carbondale: Southern Illinois University Press, 1985.

*Roster of Arab Americans in Public Service and Political Life*. Washington, D.C.: Arab American Leadership Council, 1999.

Samhan, Helen Hatab. "Arab Americans and the Elections of 1988: A Constituency Come of Age." *Arab Studies Quarterly*, Spring/Summer 1989, pp. 227-49.

Samhan, Helen Hatab. "Politics and Exclusion: The Arab American Experience." *The Journal of Palestine Studies*, Winter 1987, pp. 11-28.

Younis, Adele L. *The Coming of Arabic-Speaking People to the United States.* New York: Center For Migration Studies, 1995.

Zogby, John. *Arab America Today: A Demographic Profile of Arab Americans.* Washington, D.C.: Arab American Institute, 1990.

Zogby, John, ed. *Taking Root, Bearing Fruit: The Arab-American Experience.* Washington, D.C.: American-Arab Anti-Discrimination Committee, 1984.

## Web Sites

American-Arab Anti-Discrimination Committee (ADC). [Online} Available www.adc.org (last accessed September 21, 1999).

Arab American Institute (AAI). [Online] Available www.aaiusa.org (last accessed September 21, 1999).

National Association of Arab Americans (NAAA). [Online] Available www.naaa.net (last accessed September 21, 1999).

*Helen Hatab Samhan is Executive Vice President of the Arab American Institute in Washington D.C., a non-profit institute representing Arab American issues in politics, elections, leadership training, and public policy. She holds an M.A. in Middle East Studies from the American University of Beirut.*

# Music

15

The Arab American community hosts a dynamic musical subculture that has been part of American music since the beginning of the century. (Traditions of an ethnic or religious group within the larger society are known as a subculture.) Today large communities of Arab Americans live in Michigan, New York, California, Texas, New England, and Illinois. Arab Americans—estimated at three million in the late 1990s—are among the fastest growing minority populations in the United States. In spite of the overwhelming influence of American popular music, Arabic music continues to thrive in many Arab American communities in the United States.

## The early years

The people who made up the first wave of Arab immigrants to the United States came mostly from Syria and Lebanon, which were then part of Greater Syria (present-day Syria, Lebanon, Jordan, Palestine, and Israel). By 1914, there were at least 110,000 Arabs living in the United States (see chapter 4).

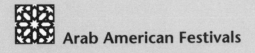

## Arab American Festivals

The mahrajanat, or festivals, that were popular among Arab Americans between the 1930s and 1960s are witnessing a revival in many Arab American communities around the country. In all of these festivals, music is the most important component that brings the community together. Local Arab American musicians, singers, and dance groups along with singers from the Arab world perform to large audiences. Most of these festivals are held over two or three days. Among the most popular Arab American Festivals are:

- Mahrajan Al-Fann in New York City

- Arabian Fest in Milwaukee, Wisconsin

- Arab World Festival in Detroit, Michigan

- East Dearborn Arab International Festival in Dearborn, Michigan

- Ana Al-Arabi Festival in Washington, D.C.

During the early years, many Arab immigrants worked in mills and factories or as peddlers. Music events were limited to friends or community gatherings, family events such as births or weddings, or simply listening to recordings of Arab music. Most immigrants either worked long days or traveled the long peddling routes they established. They did not have the time, money, or professional musicians to organize musical events such as festivals or concerts, which later became important features in the life of the Arab American communities.

In this early period Arab music was performed in nonprofessional settings by amateurs (people who play music as a hobby rather than for pay) who brought their instruments from their homeland. Sometimes people just got together for impromptu (spur of the moment) group singing, clapping, and dancing. Family memoirs and photo albums indicate that music was an important part of most family gatherings. No party, wedding, or picnic was complete without singing and dancing.

Although most immigrants in the early twentieth century came from Greater Syria, there was a distinct difference in the music traditions of those who came from the villages of Mount Lebanon and those who came from cities such as Aleppo, Damascus, and Beirut. This distinction between rural and urban has greatly influenced Arab American music. Throughout the twentieth century, there have always been some musicians who sing the traditional village songs, which encourage audience participation, including clapping, singing, and folk dancing. There are also those who perform in the urban traditions, which involve one or more singers accompanied by different musicians and instruments.

## The middle period: 1930 to 1970

By the 1930s, Arab American community groups began to organize music parties and festivals for which they hired professional musicians. Live music performances became the focus of two events in the Arab American community: the *hafla* (plural *haflat*), a cross between a concert and a party; and the *mahrajan* (plural *mahrajanat*), an outdoor festival that could last for three days, involving hundreds, sometimes thousands, of participants.

## The hafla

In the early 1930s, the hafla was held in a church hall for 100 to 200 people. The idea behind the hafla was to celebrate a community event, raise funds for a good cause, or just to have people come together and have a good time. Later, as the community grew and the haflat became more popular, they were held in hotel ballrooms that could accommodate larger groups of 1,000 to 1,500 people. Gradually the hafla evolved into a formal musical event during which the community gathered to listen to live performances of Syrian, Egyptian, and Lebanese music and to enjoy skits, poetry, and the speeches of clergymen and community leaders. The hafla became an important institution in the life of the community. It also provided the Arab American musicians with a venue where they could perform.

The musical groups that performed included singers (both male and female) and men who played the *'oud*, the *qanun* (a 72-stringed, flat wooden instrument), the *riqq* (a fancy tambourine with heavy brass cymbals), the violin, and the *derbekeh* (a vase-shaped ceramic drum). Elia Baida, Russel Bunai, Anton (Tony) Abdel Ahad, and Najiba Maurad were

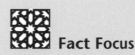 **Fact Focus**

- The 'oud, an Arabic stringed instrument, is considered the grandparent of western guitars and mandolins. It was the first instrument to have a wooden face rather than an animal-skin face.

- Among the earliest famous Arabs is the ninth-century singer and composer Ziryab. He was born in Baghdad and is said to have memorized 1,000 songs.

- The Andalusian tradition, a genre of Arabic music, was born in Spain where the Arabs ruled for nearly eight centuries (711–1492). It is still one of the most popular musical traditions among Arabs and Arab Americans.

- The mahrajan, an Arab American outdoor gathering that was popular until the 1960s, would sometimes last for four days and attracted thousands of people from around the United States.

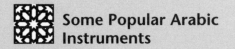

## Some Popular Arabic Instruments

- **Daff:** a tambourine, also known in Arabic as tambour.

- **Derbekeh:** a vase-shaped clay or metal drum with a skin of fish or lamb stretched over the top.

- **Kamanja:** a violin.

- **Mijwiz:** a double-reeded wooden flute that is the predecessor of the oboe, bassoon, clarinet, and other reed instruments common in the West.

- **Nay:** a flute made of dry reed that is blown from the end. It has six front finger holes and one hole underneath for the thumb. Due to the limited number of keys, musicians use several nays of varying lengths in order to play different scales.

- **'Oud:** a pear-shaped wooden instrument with eleven strings. The 'oud is called a lute in English.

- **Qanun:** a trapezoid-shaped flat board with seventy-two strings that are plucked with a finger or pick.

- **Rabbabah:** the ancestor of the violin. It is a simple, one-stringed instrument made of wood, animal hide, and hair.

among the early popular singers who performed professionally during this period. Later, singers such as Hanan, Kahraman, and Mohammed el Bakkar enjoyed enormous popularity. The talents of the 'oud player Joe Badawi, violinist Philip Solomon, and qanun player Muhammad al-Akkad were in constant demand. To please their audiences, musicians would plan their programs to include a little of everything: village songs and music for *debkeh* (group folk dancing), traditional urban music, the newest popular songs, and music for modern dancing for the younger folks, some of whom were American born. Often the highlight of the haflat took place after most of the audiences had left. About fifty people would sit in a half circle around the stage and request one song after another.

In addition to providing entertainment and a place for socializing, the hafla brought the community together to raise funds for supporting needy families in the United States and back home and building Arab American institutions such as churches, mosques, and community organizations.

## The mahrajan

The mahrajan, or community festival, started as a church picnic, where musicians would play, people would dance, and the older folks would tell stories to the young. Platforms for the musicians were constructed out of whatever was available. Later, real stages were built with some sort of roof to protect the musicians from the sun. Eventually the mahrajan grew into a three-day event sponsored by churches or large Arab American organizations.

The festive mahrajan was especially popular with children and young adults. The musical program was varied and consisted of popular tunes and music for dancing. Performances took place during the afternoon and evening and featured a number of musical groups. Both professional and amateur musicians performed. In addition to the scheduled public performances, many people got together and played and sang among themselves. The mahrajan was also a social affair where making friends, matchmaking, eating, and dancing were as important as the live music. The mahrajan was a grand event that everybody looked forward to, and people traveled hundreds, sometimes thousands, of miles to attend.

With time, the mahrajan became too large and too much of a financial gamble for those who planned and promoted them. The last large-scale, outdoor mahrajan was held in the mid-1970s.

# Recording and production

Beginning in the 1920s, Arab immigrant musicians began recording their music at the invitation of American record companies such as Columbia, Victor, and Standard. These American record companies were searching for new kinds of music to sell in the ethnic communities in America. By the 1940s, however, Arab Americans had taken charge of their own recording industry and several Arab American record labels (companies that record and produce music) emerged.

Among the record producers and importers who emerged from within the Arab American community was Farid Alam of New York, who imported and reproduced a lot of early twentieth-century Egyptian music on his label, Alamphoe. Beginning in 1934, Albert Rashid imported musical films from Egypt and arranged for public showings in cities with large Arab American communities, such as Detroit, Boston, and New York. He would also get permission to record the hit songs from these films and then sell them on his label Al Chark (Orient) Records. Rashid also took blank records to Cairo, Egypt, when commercial traffic between the United

**Hamza El Din is considered the father of modern Nubian music.** *Reproduced with permission of Jack Vartoogian.*

States and the Arab world was at a standstill. The Rashid family still owns and operates Rashid Sales Company in Brooklyn, New York, which has the largest collection of Arabic and Arab American music in the United States.

A number of Arab American musicians recorded their music in small studios and created their own record labels. Labels such as Maloof, Star of the East, Cleopatra, Nilephon, Metrophon, Arabphon, and Golden Angel, as well as Rashid's Al Chark, featured the influential and popular musicians of that period.

# The night club scene: 1960s to 1980s

Middle Eastern nightclubs have also been part of Arab American musical life. From the 1960s to the 1980s these nightclubs, which offered Arabic food and lively modern music, were found in most American cities. The nightclubs attracted a diverse population of Arab Americans and people of other ethnic backgrounds.

The nightclub music created during the 1960s and 1970s was adventurous, creative, electronic, and commercial. Many of the older, more traditional musicians, however, never made the transition to the nightclubs. They claimed that the nightclubs did not originate in the Arab American communities, but rather in the Armenian, Turkish, and Greek communities. On the other hand, young Arab American musicians of the 1960s and 1970s, who had originally played with traditional musicians, succeeded in this exciting environment.

During this period, ethnic music (music of minority populations, such as Italian or Arab Americans) became more popular and accepted in the United States. Arab American musicians worked with musicians of Turkish, Armenian, and Greek origins. Together they created new nightclub music that was suitable for a multi-ethnic audience and was popular among the younger American-born audiences who wanted to dance and have a good time.

In contrast to the hafla and to the mahrajan that were rooted in the Arab American communities, the nightclub was a public, American institution. Although the music included Arabic rhythms, it also included the use of Western instru-

## Arab American Musicians

There are a number of musicians and composers who were born in the Arab world but now reside and perform in the Unites States. They include:

- Hamza El Din: Considered the father of modern Nubian music, El Din was born in Nubia, Sudan, along the Nile River near the southern Egyptian border. He studied music in Egypt and Italy. He now resides in San Francisco and performs all over the world. His CDs include *Music of Nubia, Lily of the Nile,* and *Eclipse.*

- Hassan Hakmoun: Born in Morocco, Hakmoun integrates the traditional Moroccan music with a variety of other styles including African American jazz. His CDs include *Life Around the World* and *Gift of the Gnawa* with Adam Rudolph.

- Ali Jihad Racy: Born in Lebanon, Racy is a performer and composer of traditional Middle Eastern music. Racy is the master of many instruments, including the 'oud (lute), the rabbabah (an instrument similar to the violin), and the mijwiz (a double reeded wooden flute). His CD is called *Mystical Legacies.*

- Simon Shaheen: Born in Jerusalem, Shaheen is a composer and plays the 'oud and violin. He resides in New York and is the director of the Near Eastern Music Ensemble. He is also one of the leading organizers of New York's annual mahrajan Al-Fan, a two-day festival of Arab World culture. His CDs include *Turath* ("Heritage"), and *Saltanah*, with Vishwa Mohan Bhatt.

ments such as the saxophone, electric guitar, drums, and flute. Sometimes English lyrics and titles were integrated in the music to produce what was called *amaraba*—music with Arabic flavors, geared to the American ear. Much of the nightclub music emerged as the result of the cooperation between two Arab American musicians of the time, Muhammad al-Bakkar and Edie Kochak.

The nightclub era overshadowed the community-based musical events of earlier times. Second- and third-generation Arab Americans were more likely to enjoy the music, dance, oriental decor, and Arabic food of the nightclub rather than the traditional music that had entertained their parents in the hafla and mahrajan. Although Middle Eastern nightclubs continue to exist in many American cities, their popu-

**Simon Shaheen is a composer and plays the 'oud and violin.** *Reproduced with permission of Millard Berry.*

larity among the Arab American population has decreased since the 1970s.

## Arab American music today

The nature of the Arab American community has changed dramatically since the 1970s. The immigration quotas of 1924 that restricted Arab immigration were lifted in 1965. This resulted in an increase in the number of immigrants from Arab countries. Among the Arab immigrants who came to America since then were a new group of singers and musicians who were in touch with the popular trends of the modern Arab world.

While the early Arab American community came mostly from Syria and Lebanon, the more recent Arab American population has come from a number of Arab countries, including Morocco, Egypt, Palestine, Jordan, and Yemen. The diversity of this population is reflected in the music they perform and enjoy. This includes the traditional music of Aleppo and Damascus, the folk songs and dances of Mount Lebanon, the Egyptian popular music played on synthesizers, the ritual wedding songs, the African-influenced rhythms of Yemeni music, and the *Rai* music of North Africa. Today there are separate sub-communities of Yemenis, Egyptians, and North Africans who gather in their homes and community centers or at celebrations to enjoy their own distinct music and culture.

Today, Arab music and dance takes place in every major city in the United States. They are performed at weddings and in the haflat and mahrajanat that are once again becoming popular in Arab American communities. There are a large number of musical groups and singers who are in constant demand to perform. Some travel around the country (and sometimes to Canada and Latin America) to perform. These singers and music groups include: the Dearborn Traditional Arab Ensemble of Dearborn, Michigan, directed by the nye player Nadeem Dlaikan; Kan Zamman Community Ensemble in Los Angeles, directed by Wael Kakish; and Tarab in the Boston/Cambridge area, directed by Nabeel Atta. Among the most popular singers are: Radwan al-Hares, Naji Youssef, and Na'im Moussa in New York; Amin Al-Rawi in

New Jersey; Ahmad El-Asmar in Los Angeles; Bassam Saleh, Osama Baalbaki, and Rana and Naim in Detroit; Faysal Al-Wazzan in Orlando, Florida; Merielle Thomas and Hisham El-Mousakkat in Boston; and Albert Baba and Juliana in Chicago.

Modern Arab American musical events feature exciting pop songs and hours of music played for a lively folk line-dance called the debkeh. The debkeh and the folk music that goes with it were originally associated with the Arab countryside. Since the 1960s this music has become popular among Arab Americans of all ages and all backgrounds, both rural and urban. The lyrics of this music are about nature, village life, and romance.

## Musicians in Demand

In addition to performing in the hafla and mahrajan, Arab American musicians traveled continuously to satisfy the demands of enthusiastic audiences across the United States and Canada. For example, the husband and wife singing team Amer and Sana Khaddaj, who immigrated to the United States in 1948, performed throughout New England and in the midwestern states and made thirty-two recordings. By 1962 Amer Khaddaj estimated that he had performed in forty of the fifty states.

Some musicians and audiences prefer music for listening rather than the lively dance and pop music heard at the haflat. They favor the traditional music and the traditional Arab instruments such as the 'oud, the qanun, the nay, and the kamanja (violin). Through their teaching, performances, and recordings, musical leaders in the community, such as Simon Shaheen, Ali Jihad Racy, and Youssef Kassab, have worked hard to bring more traditional music to the attention of Arab Americans and to people outside the community.

The 1990s saw some interesting initiatives by Arab American and other ethnic musicians to create a new mix, or fusion, of music from different traditions. Arab musician Ali Jihad Racy and Spanish American guitarist Pedro Cortez have experimented with the fusion of Arabic and Spanish music. Simon Shaheen and Vishwa Mohan Bhatt have experimented with the fusion of Arabic and Indian music. Hassan Hakmoun and Adam Rodolph have attempted to join traditional Moroccan music with a variety of world music styles, including African American jazz.

There are a number of Arab American musicians who are trained in Western classical and modern musical tradi-

The Yemeni Dance Troupe performs at an Arab American street festival in Dearborn. This festival takes place every summer, drawing tens of thousands of people. *Reproduced by permission of Millard Berry.*

tions and who perform mostly in mainstream American arts institutions with large non-Arab audiences. Among them are pianist Diana Takieddiene, from Washington, D.C., and pianist and composer Waleed Howrani in Ann Arbor, Michigan. Howrani's CD is called *Lebanese Rhapsody.*

Arab and Arab American music is also gaining popularity among non-Arabs. Several American colleges and universities offer courses in the rich musical culture of the Arab world and the Middle East. Some CDs are available at mainstream record stores. A larger collection of CDs, audiotapes, and videotapes of Arab and Arab American music can be found in Arab American specialty stores. Also, most Arab American grocery and dry good stores carry the latest cassettes and videos from Arab countries.

Today Arab American music is an important part of Arab American culture. In addition to local musicians who are in constant demand to perform, famous singers from different Arab countries tour the United States regularly, sometimes bringing with them musicians and dancers. With their exciting and popular performances, Arab American musicians have helped their community stay together in America. Musical performances have become important events in which family, friends, and community members come together to enjoy music, dance, food, and storytelling and to celebrate their culture.

# For More Information

Gross, Joan, David McMurray, and Ted Swedenburg. "Rai, Rap and Ramadan Nights: Franco-Maghribi Cultural Identities." *Middle East Report,* September/October 1992.

McMurray, David, and Ted Swedenburg, "Rai Tide Rising." *Middle East Report,* March/April 1991.

Mostyn, Trevor, and Albert Hourani, eds. *The Cambridge Encyclopedia of the Middle East and North Africa.* Cambridge: Cambridge University Press, 1988.

"Music in the Making." *Detroit Free Press,* 1993.

Rasmussen, Anne. *Arab Music in the United States: An Historical Overview.* New York: Mahrajan Al-Fann, 1994.

Rasmussen, Anne. "The Music of Arab Americans: Aesthetics and Performance in a New Land." In *Images of Enchantment: Visual and Performing Arts of the Middle East,* edited by Sherifa Zuhur. Cairo, Egypt: The American University in Cairo Press, 1998.

Rasmussen, Anne. "The Music of Arab Detroit: A Musical Mecca in the Midwest." In *Music of Multicultural America: A Study of Twelve Musical Communities,* edited by Kip Lornell and Anne Rasmussen. Schirmer Books, 1997.

Shabbas, Audrey, and Ayad Al-Qazzaz, eds. *Arab World Notebook.* Berkeley, CA: Najda (Women Concerned About the Middle East), 1989.

Zuhur, Sherifa, ed. *Images of Enchantment: Visual and Performing Arts of the Middle East.* Cairo, Egypt: The American University in Cairo Press, 1998.

## Words to Know

- **Debkeh:** group folk dancing performed at weddings and community events.

- **Ethnic music:** music of ethnic groups such as African Americans or Arab Americans.

- **Ethnomusicology:** the study of music of various cultures.

- **Hafla (plural haflat):** a get-together that is a cross between a concert and a party.

- **Mahrajan:** (plural mahrajanat): an outdoor festival that lasts for two or three days involving music, dance, food, and artifacts, usually attended by thousands of people.

- **Record labels:** companies that record and produce music.

- **Subculture:** a small cultural group within the larger society.

*Adapted by Anan Ameri from a number of articles by Anne Rassmussen.*

*Anan Ameri is the Cultural Arts Director of the Arab Community Center for Economic and Social Services (ACCESS). She received her B.A. from the Jordanian University in Amman, Jordan, her M.A. from Cairo University in Egypt, and her Ph.D. in Sociology from Wayne State University in Detroit, Michigan.*

*Anne Rasmussem is a Professor of Ethnomusicology at the College of William and Mary in Williamsburg, Virginia. She is also a performer and teacher of Arab music (on the 'oud) and directs a small Middle Eastern music ensemble.*

# Fine Arts

16

Arab artists who come to the United States bring with them a diverse and rich legacy of art and culture. Whether they hail from metropolitan cities such as Beirut, Lebanon; Cairo, Egypt; Baghdad, Iraq; or from small towns and villages, many Arab artists grow up surrounded by ancient monuments and other works of art and culture produced by local artisans for thousands of years.

Because of the Arab world's position as an ancient crossroads and the extensive trade that went on there, the art and culture of the Arab world has both influenced and been influenced by many other civilizations. These include the Roman, Greek, Mongol, and European civilizations as well as the Arab/Islamic civilization that originated in what is now Saudi Arabia.

The art and monuments of the Arab world reflect this mix of cultures. Arab art includes the richly painted tombs of Egypt; the 2,500-year-old mosaics of Carthage, Tunisia; the ceramic tiles, rugs, and pottery of Morocco; the 10,000-year-old idols (some of the earliest sculptures known to humankind) of Jordan; the earliest Christian paintings in Syria; the exquisite architecture of Yemeni high rise buildings; tra-

## The International Council for Women in the Arts (ICWA)

The International Council for Women in the Arts (ICWA) and its division, the Cultural and Visual Arts Resource, is a nonprofit educational organization established in 1989 to recognize the outstanding achievements of Arab men and women in visual arts. The Council is a unique resource in that it organizes exhibitions and creates accompanying educational programs as well as maintains a database with files for more than 500 artists from the Arab world. Additionally, the Council collaborates with other art institutions at museums and universities as well as with publishers and art professionals to further appreciation and understanding of Arab art.

Exhibitions organized by the Council include Forces of Change: Artists of the Arab World and Artists' View and Rhythm & Form: Visual Reflections on Arabic Poetry. Educational programs and publications that the council sponsers include exhibition catalogues, children's and teacher's manuals, videos of interviews with artists, seminars, film series, a visiting artists program, a family day workshop, and programs exploring the visual art and cultures of the Arab world. For more information, contact: Cultural and Visual Arts Resource, International Council for Women in the Arts, PO Box 226, Lafayette, CA 94549.

ditional Bedouin weaving; intricate Palestinian embroidery; and the first molded, blown glass of Lebanon.

## Arab-Islamic art

By the thirteenth century C.E. (common era, also called A.D.), the Islamic Empire extended from Spain to the borders of China. What was unique about the Islamic Empire is that it did not impose one dominant culture on the newly conquered people. Instead, it allowed regional differences in culture to exist alongside those of the ruling Arab groups (see chapter 2). This policy of tolerance resulted in art that was Islamic in style, with regional variations. When we speak of Islamic art we do not mean a religious art, but a culture that produced art to be used by Muslims and non-Muslims alike. The artists were Muslims, Christians, and Jews living in the Islamic Empire.

Arab-Islamic art often avoids drawing living forms—especially humans and animals. Although the *Qur'an* (Koran; Muslim holy book) does not prohibit the representation of human figures in art, Islamic art avoids portraying humans, especially prophets and leaders, to prevent people from worshipping their images. Human forms are also avoided in Islamic art because of the belief that only God creates living beings, therefore the artists must try not to compete with images created by God. This is especially true for the art found on religious sites and objects. Mosques and other houses of worship are decorated with Arabesque designs—two-dimensional plantlike or geometric shapes that are repeated in patterns.

Calligraphy is another form of two-dimensional representation in Islamic art. Calligraphy is the art of stylistic handwriting. Its initial purpose was to copy religious documents, but it later became used for writing all kinds of documents and for decorating buildings and many types of objects.

Easel painting, which was popular in the West (Europe and America), did not take hold in the Arab world until the mid-eighteenth century. At the turn of the nineteenth century, the first schools of Western art opened in Egypt, and then in Lebanon and Iraq. Men and women artists were encouraged to attend these academies.

**Self portrait of Kahlil Gibran. In addition to being a famous writer and poet, Kahlil Gibran was also a painter.** *Reproduced by permission of AP/Wide World Photos.*

# Arab American fine artists

There are few records of artists among the early Arab immigrants to the United States aside from the famous Lebanese poet and artist Kahlil Gibran. Since the mid-1950s, many Arab artists—like many Arab professionals—came to study in the United States, while others immigrated to the United States after completing their studies in the arts in their own countries. At the end of the twentieth century, there are more than 300 artists of Arab origin in the United States. There are probably many more second- and third-generation American artists of Arab origin who have exhibited their work in major museums and art galleries. Unless their work represents their Arab heritage in either its form (the style of art) or its content, however, it is difficult to tell that they are of Arab origin.

Some of the most prominent Arab American artists and their works are discussed below.

# Furniture crafter Sam Maloof

Sam Maloof is an Arab American furniture maker who was born to Lebanese parents who immigrated to California in the early 1900s. He started his career as a furniture maker in 1948 and his pieces are now sought by collectors from around the world. He built a twenty-two room house for himself and filled it with pieces of furniture that he crafted with regard to beauty and function. His house is now considered a historical landmark in California. Maloof's famous rocking chair is part of the White House collection of American furniture. Other works by Maloof are exhibited at the Smithsonian Institution in Washington, D.C., the Metropolitan Museum of Art in New York City, the Los Angeles County Museum, and the Boston Museum of Fine Arts.

**Sam Maloof's famous rocking chair is part of the White House collection of American furniture.**
*Photograph by George Baramki Azar. Photo courtesy Aramco World Magazine.*

# Wasma' Chorbachi, Islamic artist and designer

Islamic designer Wasma' Chorbachi was born in 1944 in Iraq. At the age of five, Chorbachi began molding clay and baking it along with the bread in her family's traditional Arab bread ovens at thier home in Baghdad. Her parents nurtured her artistic talents, and Chorbachi went to study in Beirut, Lebanon, and Florence, Italy. She then came to the United States to study at Harvard University, where in 1989 she completed her doctorate degree in Islamic Design. Her dream was to return to the Arab world, but war in Lebanon and later in Iraq prevented her return. She now lives and works in Cambridge, Massachusetts. It was only after many years of training and working in American abstract expressionism did Chorbachi become a successful artist—working and selling her art in the Arab world. Western art forms, she felt, did not allow

**Wasma' Chorbachi,** *Profession of Faith,* **1991. Chorbachi's calligraphic designs on tiles, plaques, and plates continue a tradition that began in her homeland more than a thousand years ago.** *Photo courtesy of the International Council for Women in the Arts/Cultural and Visual Arts Resource, Lafayette, CA.*

her to present her true identity. In a 1989 interview in the *Arab Studies Quarterly*, Chorbachi stated that, "There was nothing wrong with Western styles . . . but they simply could not express what I felt . . . I had to have my own art language . . . I started making pieces that emphasized the linear and geometric designs inherent in Islamic art using Islamic media such as dyes, textiles, clay, and drawing."

Chorbachi continues to explore her own identity as an Arab and a Muslim in her art, focusing on the intersection between science and the art of design in Islamic architectural (building) decoration. She has studied old Islamic practical geometry manuscripts written for artisans and architects and has applied these ancient teachings to her modern works. Her paintings on silk and calligraphic designs on tiles, plaques, and plates continue a tradition that began in her homeland more than a thousand years ago, when Iraqi artisans perfected new methods of producing a variety of lusters and glazes in ceramics.

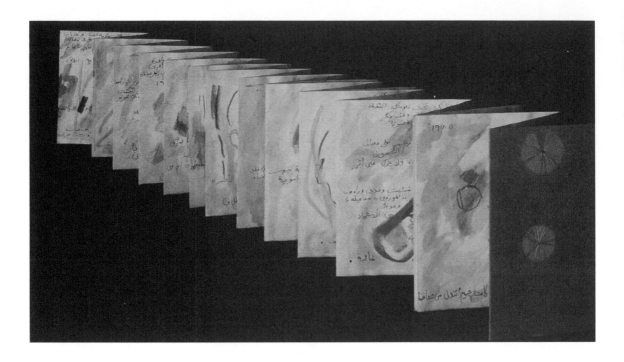

Etel Adnan, *One Linden Tree...Then Another Linden Tree,* 1975. Adnan writes texts of poetry that unfold to stretch 20 to 30 feet. *Photo courtesy of the International Council for Women in the Arts/Cultural and Visual Arts Resource, Lafayette, CA.*

# The poetry and art of Etel Adnan

Oral (spoken) poetry has been a popular form of creative expression in the Arab world since the pre-Islamic era. The Arabic language allows poets to produce harmonies of rhyme and rhythm that please the listener and ensure that the poetry is passed on from one generation to the next. Today poetry remains a popular art form in the Arab world.

Etel Adnan, an Arab American artist who has successfully combined art and poetry, was born in Lebanon in 1925 and immigrated to the United States in the early 1960s. She studied philosophy and philosophy of art at the University of Paris, the University of California at Berkeley, and Harvard Univeristy. Adnan has worked as a professor of philosophy, an art critic, and a newspaper editor. She is both a poet and a painter. Working from her home studio in Sausalito, California, Adnan writes texts of poetry on Japanese accordion-like books (made in Kyoto, Japan), that unfold to stretch 20 to 30

**Mamoun Sakkal,** *Growth,* **1994. Sakkal, a master calligrapher, started producing calligraphy in paintings using watercolors, but now uses the computer.** *Photo courtesy of the International Council for Women in the Arts/Cultural and Visual Arts Resource, Lafayette, CA.*

feet. Working according to this format for more than thirty years, she has created these "artist's books" using poetry by major contemporary Arab poets and a number of American and French poets. Adnan's books and paintings are part of permanent collections around the world, including the British Museum in London, England, and the National Museum of Women in the Arts in Washington, D.C. Her poetry has been put to music by American and British composers, and her essays and poems have been translated into six languages.

## The calligraphy of Mamoun Sakkal

Calligraphy was first developed as an art form to preserve the sacred words of the Qur'an. It later decorated buildings, mosques, rugs, clothing, and manuscripts. The art of Arabic calligraphy can be seen in many European churches, including Saint Peter's Basilica in Rome. Today this art thrives

**Doris Bitar's** *Folding Linen* **(1999) was part of an exhibition inspired by Bitar's aunt, who brought ten yards of white linen with her when she emigrated from Lebanon.** *Photo courtesy of the International Council for Women in the Arts/ Cultural and Visual Arts Resource, Lafayette, CA.*

throughout the Arab world and has many religious and commercial uses. Several Arab American artists are master calligraphers. Among them is Mamoun Sakkal, who was born in Damascus, Syria, in 1950, and immigrated to the United States in 1978. Sakkal studied art at the Aleppo Art Institute in northen Syria, and holds a degree in Architecture from the University of Aleppo as well. He later completed graduate studies in the United States. When Sakkal first began producing calligraphy he used watercolors; he later switched to the computer to produce his distinctive style. Sakkal draws in the *kufic* style.

## Doris Bitar

Painter Doris Bitar emigrated with her parents from Beirut, Lebanon, to the United States at age nine. She went on to earn a Master's degree in Fine Arts from the University of California at San Diego, where she also teaches studio art. *Fold-*

## Other Arab American Artists in the United States

Following is a list of only a handful of Arab American artists in the United States.

- Ghada Amer was born in Egypt and lives in New York. She utilizes embroidery to produce images on canvas.

- Samia Halabi was born in Palestine and lives in New York. She is an abstract artist and writes her own computer programs, producing kinetic paintings with sound.

- Nabila Hilmi, born in Palestine, lives in Philadelphia and uses mixed media to emphasize the harmony of color and form.

- Mohammad Omer Khalil, born in Sudan, now lives in New York. He works primarily in etching on metal plates and teaches at both the New School and New York University.

- Ayad el Nimr, born in Egypt and living in Monterey, California, places traditional Arab motifs onto abstract backgrounds.

- Sumaya Samaha lives in New York, but was born in Lebanon. She produces abstract landscapes on ceramics.

- Athir Shayota is of Chaldean ancestry, and was born in Iraq. He lives in New York and paints portraits and landscapes of the everyday world of his family and community.

- Rabia Sukkarieh, born in Lebanon and now living in Los Angeles, works with mixed media.

- Afaf Zurayk was born in Lebanon and now lives in Washington, D.C. He uses wood to explore shades of darkness and light.

---

*ing Linen* (1999) was part of an exhibition inspired by one of Bitar's aunts who brought ten yards of white linen with her when she emigrated from Lebanon. Bitar's aunt had planned to make a white linen suit as part of her marriage trousseau (a collection of personal and household items a bride takes to her home). But once in the United States, she gave the linen to her niece to paint on. The linen, and her aunt's story, inspired Bitar to paint themes of family life in Lebanon. "Many of the images I use originated in slides my father took," Bitar wrote in *Folding Linen: An Artist's Statement.* "They capture a close knit family at the end of 1960s, a golden period in Lebanon's history. When the civil war began in the 1970s they immigrated to the United States. In my painting I use the image of my par-

## Fact Focus

- Some of the oldest examples of artwork—including tomb paintings, mosaics, rugs, weaving, glass blowing, and embroidery—have been found in the Arab world.

- The famous Lebanese American poet and writer Kahlil Gibran was also a painter.

- A rocking chair made by Sam Maloof is part of the White House collection of American furniture. His twenty-two room home filled with furniture of his design is considered a historical landmark in California.

ents before their marriage, with family in my grandfather's backyard. My father holds a baby as he gazes at my mother. . . . I wonder what they were saying to each other and how the mountain air felt on their skin. . . . I am grateful that my grandfather took that picture."

## The photography of Lily Bandak

Photographer Lily Bandak, who was born in Jordan, was diagnosed with multiple sclerosis, a disease that affects the nervous system and causes paralysis, in 1984. After several years of rehabilitation, Bandak decided to continue her work in photography. With a camera mount attached to her wheelchair and the help of a former student, Bandak travels to Jordan and Bahrain on assignments. She spends several weeks in each country photographing the people and their land. Many exhibitions of her work have been held in these countries, as well as in Egypt and the United States. In 1994 she started the Bandak Foundation to introduce aspects of the Arab world to people in the United States. She hopes to set an example for others with disabilities. In 1996 she participated in the Very Special Arts and the Cultural Paralympic Exhibition in Atlanta and plans to present her work at the Sydney Olympiad 2000.

## For More Information

Ali, Wijdan. *Modern Islamic Art: Development and Continuity.* Gainsville: University of Florida Press, 1997.

Azar, George Baramki. "Soul of the Hardwood." *Aramco World,* March/April 1995, pp. 10-11.

Bitar, Doris. *Folding Linen: An Artist's Statement.* Lafayette, CA: International Council for Women in the Arts, 1999.

Chorbachi, Wasma'. "Profile: Wasma Khalid Chorbachi." *Islamic Arts Foundation,* Spring 1985, pp. 77-79.

Grabar, Oleg. "Architecture and Art." In *The Genius of Arab Civilization: Source of Renaissance.* New York: New York University Press, 1992.

Grabar, Oleg. *Formation of Islamic Art: New Haven and London.* New Haven, CT: Yale University Press, 1987.

Howel, Daedalus. "Etel Adnan: Artist Transforms Verse into Visual Poetry." *San Francisco Chronicle,* December 18, 1998.

Khatibi, A., and Mohamed Sijelmassi. *The Splendor of Islamic Calligraphy.* New York: Thames & Hudson, 1996.

Nashashibi, Salwa Mikdadi, ed. *Forces of Change: Women Artists of the Arab World.* Washington, D.C.: International Council for Women in the Arts and the National Museum for Women in the Arts, 1994.

## Web Sites

Kahlil Gibran's paintings. [Online] Available http://leb.net/gibran/paint.html, and http://impact.civil.columbia.edu/~fawaz/g-gallery.html (last accessed on September 21, 1999).

Sakkal Design. [Online] Available http://www.sakkal.com (last accessed on September 21, 1999).

*Salwa Mikdadi Nashashibi is the President and Founder of the International Council for Women in the Arts. She is a frequent lecturer and writer on the subject of women artists of the Arab world and is the editor of the award-winning publication* Forces of Change: Women Artists of the Arab World.

# Theater, Storytelling, and Traditional Arts

**17**

## Arab American theater

Ethnic theater emerged in the United States as a form of entertainment for new immigrants and other groups that could not speak English or did not relate to the American mainstream theater that was staged for mostly middle-class audiences of European descent. Ethnic plays often reflect the experiences of immigrants in their new country and the values that are most important to them. Arab American theater is no exception.

Because immigrants from Arab countries have been coming to the United States in the various periods since the end of the nineteenth century, their knowledge of Arabic and English varies. For new Arab American immigrants, some Arab American plays are produced in Arabic. Other plays are bilingual (using both Arabic and English), while still others are in English for general audiences, including Arab and non-Arab Americans alike.

Early Arab American theater was produced by amateurs, by people who participated as a hobby rather than to earn a living. These plays were performed in social and cultural clubs. The audiences were mostly members of the club or the immediate community, such as people who belonged to the same church or came from the same village, town, or homeland. These types of plays have been performed throughout the twentieth century by newly arrived Arab American immigrants who needed to create their own forms of entertainment.

# Contemporary Arab American theater

The 1980s and 1990s witnessed a large increase in the number of Arab American theatrical performances. This was the result of the rapid increase in the number of immigrants from Arab countries to the United States since the 1970s. As the size of Arab American communities grew in urban areas such as Detroit, New York, Los Angeles, and Chicago, the production of their newspapers, radio and television shows, and theater increased dramatically.

The two most important cities for Arab American theater are Detroit and Los Angeles. Both have large concentrations of Arab Americans. In Detroit, Arab American theater has been performed mostly in Arabic, while in Los Angeles, plays tends to be either bilingual or in English. In cities such as Chicago and San Francisco, Arab American theater tends to be mostly in English.

## Detroit

In the Detroit area, a number of amateur and professional theatrical groups have been established since the 1980s. Among the most popular in the Iraqi community are the Baghdad Theater, founded in 1985 by Salah Kulato, who had produced fifteen plays by 1999, and Firqat al-Yaoum (Today's Cast), founded in 1987 by Hussam Zoro, who as of 1999 produced eight plays. Most of these plays are in the Iraqi dialect of Arabic and deal with the experience of immigration and the difficulties immigrants face as they try to adjust to their new life in the United States. The plays also address some of the community's concerns, such as crime and drugs, and focus on the need to preserve important cultural values, such as extended family and work ethics. Many of these plays have toured other U.S. cities with large Iraqi communities, including Chicago and San Diego. Among the most popular plays are Salah Kulato's 1983 play *Party Store* (many Arab Americans in Michigan work in party stores) and his 1988 production *Matlub Za'im Lil-Jaliyah* (*Wanted: A Leader for the Community*) and Hussam Zoro's 1986 play *Shuf al-Lotto Esh Sawwa* (*See What the Lotto Has Done*).

In the 1990s, Najee Mondalek emerged as one of the most popular theater producers and directors in the Detroit area, especially among Lebanese Americans. Mondalek, the founder of AJYAL (Generations), started producing dramas in 1989, while still in college. Since then he has produced a number of plays: *Smile, U R in Dearborn* in 1993; *Smile, U R in America* in 1994; *We Become American, Finally* in 1996; and *Come See . . . Come Saw* in 1998. Mondalek's humorous plays—which have toured cities that include New York, San Francisco, Los Angeles, and Toronto and Montreal, Canada—are about the daily experiences of Arab immigrants.

Abdulrahmen "Ray" Alcodray founded the Arab Theatrical Arts Guild (ATAG) in 1998 to promote an interest in the performing arts within the Arab American community. ATAG has produced *Thaalab El-Muhtal*, a translation of the play *Sly Fox* by the American playwright Larry Gelbart, and *Rassasa fi Al-Qalb*, a 1999 play by the famous Egyptian writer Tawfiq el-Hakim.

## California

A large Arab American community lives in California. Since the late 1980s, some Arab Americans have been producing bilingual plays and musicals. A pioneer in this area is Hammam Shafie. Among his most popular work is *Where to*

*Ramallah,* a 1987 play about the history of the Palestinian people. (Ramallah is a village on the West Bank of the Jordan River in Palestine, and "Where to Ramallah" is a very popular Palestinian song.)

In 1989 Shafie founded the Arab-American Children's Theater Company. The theater aims to encourage young Arab Americans to be proud of their culture and heritage. The first production of this company was *Festival: A Musical Play in Two Acts,* produced by Fereal Masre. *Festival* combines the talents of many Arab Americans, including those of twenty-five children. It portrays the experiences of children growing up in the United States in Arab American families and the difficulties new immigrants face.

Another bilingual theater group in California is *Al-Funun Al-Arabiya* (Arab Arts), founded in 1992 by the Arab American anthropologist and filmmaker Fadwa El Guindi. *Al-Funun Al-Arabiya* has produced *Qala al-Rawy* (*Said the Story-*

*teller*), a play about Arab-Bedouin women's storytelling and poetry, and *Mahjar,* about life in America as told by members of Arab American communities. *Mahjar* blends the poetry of Arab American Kahlil Gibran and African American Maya Angelou with the music of Arab American Jihad Racy and Lebanese singer Marcel Khalife.

## Chicago

The works of Arab American playwright and actor Fareed Al-Oboudi target the general public rather than Arab Americans. His play *Portrait of a Suspect* was produced at the Chicago Actor's Project Theater in 1989. The play explores the discrimination and stereotyping of Arab Americans and the destructive impact of discrimination on human life.

In Chicago, Jamil Khoury, a young Arab American, is emerging as a serious playwright. His first play, *Fitna,* was produced at the University of Chicago in 1995. *Fitna* examines the role of women in Arab society today. Another Arab American playwright is Kathleen Haddad. Two of her plays, *With Love from Gaza* and *The Arabs in My Head,* have been produced in the Minneapolis-St. Paul, Minnesota, area.

# Storytelling

Storytelling is an ancient Arab tradition. Until writing became widespread, it was the most common way stories were passed from one generation to the next. Mothers, aunts, and grandmothers often gathered children in the evening to tell them stories that they themselves had learned as children. Usually stories begin with the phrase *"Kan ya ma kan, fi qadeem al-zaman, kan fi . . ."* ("Once upon a time, an old, old time, there was . . ."). Most stories have moral lessons, such as the importance of honesty or the importance of family.

In California, a number of Arab Americans have revived the storytelling tradition. They perform in English, and are popular with both Arab American and non-Arab audiences. Stories often focus on the history and culture of Arabs and Arab Americans.

Elmaz Abinader, a Lebanese American, and Emily Shihadeh, a Palestinian American, are two significant storytellers in San Francisco. Abinader is a poet and performer as well. One of her works, *Country of Origin,* tells the story of three generations of Arab American women who fight racism and ignorance and strive to preserve their own identity and culture. By talking about the experience of these Arab American women, Abinader shows how a person's name, country of origin, and appearance are part of his or her identity.

Emily Shihadeh is a professional storyteller whose talent lies in her ability to present tragic events in a comic way without trivializing them, or making them seem less important than they are. Her one-person shows are usually derived from her own life and the tragedies of the Palestinian people. In 1995 she produced *Grapes and Figs Are in Season,* based on her experiences as a Palestinian American and her family's flight from Jerusalem in 1948. Shihadeh established herself as a talented performer during her work with the famous San Francisco Mime Troupe.

In Los Angeles, Tamadhur Al-Aqeel is an emerging young Arab American writer and storyteller. Al-Aqeel and Ismael Kanater formed the Kanaaqeel Theater Company, which is dedicated to exploring Arab culture and examining important values that thrive in Arab American communities. Kanaaqueel's first production was the 1998 play *Shahrazad and the Arabian Nights*. In Minneapolis, Arab American writer and musician Joanna Kadi performs stories while playing the traditional Arabic drum called the *derbekeh.*

# Films

Due to the high cost of film production, it has been rather difficult for Arab Americans to produce their own movies. The few films and videos produced by Arab Americans tend to focus on two issues: events in their country of origin and the life experiences of the Arab immigrant communities in the United States.

Anthropologist Fadwa El Guindi has produced a number of documentaries about Egyptian traditions. *El-Sebou': Egyptian Birth Rituals* is a 27-minute film produced in 1986. *El-Sebou',* which means "the seventh," is an Egyptian celebration that happens on the seventh day following the birth of a child.

*El-Mouild: Egyptian Religious Festival* is a 38-minute film produced in 1995 about an Egyptian religious festival that celebrates the birth of the Muslim prophet Mohammad. El Guindi is in the process of producing two new films about Arab Americans, *The Wedding of Nevine* and *Pizza or Kushari* (*kushari* is a popular Egyptian dish made of rice, lentils, pasta, and tomatoes).

The first Arab American commercial film, *Nahr el-Hayat* (River of Life), directed by Hazim Bitar, was released in 1999. This film was written, produced, and performed by a team of emerging Arab American artists in the Washington, D.C. area.

Tiny Leaps Productions produced a feature film, *Adrift in the Heartland,* about a young Palestinian woman's adaptation to life in the United States and her friendship with an African American woman in Chicago. *Adrift in the Heartland* was written and directed by Brigid Maher and produced by Mahasen Nasser-Eldin and Yaser Tabbara. Tiny Leaps Productions is a nonprofit company based in Chicago that promotes innovative projects in the media arts and theater in order to project positive images of people of diverse racial, ethnic, and cultural backgrounds.

Nasir Zacharia is a cinematographer who has worked on several films, including Rod Gailes's award-winning *Twin Cousins.* He is currently completing *The Tale of Three Mohammads,* a film about three Arabs wrongly accused of a terrorist bombing.

# Videos

Since video production is much more affordable than film, many Arab Americans have produced valuable videos on a variety of topics. Jocelyn Ajami of Boston has produced three videos: *Jihad* (1999), a short informational video on the

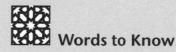
## Words to Know

- **Amateur:** a person who is engaged in an art or a sport as a hobby rather than to make a living.
- **Bilingual:** fluent in two languages.
- **Henna:** a dye made from henna tree leaves, which is used to color hair and to decorate hands and feet.
- **Kushari:** a popular Egyptian dish, made of rice, lentils, pasta and tomato sauce.
- **Mainstream:** pertaining to the dominant or the majority culture.

Gulf War; *Oasis of Peace,* a story about a village where Palestinians and Israelis live in peace; and *Gypsy Heart* (1998), a documentary about Flamenco dancers. Hakim Belabbes, a Moroccan American living in Chicago, has produced two videos, including a documentary about his family and village in Morocco.

Another popular video is *Tales from Arab Detroit,* a 1994 documentary produced by Joan Mandell and co-produced by Sally Howell and the Arab Community Center for Economic and Social Services (ACCESS). The film portrays the Arab American community in Detroit and the conflicts between different generations of Arab Americans. *Banat Chicago* (Chicago Girls), produced by the American Friends Service Committee, portrays the life of Palestinian women and young adults in the city of Chicago.

**A Palestinian embroidered gown by Halima Abdel Fatah.** *Reproduced by permission of the Arab Community Center for Economic and Social Services (ACCESS).*

# Traditional arts

Throughout a century of immigration to the United States, immigrants from different Arab countries have brought with them some important traditional art forms, which have survived many generations. Among the most popular of these are embroidery, henna design, and calligraphy.

## Embroidery

One way women of the Arab world have traditionally expressed their creativity and identity is through various hand-embroidered patterns. Styles of needlework vary considerably throughout the Arab world. Each region, village, and family has its own unique designs. In parts of Saudi Arabia, the use of gold and silver threads with beads is very popular. During the winter in Yemen, it is common to see men's head scarves embroidered with floral patterns.

The art of elaborate embroidery tends to be very well preserved among Palestinian women. Traditional embroidery, which became a symbol of Palestinian identity, continues to thrive in many Palestinian villages, as well as among Palestinian Americans. Women take pride in preserving this tradition and passing it from one generation to the next. In recent years, new designs have emerged that reflect the sentiments and values of present-day Palestinians. For instance, the names of cities and villages in Palestine embroidered in stylized calligraphy patterns are popular.

In the United States, Palestinian American women continue to produce hand-made, cross-stitched dresses and decorative household items such as pillowcases, tablecloths, and wall hangings. Some Palestinian American women, especially those who come from villages, continue to wear their *thoub* (long dresses, usually black, with elaborate and colorful embroidery). It is not unusual to see women in the streets and shops of Arab communities wearing these dresses. It is also very common to see these beautifully embroidered dresses at weddings and other festive occasions.

The Palestinian Heritage Foundation, founded in 1987 by Hanan and Farah Munayyer of New Jersey, has more than 250 traditional Palestinian and Syrian embroidered bridal costumes. Theirs is considered one of the largest and best collections in the world. The collection has been exhibited to audiences across the country in museums, public libraries, festivals, and universities.

## Calligraphy

Arabic calligraphy (handwriting in beautiful patterns and geometric designs) is one of the most important art forms in the Arab world. It is used for writing texts, as well as for decorating objects and buildings. Calligraphy is an art form that is still very much alive in the United States. Arabic calligraphy is utilized in art and decorations, as well as in advertising signs, wall posters, and banners. The most famous calligrapher in the United States is Mohammed Zakariya. He is a European American who learned calligraphy in Turkey. His student, Eleanor Aishah Holland, has also emerged as a talented calligrapher. Among the most talent-

"Thanks to God the Lord of the Universe." Calligraphy by Aziz Mohammed Al Shabli. *Reproduced by permission of the Arab Community Center for Economic and Social Services (ACCESS).*

ed Arab American calligraphers are Nihad Dukhan in Toledo, Ghassan Jabr in Los Angeles, George Allam in Chicago, Ali Majed and Yousef Phenny in Detroit, and Mamoun Sakkal (see chapter 16).

## Henna design

Henna (a natural dye made from the dried leaves of the henna plant) is a popular cosmetic used throughout the Arab world. It is used to color hair and create temporary tattoos. This traditional art form is especially popular among Arab Americans from Yemen, North Africa, and Palestine.

On special occasions, such as weddings and religious holidays, Arab American women decorate each other's hands and feet with intricate henna patterns (see Chapter 11). These patterns include flowering vines and geometric shapes. Some people believe henna designs act as a good-luck charm for the person who wears them.

Henna is sometimes used with another substance called *khudab*. While the henna produces a reddish or orange color, khudab is black and similar to ink. A pointed tool, such as a toothpick, is used to draw a variety of designs on the hands and feet with khudab.

# For More Information

Abbas, Jailan. *Festivals in Egypt.* Cairo, Egypt: Hoops Books, 1995.

Ali, Wijdan. *Modern Islamic Art: Development and Continuity.* Gainesville: University of Florida Press,1997.

Bushnaq, Inea. *Arab Folktales.* New York: Pantheon Books, 1986.

Chorbachi, Wasma'. *Arts and the Islamic World,* Spring 1985.

Fa'ik, Ala. "Issues of Identity: In Theater of Immigrant Community." *The Development of Arab American Identity,* edited by Ernest McCarus. Ann Arbor: University of Michigan Press, 1994.

Grabar, Oleg. "Architecture and Art." In *The Genius of Arab Civilization: Source of Renaissance,* edited by John Hayes. New York: New York University Press, 1992.

Grabar, Oleg. *Formation of Islamic Art.* New Haven: Yale University Press, 1987.

Howell, Sally. "The Art and Artistry of Arab Detroit: Changing Traditions in a New World." In *Arab Detroit: From Margin to Mainstream,* edited by Nabeel Abraham and Andrew Shryock. Detroit: Wayne State University Press, in press.

Khatibi, A., and Mohamed Sijelmassi. *The Splendor of Islamic Calligraphy.* New York: Thames & Hudson, 1996.

Nader, Rose B., and Nathra Nader. *It Happened in the Kitchen: Recipes for Food and Thought.* Washington, D.C.: Center for the Study of Responsive Law, 1991.

Shabbas, Audrey, and Ayad Al-Qazzaz, eds. *Arab World Notebook.* Berkeley, CA: Nadja (Women Concerned About the Middle East), 1989.

Shihab Nye, Naomi. *Habibi.* New York: Simon and Schuster, Books for Young Readers, 1997.

**On special occasions Arab American women decorate each other's hands and feet with intricate henna patterns.** *Photograph by Hajer Mitchell. Reproduced by permission of the Arab Community Center for Economic and Social Services (ACCESS).*

*Tales from Arab Detroit* (video). Directed by Joan Mandell, produced by The Arab Community Center for Economic and Social Services (AC-CESS) and Sally Howell. Ho-ho-Kus, NJ: New Days Films, 1995.

Weir, Shelagh. *Palestinian Embroidery: A Village Arab Craft.* London: The British Museum, 1970.

## Web Sites

Al-Funun Al-Arabia. [Online] Available http://www-bcf.usc.edu/~elguindi/funun.htm (last accessed on September 21, 1999).

Casey Kasem. [Online] Available http://www.arabmedia.com/achievers.html (last accessed on September 21, 1999).

Tiny Leaps Productions. [Online] Available http://www.tinyleaps.com/ (last accessed on September 21, 1999).

*Anan Ameri is the Cultural Arts Director of the Arab Community Center for Economic and Social Services (ACCESS). She received her B.A. from the Jordanian University in Amman, Jordan, her M.A. from Cairo University in Egypt, and her Ph.D. in Sociology from Wayne State University in Detroit, Michigan.*

# Literature

## 18

**A**rabs have been immigrating to the United States in significant numbers since the late 1800s, and Arab American literature began with these early immigrants. One of the first genres, or types, of literature to appear was journalism. The first Arab American newspaper, *Kawkab Amrika* (Star of America), began publishing articles by Arab American writers in 1892 (see Chapter 19). By the early 1900s, there were a number of authors publishing in both Arabic and English. The first Arab American literary group, the Pen League, began in 1920.

## Genres of Arab American literature

Arab American literature includes many genres, or forms, of writing, including poetry, short stories, novels, travel accounts, autobiographies, journalism, academic books, and articles. Many Arab American writers have written works in a variety, if not all, of these genres.

The first Arab American novel was Ameen Rihany's 1911 work *The Book of Khalid.*

Poetry is a significant form of Arab American literary expression and has a long history in the Arab world. Poetry was a prestigious form of oral (spoken) expression among Arabs before the Arabic language became a common written language (just as storytelling and ballads were in other societies). It continues to be an important art form in the Arab world today. *Grapeleaves* was the first Arab American anthology, or collection, of Arab American poetry to be published.

Autobiographies are true stories from the author's life and are also an important form of writing for Arab Americans. In addition to book-length autobiographies, many poems, short stories, novels, and essays deal with an author's life and memories of growing up. Autobiography is an important literary genre for all immigrant communities because it allows writers to explore issues of their ethnicity—their religious, national, or cultural identity (the cultural group they feel that they belong to). It also allows them to explore the history and culture of their parents and grandparents.

There are a few Arab American novels (book-length works of fiction), including Ameen Rihani's 1911 novel *The Book of Khalid* and Diana Abu-Jabar's more recent (1993) novel *Arabian Jazz.* Short stories are more common, although many of them are more autobiographical than fictitious (made up), and weave personal stories of the author's life into the narrative (story).

Many Arab American writers also publish scholarly, or factual, essays, books, and articles on a variety of topics. Some write mostly about Arab Americans. Others write about topics completely unrelated to Arab or Arab American issues. Many do both.

# Early Arab American writers

The earliest Arab American writers were immigrants from what is today Syria and Lebanon. Well-known writers of the early twentieth century included the poets of New York City's Pen League and essayists, novelists, journalists, and scholars. Many of these writers wrote in Arabic, and some wrote in both Arabic and English.

The writings of these early immigrants cover a variety of topics, including love of family, a nostalgia for the homelands of Syria and Lebanon, philosophy and religion, a concern with human justice and the suffering caused by war, and an amazement of what the United States had to offer. Many of these authors expressed excitement about the economic opportunities and political freedom in the United States while at the same time were eager to share the positive aspects of the Arab world with Westerners.

 **Fact Focus**

- Arab American literature began in the late 1800s when the first Arab-language newspapers in the United States started publishing articles by Arab American writers.

- The first Arab American novel was Ameen Rihany's 1911 work *The Book of Khalid.*

- Afifa Karem was the first Arab American woman to become a well-known journalist and publisher. Her articles began appearing in Arab-language newspapers by 1905.

- Before writing his bestseller *The Exorcist,* William Peter Blatty published *Which Way to Mecca, Jack?*, a humorous account of his life growing up as an Arab American.

The first Arab American woman to publish a book was Lila Barakat. *A Message from Mount Lebanon* (1912) is an autobiographical account of her life. Another early autobiography is Abraham Rihbany's *A Far Journey* (1914). Rihbany, a well-known clergyman, attempted to explain the Arab world in a way that would be understandable to Americans. Both he and Barakat used references from the Bible, since the Christian holy lands familiar to Americans lay in the Arab world.

Afifa Karam (1883–1924) was the first well-known Arab American woman journalist. Born and raised in Lebanon, she immigrated to the United States at age fourteen with her husband. She began her career as a journalist by the age of twenty and wrote articles for Arab-language newspapers and journals, including *al-Huda* (*The Guidance*) and the *Syrian Woman.* She was publisher and editor of *The New*

**Kahlil Gibran is the most famous of the early Arab immigrant writers.**
*Reproduced by permission of Corbis Corporation (Bellevue).*

*World: A Ladies Monthly Arabic Magazine.* Karam authored three novels and translated five books into Arabic. Karam was highly concerned about the condition of Arab and Arab American women and much of her writing argued for an improvement in women's status.

A positive portrayal of the United States can be found in Salom Rizhk's (1909–1973) autobiography *A Syrian Yankee* (1942). Rizhk's book expresses his admiration for the freedom and opportunity he found in the United States. He describes the United States as "a country like heaven, the land of peace, contentment, liberty, brotherhood, plenty."

## The Pen League

The Arab literary group the Pen League (*al-Rabitah al-Qalamiyah* in Arabic) was founded in New York City in 1920. Its members, some of the most well-known writers of the time, have had a great influence on literature in the Arab world and on Arab American writers.

Kahlil Gibran (1883–1931) is the most famous of the early Arab immigrant writers. Like his friend Rihany, Gibran came to the United States at the age of twelve from Lebanon. He wrote and published in both English and Arabic. Gibran earned fame from his book *The Prophet* (1923), which has been translated into numerous languages and has sold more than eight million copies. Gibran was also an artist.

Ameen Rihani (Rihany); (1876–1940) came to the United States from Lebanon in 1888. Although he lived in New York City, he traveled throughout much of the Arab world and maintained a second home in Freike, Lebanon, the town of his birth. Rihany published in both Arabic and English. His works include news and magazine articles for both Arab- and English-language journals, novels, short stories, essays, poetry, travel books, and translations. His works in Arabic are concerned with improving the situation of the Arab world. His English-language publications sought to explain the Arab world, and its historical contributions, to the West. In both cases he emphasized that both the East (the Arab world and Asia) and the West (Europe and the Americas) had much to learn from each other. Rihany wrote the first English-language Arab American novel, *The Book of Khalid* (1911), which follows the journey of an immigrant from Lebanon to the United States and back home again.

Elia Madi (Madey); (1890–1957) was born in Lebanon, educated in Cairo, Egypt, and moved to New York City in 1916. Unlike the other influential members of the Pen League, Madi wrote only in Arabic. While his work is very well known in the Arab world, the lack of English translations has kept him rather unknown in the United States. In addition to writing a number of volumes of poetry, he also published the newspaper *Mirat al-Gharb* (*Mirror of the West*), which he took over from his father-in-law. He later began his own newspaper, *Al-Samir,* which was published in Brooklyn until his death in 1957.

Mikhail Naimy; (1889–1988) was a highly acclaimed writer in the Arab world, but remains virtually unknown in the United States, though he lived in America for twenty years and was an active member of the Pen League. His works include the *Book of Mirdad, Memoirs of a Vagrant Soul,* and a biography of his friend Kahlil Gibran.

# Contemporary Arab American literature

Arab American literature has changed since the first half of the twentieth century. Not only is there a larger number of writers, but there is also a greater diversity in today's Arab American communities that is reflected in contemporary Arab American literature. While we still have recent immigrants who speak and write Arabic, we also have a number of American-born second- and third-generation Arab Americans who write mostly in English. Unlike the early writers, who came almost entirely from Lebanon and Syria, today's Arab American writers can trace their ethnic heritage to any of the countries of the Arab world, and some

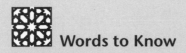

## Words to Know

- **Anthology:** a collection of stories or poems by different authors.

- **Autobiography:** a work based upon the life of the author.

- **Ethnicity** or **ethnic identity:** the cultural group that a person feels he or she belongs to.

- **Fiction:** something that didn't really happen; made up.

- **Genres:** a style of writing, such as poetry, prose, or essay.

- **Memoir:** like an autobiography, it is the story of the author's life.

- **Prose:** unlike poetry, something written in complete sentences rather than free verse.

- **Scholarly:** something academic, or based upon facts and research rather than fiction.

also have a parent or grandparents of non-Arab backgrounds.

Contemporary Arab American writers are similar to those of the first half of the 1900s in that they are also concerned with bridging the gap between the land of their ancestors and the United States. The writing of today's authors, however, presents a more realistic picture of the United States. Whereas the early writers tended to portray the United States as a land of freedom and opportunity, contemporary writers depict it as a place where poverty, racism, and injustice exist alongside economic opportunities and social freedom.

These writers are also more critical of the role that the United States has played in the political events of the Arab world. This includes the United States' financial and military support of the state of Israel from Palestinian lands. Many Arab American writers speak of the wars between Israel and the surrounding Arab countries, the mass expulsion of Palestinians upon the creation of the state of Israel in 1948, and the Israeli invasion and occupation of southern Lebanon. Another important political event that has shaped Arab American political identity, and which is reflected in Arab American writing, is the United States-led Gulf War against Iraq. Arab American writers not only focus upon these political events themselves, but also write about the anti-Arab sentiments that emerge during these times of crises.

But writings of Arab Americans are also full of positive images associated with being Arab: food, gardens, close-knit families, music, and dancing. Many of the autobiographical writings contain humorous stories about the difficulties of finding a balance between being Arab and being American: the embarrassment at having one's father stop the car along the highway to pray, or at showing up at school with falafel sandwiches in pita bread when everyone else is eating peanut butter and jelly sandwiches.

## Autobiographical works and novels

In recent decades, a number of books have been published that are similar to novels but are often based more on true stories from the authors' experiences than pure fiction. One of the earliest of these, Vance Bourjaily's *Confessions of a Spent Youth* (1960), tells the author's life story, although the issue of his Arab heritage only surfaces in one chapter about his return to the village of his grandparents.

In 1960 William Peter Blatty published his own life story, *Which Way to Mecca, Jack?* This book, and a later work dedicated to his mother (*I'll Tell Them I Remember You,* 1973), both contain humorous accounts of growing up as an Arab American. Blatty is best known, however, as the writer of the novel *The Exorcist* (1971).

More recently, Joseph Geha published *Through and Through: Toledo Stories* (1990), a book of short stories that portray the lives of three generations of a Lebanese American family. Raymond Hanania authored the 1996 work *I'm Glad I Look Like a Terrorist,* a book of essays that contains humorous accounts of growing up Arab American in Chicago. Hanania is a journalist and scholar who has published a number of other works and has a web page dedicated to Arab American writing.

A book-length work that depicts the life experiences of Arab Americans from a more serious perspective is Gregory Orfalea's *Before the Flames* (1988). This work tells one hundred years of Arab American history though personal stories and research about Arab Americans across the United States.

**William Peter Blatty published his life story, *Which Way to Mecca, Jack?*, in 1960. Blatty is best known, however, as the writer of the novel *The Exorcist* (1971).**

## Arab American Magazines and Associations

- *Al Jadid*, edited by Elie Chalala, is a journal of Arab and Arab American culture and arts that features the works of many Arab American writers.

- *Graffiti Rag*, a journal of urban writing edited by Arab American poet Hayan Charara, features many Arab American writers.

- *Jusoor* is a multilingual journal featuring Arab writing.

- *Mizna* is a literary journal dedicated solely to Arab American writing. It contains poetry, fiction, essays, and art.

- RAWI (Radius of Arab-American Writers, Inc.) is an Arab American writers group that provides members with a newsletter and a directory of writers.

One of the latest Arab American memoirs to be published is Jane Brox's *Five Thousand Days Like This One: An American Family History* (1999). The book tells the story of her family's life in the Merrimack Valley of Massachusetts. Born in 1956 to a Lebanese American father and an Italian American mother, Brox has published a number of poems and essays, along with her earlier book *Here and Nowhere Else: Late Seasons of a Family Farm* (1996).

In addition to these autobiographical books, recent years have seen the emergence of a few Arab American novels. While these contain fictitious characters and events, they often still retain an autobiographical bent, drawing heavily upon the life experiences of the authors.

Elmaz Abinader is both a poet and prose writer. Her novel, *Children of the Roojme, A Family's Journey* (1991) depicts the lives of three generations of a family as they move from Lebanon to South America to the United States. Abinader also gives storytelling performances. *Country of Origin* depicts the lives of different generations of Arab women through their personal stories.

Kathryn Abdul-Baki is the author of a collection of short stories, *Fields of Fig and Olive* (1991), and the 1994 novel *Tower of Dreams*.

Diana Abu-Jabar is one of the first of the contemporary Arab American novelists. *Arabian Jazz* (1993), centering on a Jordanian American family in upstate New York, portrays the struggle between Arab culture and American culture.

Rabih Alameddine is both a painter and a writer. Alameddine's *Koolaids: The Art of War* (1998) travels between San Francisco and Lebanon during its civil war. *Peru* (1999) is a collection of short stories about a Lebanese family.

## Other Poets and Essayists

In addition to the poets featured in *Grapeleaves* and *Food for Our Grandmothers,* a number of other Arab Americans have published their own collections of poetry and essays.

- Hayan Charara's poetry, essays, and short stories have been featured in a number of journals. He has an upcoming book of poetry, *Every Blessed Day,* and is currently working on a novel.

- One of the youngest Arab American poets to publish a book of poetry is Suheir Hammad. Both her collection of poems, *born Palestinian, born Black* (1996), and her memoir *Drops of this Story* (1996), draw upon her life experiences and the themes of racism, violence against women, drug abuse, poverty, and Zionism. Hammad was born in Jordan and after living briefly in Beirut, Lebanon, and grew up in Brooklyn, New York.

- Khaled Mattawa was born in Libya, and came to the United States at the age of fifteen. His poems have appeared in a variety of journals and anthologies, and the first collection of his poetry, *Ismailia Eclipse,* was published in 1995.

- Haas Mroue is a poet whose first book, *Beirut Seizures,* deals with the sadness of war and exile.

- David Williams is the author of *Travelling Mercies* (1993), a collection of poems that touch upon the themes of his Arab heritage and the issues of immigrant groups and oppressed peoples in the United States and elsewhere.

Shaw Dallal, a Palestinian American, is one of the newest Arab American novelists. *Scattered Like Seeds* (1998) is his first novel, a semi-autobiographical account about a Palestinian uprooted from his homeland by the Arab-Israeli conflict.

Mona Simpson is a critically acclaimed author. Her first novel *Anywhere But Here* (1987) was a bestseller. Her other novels include *The Lost Father* and *A Regular Guy.*

# Poetry, short stories, and essays

The works of contemporary Arab American writers can be found in a variety of books, magazines, and journals. In addition, two anthologies (books that contain the writings

One of the most famous Arab American poets, Naomi Shihab Nye has published a number of volumes of poetry and books for children and young adults.
*Reproduced by permission of Bill Kennedy.*

of many authors) of Arab American poetry and essays have come out since the late 1980s.

The first of these is *Grapeleaves: A Century of Arab-American Poetry* (1988). Edited by Gregory Orfalea and Sharif Elmusa, *Grapeleaves* contains the works of twenty poets, beginning with the early Arab American writers and continuing through the poets of the late 1990s. Some of the more recent poets featured by *Grapeleaves* include:

Etel Adnan, artist and poet, who was born in Beirut, Lebanon in 1925. She has published numerous collections of poetry in both English and French, as well as *Sitt Marie Rose* (1977), a novel about the Lebanese civil war (see chapter 16).

Born in Pittsburgh, Pennsylvania in 1928, Samuel Hazo is a well-known poet and novelist. Hazo has published more than twenty books and was named Pittsburgh's Man of the Year for the Arts in 1984.

Lawrence Joseph, a Lebanese American, was born in Detroit, Michigan, in 1948. His books of poetry *Shouting at No One* (1983), *Curriculum Vitae* (1988), and *Before our Eyes* (1993), describe his experiences growing up as an Arab American in Detroit. Joseph is also a lawyer and a scholar and has published a book about lawyers—*Lawyerland: What Lawyers Talk About When They Talk* (1997).

Jack Marshall is an Iraqi Jewish American. He was born in Brooklyn, New York, in 1937. Marshall has written numerous volumes of poetry, including *Sesame* (1993), *Arabian Nights* (1987), and *Arriving on the Playing Fields of Paradise* (1984).

D. H. Melhem was born in Brooklyn, New York, in 1926, and is part Greek American, part Arab American. Melhem has published various books of poetry and essays, including *Rest in Love* (1975), and a novel, *Blight* (1995).

Eugene Paul Nassar was born in Utica, New York, in 1935. His memoir, *Wind of the Land* (1979), celebrates the Lebanese American community in which he grew up and has been described as one of the best portrayals of the experience of growing up Arab American.

Born in St. Louis, Missouri, in 1952, Naomi Shihab Nye is one of the most famous Arab American poets. Nye has published a number of volumes of poetry (including *Red Suitcase,* 1994, and *Fuel,* 1998). She has also published children's books (*Sitti's Secrets,* 1994),  and *Habibi,* 1997, a novel for young adults.

Fawaz Turki was born in Haifa, Palestine, in 1940. In addition to his poetry, Turki has written essays and prose on the fate of the Palestinian people. He published the first English-language memoir of a Palestinian raised in the refugee camps, *The Disinherited: Journal of a Palestinian Exile,* in 1972.

# Food for Our Grandmothers

A second anthology, *Food for Our Grandmothers: Writings by Arab-American and Arab-Canadian Feminists* (1994), contains poetry and essays by more than forty women. These writers discuss both the beauty and the difficulties of being Arab American. They reminisce about the Arab world—its food, traditions, and natural beauty—and family members who have passed away. They also lament the sufferings of Arabs and Arab Americans caused by political injustice, war, racism, and discrimination.

In addition to some of the poets whose works appear in *Grapeleaves, Food for Our Grandmothers* contains the works of a number of younger poets and essayists. These include Adele Ne Jame, whose work draws upon both her Arab heritage and her experience growing up in Hawaii; Pauline Kaldas, who was born in Egypt; Lisa Suhair Majaj, a Palestinian American writer and scholar of Arab American literature; and Therese Saliba, a scholar of English and Arabic literature.

The editor of *Food for Our Grandmothers,* Joanna Kadi, has made a major contribution to Arab American literature by publishing this anthology of women's writings. Kadi has also published *Thinking Class: Sketches from a Cultural Worker*

Edward Said, a scholar at Columbia University, is one of the best-known Arab American scholars today. *Reproduced by permission of Corbis Corporation (Bellevue).*

(1996), a book of personal essays about her own experience growing up Arab American in a working class environment.

## Arab American scholars and scholarship on Arab Americans

Many Arab American writers are scholars who publish factual, or nonfiction, books about Arab Americans and the issues that concern them. One of the first well-known Arab American scholars was Philip K. Hitti (1886–1978). He wrote a number of books, including *The Syrians in America* (1924), *The History of the Arabs* (1937), and *Islam: A Way of Life* (1962).

One of the best-known Arab American scholars today, both among Arabs and non-Arabs, is Edward Said, a scholar at Columbia University. Said (pronounced sagh-eed) is a Palestinian American who has written extensively about the Arab world, U.S. foreign policy, and social justice. His most famous book, *Orientalism,* talks about how the Arab world and other colonies of Europe were portrayed in colonial literature—literature that was written by Europeans about the people in the countries they controlled. This research is important because it has made scholars and others more aware of how negative stereotypes are often embedded in literature which we assume is objective, or without bias.

## For More Information

Abinader, Elmaz. *Children of the Roojme: A Family's Journey.* New York: Norton, 1991.

Charara, Hayan. "Growing up Arab in Detroit." *Forkroads: A Journal of Ethnic-American Literature*, Winter 1996.

Gibran, Jean, and Kahlil Gibran. *Kahlil Gibran: His Life and World.* New York: Interlink Books, 1991.

Kadi, Joanne, ed. *Food for Our Grandmothers: Writings by Arab-American and Arab-Canadian Feminists.* Boston: South End Press, 1994.

Majaj, Lisa. "Arab-American Literature and the Politics of Memory." In *Memory and Cultural Politics: New Essays in American Ethnic Literatures,* edited by Amritjit Singh, Joseph Skerrett, Jr., and Robert E. Hogan. Boston: Northeastern University Press, 1996.

Majaj, Lisa. "Two Worlds Emerging: Arab-American Writing at the Crossroads." *Aljadid,* March 1997.

Najor, Deborah. "Selma's Weddings." *Michigan Quarterly Review,* Fall 1992.

Nye, Naomi Shihab. *Habibi.* New York: Simon and Schuster, 1997.

Orfalea, Gregory. *Before the Flames: A Quest for the History of Arab Americans.* Austin: University of Texas Press, 1988.

Orfalea, Gregory, and Sharif Elmusa, eds. *Grapeleaves: A Century of Arab-American Poetry.* Salt Lake City: University of Utah Press, 1988.

Selim, George. *Afifa Karem: The Voice of al-Huda's Most Prominent Woman Contributor.* Arab-American Institute Press, 1999.

Shakir, Evelyn. "Arab Mothers, American Sons: Women in Arab-American Autobiographies." *MELUS,* Fall 1991-92.

Shakir, Evelyn. "Mother's Milk: Women in Arab-American Autobiography." *MELUS,* Winter 1988.

Suleiman, Michael. "Early Arab-Americans: The Search for Identity." In *Crossing the Waters: Arabic-Speaking Immigrants to the United States before 1940,* edited by Eric Hooglund. Washington, D.C.: Smithsonian Institution Press, 1987.

## Other Important Arab American Scholarly Writers and Some of Their Works

- Anthropologist Nabeel Abraham: *Arab Detroit: From Margin to Mainstream* (2000) and *Arabs in the New World: Studies on Arab-American Communities* (1983).

- Historian Yvonne Haddad: *Muslim Communities in North America* (1994) and *The Muslims of America* (1991).

- Historian Alixa Naff: *The Arab Americans* (1998) and *Becoming American: the Early Arab Immigrant Experience* (1985).

- Jack Shaheen: *The TV Arab* (1984).

- Literary critic and oral historian Evelyn Shakir: *Bint Arab: Arab and Arab-American Women in the United States* (1997).

- Political scientist Michael Suleiman: *Arabs in America: Building a New Future* (1999), *Arab Americans: Continuity and Change* (1989), and *The Arabs in the Mind of America* (1988, with Baha Abu Laban).

- Adele Younis: *The Coming of the Arab Speaking People to the United States* (1995).

## Web Sites

Arab American Writers. [Online] Available http://www.hanania.com/arablit.htm (last accessed September 21, 1999).

Mona Simpson. [Online] Available http://www.randomhouse.com/vintage/read/simpson (last accessed September 21, 1999).

Naomi Shihab Nye. [Online] Available http://www.cs.uiowa.edu/~bonak/nye.html and http://www.wnet.org/archive/lol/nye.html (last accessed on September 21, 1999).

*Dawn Ramey is a Ph.D. candidate in Anthropology at Indiana Univeristy. She worked with the Arab Community Center for Economic and Social Services (ACCESS) from 1995 to 1999 and is currently conducting research on social justice issues for the Arab American community.*

# Media

**B**efore radio and television, people relied on newsprint for their information and entertainment. Newsprint includes newspapers, magazines, newsletters, and other forms of printed material. Early on, people referred to the institutions that published newsprint as the press. Today, the press has evolved to include radio, television, and the internet. We refer to these different forms of mass communications collectively as the media.

Most American media, such as a local newspaper or television station, uses the English language, but there are also many newspapers and broadcasts in other languages, including Spanish, Polish, Yiddish, and Arabic. This chapter is about Arab American journalism, press, and media, which, in 1992, celebrated its centennial—one hundred year anniversary. The first Arabic language newspaper in the United States was founded in 1892. It was called *Kawkab Amirka*, or *Star of America*. It was published in New York by Najeeb Arbeely, one of the founding fathers of Arab American journalism.

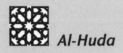

## Al-Huda

Although there were many publications in the early days of the Arab American community, the story of *Al-Huda* (*The Guidance*) is among the most interesting. *Al-Huda* was published by Na'uum Moukarzil, a teacher by training, who sought not only to inform his readers but also to educate them in the ways of the United States. His mission was to cover three main areas: social, cultural, and political news. On the social and cultural levels, the aim of the paper was to instill a sense of identity within the new community—a sense of who Syrians and Lebanese were in America. Moukarzil developed his newspaper as a forum for the discussion of political ideas that impacted Arabs in America and back home. Thus, the newspaper focused upon events in the Arab world, particularly Lebanon as well as politics in the United States. Although *Al-Huda* stopped publishing in the early 1990s, it remains the longest surviving pioneer Arabic newspaper in America.

# The early Arabic press

The need for Arab American media originated from the trauma of immigration and early Arab Americans' need to deal with the problems of adjusting to the culture of the United States. Arab Americans founded the early newspapers for two major reasons. First, they wanted to assist other Arab immigrants in the process of integrating into (becoming part of) the social, economic, and political life of their new country. Second, they wanted to help them maintain a sense of community by focusing on issues that were important to Arabs in America. Today's Arab American media continues to serve similar functions—offering news, views, and entertainment that is not otherwise readily available to the community.

The early Arab immigrants largely came from an area called Greater Syria (which includes present-day Lebanon, Syria, Jordan, Palestine, and Israel). They identified with the villages, towns, and cities they came from, and often kept close ties with these communities. As a result, the early Arab American press often covered issues of importance in the communities the publishers came from. In addition, they may have represented a particular religious community, including eastern Catholics, the Orthodox Christians, the Druze community, and the smaller Muslim community.

Najeeb Arbeely founded the first Arabic newspaper in New York City in 1892. *Kawkab Amirka* (*The Star of America*) consisted of one English and three Arabic pages. The focus of the paper was local community and homeland news. *Al-Asr* (*the Mid-day*) followed in 1894, published by Na'uum Moukarzil, who began *Al-Huda* (*The Guidance*) in 1896. In

1903, *Al Huda* moved to New York and was published by Salloum Moukarzil, brother of the original publisher. Not long afterwards, *Al-Bayan* (*The Explanation*) began publication.

Many of the first Arabic papers were published in New York City because, as with many other immigrants, New York was the gateway to America for Arab immigrants. They established a mother colony there before relocating to other parts of the country.

Many other publications followed the three pioneering Arab American newspapers, and by 1907, twenty-one newspapers were established—in New York City, Philadelphia, St. Louis, and Lawrence, Massachusetts. By 1930 there were fifty Arab American newspapers, and each small community had a news outlet serving its particular needs.

This rapid growth in Arabic-language newspapers did not last, however, because the Arab American community was not large enough to support so many papers. As time passed the early Arabic press began to decline. Members of the community who could read Arabic were aging and dying, and new U.S. laws restricted the flow of new immigrants from the Arab world who could read the Arabic language. In addition, the old Arabic press heavily favored cultural assimilation and Americanization (integration into mainstream American society) over the maintenance of Arabic language and culture. As a result, younger generations of Arab Americans often could not speak or read Arabic. As a consequence of these factors, the Arabic-language newspapers began to lose their readership.

Although the younger generations of Arab Americans could not read Arabic, many still had a connection to their ancestral culture. To that end, *The Syrian World* was founded in 1926 to meet the challenge of connecting the new English

 **Fact Focus**

- The first Arabic-language newspaper in the United States was founded in 1892. It was called *Kawkab Amirka,* or *Star of America.* It was published in New York by Najeeb Arbeely, one of the founding fathers of Arab American journalism in this country.

- Arab Americans now have a number of local and national print media (newspapers and magazines) and electronic media (television, radio, and the internet) that allows them to stay in touch with each other and with events in their countries of origin.

- Many of the first Arab American newspapers were published in New York City.

- In 1930, there were fifty Arab American newspapers.

speaking generation with the old country. *The Syrian World* was an English-language monthly magazine established by Na'uum Moukarzil to serve readership across the country. The magazine focused on the issues of culture and heritage of Syrian Americans.

## Origins of the contemporary press

In the years following World War II (1939-45), many Arabs came to the United States. The new immigrants were mostly Muslim (believers in Islam) and pan-Arab (nationalists who believed in Arab unity and solidarity). These newcomers felt that the mainstream American press did not represent their concerns and looked toward the Arabic press as a source of unbiased news about the Arab world (particularly the Arab-Israeli conflict) and their situation in this country.

American-born Arabs who felt connected to their ancestral homelands needed a press that could communicate to them in English. As a result, the new press tended to be bilingual (in English and Arabic) and focused on national Arab and Arab American issues. The new demands on the press revived Arab newsprint and paved the way for other forms of media later in the century. The publishers and editors of the new press worked to develop Arab American community solidarity by providing information through a bilingual format.

Nowadays, every geographic area of major Arab American presence in the country has the benefit of a newspaper or magazine. Southern California has *Beirut Times* (a news-oriented publication published by Michel Bou Abssi), *Al-Jadid* (a quarterly newspaper published by Elie Chalala and devoted to culture and the arts), and *The News Circle*, a magazine established by Joseph Haiek in 1972 to serve the information needs of the growing community. (Along with covering Arab-American affairs, *The News Circle* offers a wide variety of publications, including books and the *Arab-American Almanac,* a national guide on the community.)

In Detroit, Michigan, many newspapers and magazines can be found. One of the oldest newspapers there, *Sada al-Watan* (the Homeland's Echo, founded in 1984) is a nation-

al tabloid that focuses on political news, published by Osama Siblani. *Detroit Chaldean Times* (founded by Amir Denha in the early 1990s) serves the Chaldean sub-community in metropolitan Detroit. The newest addition to the world of newspapers in Detroit is the *Arab-American Journal* (founded in 1997 by Nuhad El-Hajj and Mohamad Ozeir), which deals with issues of national concern from the perspective of Arab Americans in Detroit and southern California.

Although southeastern Michigan and southern California have the two largest areas of Arab concentration, Arab Americans are found in other parts of the country and have established media outlets. Arab American media presence is also strong in Washington, D.C., with several newsprint outlets, including *Al-Nashra* (*The Report*), a monthly newspaper published by Hikmat Beaini, and *Al-Hewar* (*Dialog*) magazine, founded by Subhi Ghandour in the late 1980s to address the national community's concerns in the nation's capital.

**Nowadays, every Arab American community in the United States has the benefit of a newspaper or magazine.** *Reproduced by permission of Corbis Corporation (Bellevue).*

In Chicago, *Al-Bostaan* (*The Orchard*) is edited by Ghassan Barakat and is dedicated to local news. Two other Illinois newspapers include *Al-mahjar* (*The Diaspora*), which is published by Khaled Damisi in Burbank, and *Al-Ufuq al-Arabi* in Bedford Park. In Clifton, New Jersey, there is *Al-itidal* (*Moderation*), edited by Abdalla Tahan, and *Phoenicia Newspaper* (published by Ali Ballout) in Princeton, Florida. Of course, this account of the U.S. Arab newspapers is not exhaustive—only a sampling of the newspapers and magazines being published.

In addition to local or regional newspapers and magazines, some national Arab American organizations have publications that are widely read across the country. These national publications are often the newsletters or papers of organizations such as the ADC (American-Arab Anti-Discrimination Committee) and the AAUG (Association of Arab-American University Graduates). *ADC Times* is a twenty-page monthly newsletter with a circulation of 10,000. AAUG publishes a newsletter and the *AAUG Monitor,* which provides articles on current events and issues of concern to Arab Americans. Through these and many other newsletters, Arab Americans stay informed of organizing and community events around the country along with events in the United States and the Arab world of importance to them.

# Electronic media

Before the beginning of Arab American radio and television, Arabic speakers in the United States were able to listen to Arabic language programs on short wave radio. One of the programs available in the Arabic language was the "Voice of America." The United States Information Agency broadcast the "Voice of America" in many languages in order to represent the policies and political aims of the U.S. government to the world. It was established during the Cold War, a period of hostility between the United States and the Soviet Union following World War II, in order to inform listeners from different international backgrounds on issues of importance to the United States and to influence world public opinion.

Although "Voice of America" was mainly aimed at broadcasting information to outside the United States, before the beginning of Arab American broadcasting it was a source of news and entertainment for Arab Americans, too. Because it was broadcast over short wave radio, it could be picked up in the United States as well as in the Arab world. But now, given the explosion in the availability of other Arabic media sources (and the decline of the popularity of short-wave radios), "Voice of America" is no longer a popular form of information and entertainment for Arab Americans.

## Arab American radio and television

The history of Arab American radio and television is linked to technological developments in the electronic media. As is true with the mainstream American electronic media, Arab American radio broadcasting preceded all other forms. As early as the 1960s, and across the nation, there were Arabic-language radio programs on ethnic radio stations devoted to informing and entertaining members of the community. The format of these programs followed a prescribed course of musical entertainment, including radio dramas, news, and commentary. Some programs were bilingual and a small number were in English only.

### Locally produced programs

Detroit remains the largest Arab American market for radio broadcasting. Since the 1960s, Detroit has had strong and continuous Arabic-language radio programming. "The Arab Voice in Detroit," the best known and longest running show of its genre, began broadcasting in the mid-1960s and ceased production in the early 1990s, when its producer, media pioneer Faisal Arabo, retired. Other cities also have Arab radio programs. Boston's "Arabian Night" show was founded fifty years ago by Charles Shaqouri and continues to air on Sunday mornings. Chicago also has a live call-in talk show, "Arab-American Radio," hosted by Yusef Shibley, and "Arabic Chicago."

 **Afifa Karam (1883–1924)**

Afifa Karam was the first well-known Arab American woman journalist. Born and raised in Lebanon, she immigrated to the United States at age fourteen with her husband. She began her career as a journalist at the age of twenty and wrote articles for Arab-language newspapers and journals such as *Al-Huda* (*The Guidance*) and the *Syrian Woman*. She was publisher and editor of *The New World: A Ladies Monthly Arabic Magazine*. Karam was highly concerned about the condition of Arab and Arab American women and much of her writing argued for an improvement in women's status.

Video editor Samira Atris works at the editing desk of *Sada Al Arab,* a cable television production company that produces shows for Dearborn, Michigan's Arab American community. *Reproduced with permission of Millard Berry.*

Faisal Arabo also explored the television medium in the late 1970s. He developed a show with the same name as his Detroit radio program ("The Arab Voice in Detroit"), which was aired on WGPR, an independent TV station. The program was broadcast weekly on Saturdays and represented the most successful attempt of its kind at the time. Another show, *Middle East Television,* was produced by Gregory Mitri in the 1980s and early 1990s and was aired on the same channel. Both shows went off the air when the TV station was bought out by CBS in the Detroit market.

Although Arab American programs on regular "air-broadcasting" began to decline, the new cable technology allows for locally produced Arab American programming to continue to flourish. In the suburb of Dearborn, Michigan (where 20 percent of the population is of Arab background), the local cable carrier offers an ethnic programming channel that has a full line-up of locally produced Arabic-language shows. *TV Orient,* which began airing in 1987, was the first syndicated cable show in the Detroit area that was telecast on a nightly basis by several major local cable companies. Other shows include *Arabic Hour* in Boston, the *Arabic TV Program* in Chicago, and the *Arab-American Television* in Los Angeles. These and other similar shows around the country follow the same format as radio broadcasting: news, views, entertainment, and commentary. Arab American TV producers have met with success because television naturally appeals to Arabic speakers and to Arab American English speakers, regardless of their competence in either language.

## National and international Arab American programming

The creation of the Arab Network of America (ANA) in the late 1980s revolutionized the Arab American world of media and mass communication. ANA is a national broadcaster and cable-caster that covers not only the United States, but also Canada and parts of Central and South America. Its creation marked a giant leap for Arab Americans in media, going from only locally produced programs with small audiences to an international and fully professional national network. ANA began its operation as a radio broadcaster centered in the vicinity of Washington, D.C., in 1988. ANA TV was inaugurated in 1991. Both ANA Radio and Television represent a major breakthrough for Arab Americans, since they provided the first national and international programs to present Arab American entertainment, information, and discussions. ANA has helped Arab Americans forge a national community aware of itself and its assets. The ANA broadcast signal covers all Arab American communities through local cable systems or direct satellite broadcasting. ANA Radio is syndicated in major U.S. cities such as Detroit, Chicago, New York, and Houston.

In addition to local programming, some Arab Americans watch Arabic-language programs via satellite television. These programs come from the Arab world, and are available twenty-four hours a day. For non-English speakers, this is a welcome addition to the limited programs that are available on local cable stations.

# Internet resources

Today, the internet is a major source of information dissemination. Along with the more general web sites and search engines (web sites, such as Yahoo!, that help you to find other web sites), there are some that specialize in serving Arab Americans. One advantage that the internet has over other kinds of electronic media is that anyone in any geographic area has access to it if they have a computer and an internet connection. This means that you don't have to live in an area with a large Arab-American community to access news and information, as you do for radio and television.

The first Arab American internet service provider, Visitus.net, is a Dearborn, Michigan, company whose website offers Arab-related links. Another interesting innovation on the internet is the creation of the first electronic community newspaper, the *Arab-American Mirror,* edited by Adham Rashidi. There are several Arab American-related chat rooms, including ArabChat and Arab Zone. In addition, a number of Arab American web pages provide multiple services, including bulletin boards, discussion forums for current events and social issues, and links to other Arab American and Arab world websites. Two popular sites include Café Arabic and Lebnet.

# Film and video

## Films from the Arab world

The Arab American film industry is in its infancy. So, Arab immigrants hungry for scenes of their homelands have to watch movies produced in the Arab world. Before the invention of the videocassette recorder (VCR), some enterprising Arab Americans experimented with the idea of showing Arabic-language movies at movie houses in Arab American communities by special arrangement. The practice was generally successful and drew an audience of Arab immigrants that longed to see scenes of Arab life on the silver screen. The growth of the Arab American population in the 1970s and 1980s, which gave rise to the success of radio and TV broadcasting, also promoted the growth of video-renting establishments in Arab communities. Renting and buying Arabic films is now a big industry.

In the early 1990s, Arab Film Distribution, a film library company based in Seattle, Washington, was established to promote and provide good Arab films to American and Canadian theaters, universities, museums, and media centers and outlets. The company, which grew out of the Arab Film Festival at the 1990 Goodwill Arts Games in Seattle, also provides films on video for private home use.

### Arab American filmmaking

Independent Arab American movie-making made its debut with the production of *Nahr el-Hayat* (River of Life) in April 1999. Produced in Washington, D.C., by a team of Arab American artists, the movie marks a turning point in Arab American entertainment. This short Arabic-language film is a drama based on the lives of real people and real situations, which speaks to the experience of Arab immigrants in the United States. The movie was produced and directed by filmmaker Hazim Bitar.

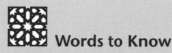 **Words to Know**

- **Americanization:** the process of integrating into mainstream American society.

- **Bilingual:** fluent in two languages.

- **Integration:** the process by which immigrants adapt to and become part of their new society.

- **Media:** a means of mass communication, including different types of information broadcasting, such as printed materials (newspapers and magazines), television and radio, and the internet.

- **Press:** the printed news media, including newspapers and periodicals (magazines).

## The importance of community media

The Arab American media is very important to members of the communities because it provides people with information (in Arabic and English) on important events and issues that the mainstream media does not cover. It provides information on cultural events such as conventions, concerts, festivals, and holiday celebrations. It also gives practical information for Arab Americans on matters such as the availability of bilingual education or social services. It reports news relevant to Arab Americans, such as incidents of discrimination or changes in immigration laws. It also provides news on events in Arab countries, which is very important for recent immigrants and those who still have family in the Arab world.

The Arab American media also serves as a source of entertainment. People listen to talk shows and music on their radios. They watch soap operas, situation comedies, and variety shows on the television. They converse with one another in internet chat rooms. Additionally, the Arab American media promotes Arab-run businesses through advertising.

As in the past, the Arab American media continues to help create a sense of community among Arab Americans who may live in different parts of the country and speak different languages. All of the different functions of the Arab American media allow the diverse members of Arab American communities throughout the United States to communicate and support each other in ways that were not possible one hundred years ago.

## For More Information

Ajami, Joseph. *The Arabic Press in the United States Since 1892: A Socio-Historical Study.* Ph.D. Dissertation, Ohio University, 1987.

Grame, Theodore C. *Ethnic Broadcasting in the United States.* Washington, D.C.: Library of Congress Folklore Center, 1980.

Haiek, Joseph. *Arab-American Almanac.* 4th ed. Glendale, CA: News Circle Publishing House, 1992.

Hitti, Philip K. *The Syrians in America.* New York: George H. Doran, 1924.

Naff, Alixa. "Arabs." In *The Encyclopedia of America Ethnic Groups,* edited by Stephen Thernstrom. Cambridge: Harvard University Press, 1980.

Selim, George. *Afifa Karam: The Voice of al-Huda's Most Prominent Woman Contributor.* Arab-American Institute Press, 1999.

Suleiman, Michael. "The Mokarzel's Contribution to the Arabic-Speaking Community in the United States." *Arab Studies Quarterly,* Spring 1999.

Tayash, Fahad A. *Ethnic Media in the United States: A Descriptive Study of Arab-American Media.* Ph.D. dissertation, Wayne State University, 1988.

Wilson, Clint C., and Felix Gutierrez. *Minorities and Media Diversity and the End of Mass Communication.* Beverly Hills, CA: Sage Publications, 1985.

## Web Sites

*Arab American Mirror.* [Online] Available http://www.alif.com/mirror (last accessed September 21, 1999).

ArabChat. [Online] Available http://www.ArabChat.com/ (last accessed September 21, 1999).

Arab Zone. [Online] Available http://www.Arabic-words.com (last accessed September 21, 1999).

Café Arabica. [Online] Available http://www.cafearabica.com (last accessed September 21, 1999).

Lebnet. [Online] Available http://www.lebnet.com (last accessed September 21, 1999).

*Nahr el-Hayat* (*River of Life*). [Online] Available http://www.alif.com/film (last accessed September 21, 1999).

*Kenneth K. Ayouby is a doctoral student in Education and Cultural Studies at Wayne State University in Detroit, Michigan. Additionally, he is an adjunct lecturer in Arabic Studies at the University of Michigan at Dearborn and a contributing writer and editorial board member of the* Arab American Journal.

# Where to Learn More

The following list of general resources focuses on material appropriate for middle school or high school students. For books, periodicals, and web sites about the specific topics covered in each chapter of *Arab American Encyclopedia,* refer to the "For More Information" section at the end of each chapter. Please note that the web site addresses were verified prior to publication, but are subject to change.

## Books:

Abraham, Nabeel, and Andrew Shryock, eds. *Arab Detroit: From Margin to Mainstream.* Detroit: Wayne State University Press, in press.

Abraham, Nabeel, and Andrew Shryock, eds. *Creating Identities: Arab Americans in Detroit.* Detroit: Wayne State University Press, in press.

Abraham, Sameer, and Abraham Nabeel, eds. *Arabs in the New World: Studies on Arab-American Communities.* Detroit: Wayne State University Press, 1983.

Abu-Laban, Baha, and Michael Suleiman, eds. *Arab Americans: Continuity and Change.* Belmont, MA: Association of Arab-American University Graduates, 1989.

Ashabranner, Brent. *An Ancient Heritage: The Arab-American Minority.* New York: Harper Collins, 1991.

Aswad, Barbara, ed. *Arabic Speaking Communities in American Cities*. Staten Island, NY: Center for Migration Studies, 1974.

Aswad, Barbara, and Barbara Bilgé, eds. *Family and Gender among Muslims in America: Issues Facing Middle Eastern Immigrants and Their Descendants*. Philadelphia: Temple University Press, 1996.

Cainkar, Louise. *Meeting Community Needs, Building on Community Strengths*. Chicago: Arab American Action Network, 1998.

Hagopian, Elaine C., and Ann Paden, eds. *The Arab-Americans: Studies in Assimilation*. Wilmette, IL: Medina University Press International, 1969.

Haiek, Joseph R. *Arab-American Almanac*. 4th ed. Glendale, CA: News Circle Publishing House, 1992.

Harik, Elsa Marston. *The Lebanese in America*. Minneapolis: Lerner Publication Company, 1987.

Hitti, Philip. *The Syrians in America*. New York: George H. Doran, 1924.

Hooglund, Eric, ed. *Crossing the Waters: Arabic-Speaking Immigrants to the United States before 1940*. Washington, D.C.: Smithsonian Institution Press, 1987.

Hooglund, Eric, ed. *Taking Root: Arab-American Community Studies*. Washington, D.C.: American-Arab Anti-Discriminatory Committee, 1985.

Kadi, Joanne, ed. *Food for Our Grandmothers: Writings by Arab-American and Arab-Canadian Feminists*. Boston: South End Press, 1994.

Kayal, P. M., and J. M. Kayal. *The Syrian-Lebanese in America: A Study in Religion and Assimilation*. Boston, MA: Twayne Publishers, 1975.

McCarus, Ernest, ed. *The Development of Arab-American Identity*. Ann Arbor: University of Michigan Press, 1994.

Naff, Alixa. *Becoming American: The Early Arab Immigrant Experience*. Carbondale: Southern Illinois University Press, 1985.

Naff, Alixa. *The Arab Americans*. New York: Chelsea House Publications, 1988.

Orfalea, Gregory and Sharif Elmusa, eds. *Grapeleaves: A Century of Arab American Poetry*. Salt Lake City: University of Utah Press, 1988.

Orfalea, Gregory. *Before the Flames: A Quest for the History of Arab Americans*. Austin: University of Texas Press, 1988.

Shabbas, Audrey, and Ayad Al-Qazzaz. *Arab World Notebook*. Berkeley, CA: Najda (Women Concerned About the Middle East), 1989.

Shakir, Evelyn. *Bint Arab: Arab and Arab American Women in the United States*. Westport, CT: Praeger, 1997.

Suleiman, Michael, ed. *Arabs in America: Building a New Future*. Philadelphia: Temple University Press, in press.

Suleiman, Michael. *The Arabs in the Mind of America*. Brattleboro, VT: Amana Books, 1988.

Wormser, Richard. *American Islam: Growing Up Muslim in America*. New York: Walker and Company, 1994.

Younis, Adele. *The Coming of the Arabic-Speaking People to the United States*. New York: Center for Migration Studies, 1995.

Zogby, John. *Arab America Today: A Demographic Profile of Arab Americans*. Washington, D.C.: Arab American Institute, 1990.

Zogby, James, ed., and Pat Aufderheide and Anne S. Mooney, asst. eds. *Taking Root Bearing Fruit: The Arab American Experience*. Washington, D.C.: American-Arab Anti-Discrimination Committee, 1984.

## Periodicals:

"The Arab Immigrants." *Aramco World Magazine,* September/October 1986.

Charara, Hayan. "Growing Up Arab in Detroit." *Forkroads: A Journal of Ethnic-American Literature,* Winter 1996.

## Web Sites:

American-Arab Anti-Discrimination Committee. [Online] Available http://www.adc.com (last accessed September 21, 1999).

Arab American Institute. [Online] Available http://www.aaiusa.org (last accessed September 21, 1999).

National Association of Arab Americans (NAAA). [Online] Available http://www.naaa.net (last accessed September 21, 1999).

Casey Kasem. "Arab Americans: Making a Difference." [Online] Available http://arab-media.com/achievers.html (last accessed September 21, 1999).

ArabChat. [Online] Available http://www.ArabChat.com/ (last accessed September 21, 1999).

Arab Zone. [Online] Available http://www.Arabic-words.com/ (last accessed September 21, 1999).

Café Arabica. [Online] Available http://www.cafearabica.com (last accessed September 21, 1999).

Lebnet. [Online] Available http://www.lebnet.com (last accessed September 21, 1999).

## Other

*Tales from Arab Detroit* (video). Directed by Joan Mandell and produced by the Arab Community Center for Economic and Social Services (ACCESS) and Sally Howell, Ho-Ho-Kus, NJ: New Day Films, 1995.

*Benatt Chicago (Daughters of Chicago): Growing Up Arab and Female in Chicago* (video). Directed and produced by Jennifer Bing-Canar and Mary Zerkel. Chicago: American Friends Service Committee, 1996.

# Index

Illustrations are marked by (ill.).

A "d" after a page number represents a definition, a "t" after a page number represents a table.

# T

Tabbara, Yaser, 251
Tabbouleh, 152t, 165d
Tahan, Abdalla, 276
Takieddiene, Diana, 230
*The Tale of Three Mohammads* (Gailes), 251
*Tales from Detroit* (Mandell and Howell), 252
*Tales of the Arabian Nights,* 14
*Tamazight* (Berber languages), 86
*Taqiya* (men's cap), 140
Tarab, 228
*Taraneem,* 160
Teenagers, 126–127, 145, 192
Television (Arab American), 277–279
Telkaif (in modern-day Iraq), 41
Tenement houses, 171
Terrorist(s), in news media, 187–188
Terrorist stereotype, 186, 192
Textile (clothing) industry, 58–59
*Thaalab El-Muhtal* (ATAG), 247
Theater, 245–249
    in California, 247–248
    in Chicago, 249
    in Detroit, 246–247
*Thinking Class: Sketches from a Cultural Worker* (Kadi), 267
Third-generation immigrants, 7d, 70d
    ethnic identity of, 57
Thomas, Danny, 247
Thomas, Helen, 207t
Thomas, Merielle, 229
*Thoub,* 253
*Through and Through: Toledo Stories* (Geha), 263
Timurlane, 16
Tiny Leaps Productions, 251
Torah (Old Testament), 90
*Tower of Dreams* (Abdul-Baki), 264
Town and family reunions, 166–167
Traditional arts, 252–254
*Travelling Mercies* (Williams), 265
Tribal nomads (Bedouins), 10, 186
Tuberculosis, 173
Turki, Fawaz, 267

Turkish/Muslim dynasty (Ottoman Empire), 17 (ill.), 17–19
*TV Orient,* 279
TWA Flight 800 (1996), 195
*Twin Cousins* (Gailes), 251

# U

U.A.W. (United Auto Workers), 67, 68 (ill.)
*Al-Ufuq al-Arabi,* 276
Umayyad Caliphate, 14
*Umma,* 96
Unionize, 70d
United Auto Workers (U.A.W.), 67, 68 (ill.)
United Farm Workers, 180
United Nations, and Arab-Israeli conflict, 28–29
United States
    Arab immigration to, 2–3
    Arab population distribution in, 58
    Arabs born in, 83–84
    Californian Arab American communities, 71–72
    citizenship, 200–201
    and Cold War, 29–30
    first Arab immigrants to, 3, 5–6, 35
    foreign policy in Arab world, 191–192, 204, 262
    gender roles in, 147–148
    immigrations laws *See U.S. immigration laws*
    marriage in, 162–163
    Midwestern Arab American communities, 64–69
    Northeastern Arab American communities, 58–64, 63 (ill.)
    official agencies of, 192–193
    Southwestern Arab American communities, 70–71
United States Information Agency, 276
Urban, 70d, 180d
Urban life
    health issues and, 176–179
    preferred by Arab Americans, 58

Arab world and, 24–27
racial identity during, 200–201
World War II, 175
immigration of Arabs after, 43
immigration of Christian Arabs
after, 100–101
Writers
contemporary, 261–263
early, 259–260
of the Pen League, 260–261
of poetry, short stories, and essays, 265–267
scholarly, 268, 269t
women, 267–268
Writers (Arab American) *See also
Literature (Arab American)*
of autobiographical works and
novels, 263–265
Writing school (*kuttab,* or *maktab*), 130
Written Arabic, 77, 78 (ill.)

# Y

Yarmuk, Battle of, 12–13

"Yellow Race Crisis," 201
Yemen, poverty in, 31
Yemeni Arabic, 79
Yemeni Dance Troupe, 230 (ill.)
Yemeni immigration, 41, 52–53,
61, 178
Younis, Adele, 269t
Youssef, Naji, 229

# Z

Zacharia, Nasir, 251
Zakariya, Mohammed, 253
*Zakat* (charity), 95
Zionists (Jewish nationalists),
25–26, 27, 28–29, 43
Ziryab, 221t
Zogby, James J., 207t
Zogby International, population
estimates by, 57
Zoro, Hussam, 246, 247
Zurayk, Afaf, 241t